Supply Management and Procurement

From the Basics to Best-in-Class

Robert W. Turner

ISBN: 978-1-60427-063-1

Printed and bound in the U.S.A. Printed on acid-free paper.

10 9 8 7 6 5 4 3 2 1

Library of Congress Cataloging-in-Publication Data

Turner, Robert W., 1947–
    Supply management and procurement : from the basics to best-in-class /
by Robert W. Turner.
        p. cm.
    Includes index.
    ISBN 978-1-60427-063-1 (hardcover : alk. paper)
    1. Industrial procurement. 2. Business logistics.
I. Title.
    HD39.5.T87 2011
    658.7—dc23

                           2011034008

Direct all inquiries to J. Ross Publishing, Inc., 5765 N. Andrews Way, Fort Lauderdale, FL 33309.

Phone: (954) 727-9333
Fax: (561) 892-0700
Web: www.jrosspub.com

Contents

Preface

Business is an amalgamation of combined business functions and activities operating in unison with one another to accomplish a specific goal. Whether a company is a manufacturing, service, marketing, or other type of business, the goal for all of them is the same—be successful in what they do. There are different degrees of success, of course, and the level of success that a company achieves is dependent on several factors. The factors that determine the level of success a company achieves are:

(a) The level of knowledge and expertise the organization has in its core functions.
(b) The level of knowledge and experience its management and employees have in fulfilling their specific roles and responsibilities within the company.
(c) The level of education and training employees have and receive.
(d) The culture that exists in the company.
(e) The level of desire employees have to do a good job and to be the best they can be at what they do.
(f) The degree to which all departments, employees, business functions, and activities work together and complement each other to accomplish the common goals and objectives of the company.

To be successful in any endeavor, there has to be a desire to be successful. As mentioned, the degree of success a company achieves is also dependent on how well departments and employees work with one another in performing their assigned duties and tasks. Business might be compared to a clock or piece of machinery. Each is made up of gears, cogs, and movements that, when working efficiently together, produce energy, forward movement, and accomplish a specific objective. Each component is important to and dependent on the operation of the whole. If one component does not perform its appointed job to expectation, the whole is less likely to obtain the level of success desired. This equates to cross-functionality; understanding the importance of other business functions within the organization and understanding how they work and the sharing of information between departments and work groups. In other words, communication between individuals and other entities within the organization is important to the degree of success of the organization.

Fundamental Objective

There are three main goals of *Supply Management and Procurement: From the Basics to Best-In-Class*:

1. To offer the readers an extended source of knowledge, tools, and techniques to better understand the philosophy of strategic supply management and procurement and master those concepts. With knowledge comes power, the power to improve processes, efficiencies, and profitability that all equate to greater success.
2. To help the readers apply specific philosophies and concepts to improve individual performance as well as that of their operations and thereby add additional value to their organizations.
3. To promote an ongoing and lasting interest in supply management and procurement as a fundamental and important value adding resource as well as a desire to adopt new philosophies and concepts for continuous process improvement.

Discussions and Examples

Supply Management and Procurement: From the Basics to Best-In-Class contains topics and concepts that will be familiar to some readers but may be entirely new to many others. It presents discussions of each topic and concept in an effort to lead the reader to a better and fuller understanding of the importance and benefit of practicing strategic supply management and procurement. Here are a few of the things that are discussed:

- What supply management is
- The conceptual difference between strategic supply management and basic procurement practices
- Effectively managing supply management
- Identifying, planning, designing, and mapping supply chains
- What value chains are and their importance to strategic supply management
- Setting strategic goals by benchmarking
- Identifying, planning, designing, and mapping activities and processes of individual links within the supply chain
- Advantages of strategically organizing and prioritizing projects
- How to create competitive advantage for your organization through practicing strategic supply management
- Developing a strategic sourcing model
- How to think creatively and critically to develop strategic goals

- Using environmental scans for strategic planning
- Identifying risks and developing risk management plans
- Using forward forecasting to make strategic decisions
- Developing and using sensitivity analysis
- Writing requests for proposals to satisfy strategic goals
- Negotiating strategic agreements
- Managing contracts effectively
- Supply management's new role and importance in international trade
- Make versus buy and breakeven analysis decisions
- Tools and techniques to attain best-in-class supply management and procurement
- Facilitating, implementing, and managing philosophical supply management change

Distinguishing Features of This Book

Comprehensive Examples at Appropriate Levels

This book is challenging, comprehensive, and analytical in its approach to the subject of strategic supply management and procurement. It is presented in an easily understandable manner and is accessible to a wide range of readers, from the C level executive planner to the procurement practitioner performing daily tasks. It attempts to be thorough in its presentations of concepts and philosophies with emphasis placed on real world examples.

Fundamentals and Basics of Supply Management

Driven by a down economy and simple economic realities, many organizations are discovering that what worked well in the past may not necessarily be what is now needed to not only survive, but move forward. Several chapters contain excellent examples of how practicing basic and fundamental procurement can lead to disastrous consequences. Throughout the other chapters, comparisons are drawn between practicing basic procurement and more advanced principles of strategic supply management.

Integration of New Concepts, Tools, Techniques, and Philosophies

Throughout the book, an emphasis is placed on the value and benefit of integrating new concepts and philosophies into current operations to bring more value to an organization through cost reduction, process improvement, and increases in efficiencies that equate to higher profit margins and higher levels of competitive advantage. Chapter 19 examines the various analysis, tools, and techniques used by best-in-class strategic supply management departments and elaborates on each one to demonstrate how the use of these tools and techniques might be used in real world situations.

Emphasis on Technological and Philosophical Change

Technology upgrade examples are offered throughout the book to illustrate the activity cost reductions and efficiency improvements that yield benefits in instituting a change philosophy. Chapter 20 discusses how to facilitate, implement, and manage change from a basic procurement philosophy to a strategic supply management philosophy. Cases are made that offer opportunities for internal discussions within an organization to identify current directions and goals and how movement toward changing current procurement culture and procedures to a strategic supply management and best-in-class culture can and should be made.

Step-by-Step Approach to Strategic Supply Management

Each chapter builds upon the preceding chapters and offers sequential tools and techniques that can be added at an appropriate pace. Rome was not built in a day, and it will take time to promote change in an organization's culture and procurement philosophy, policy, and procedures. Not all concepts discussed in the book will be valuable or appropriate for all organizations and situations. The analysis, tools, and techniques presented represent those that are currently available to procurement to implement in their own operations. It will be up to individuals and organizations to decide which ones offer the most value and make the most sense for them.

Focus on Strategic Philosophies

There is a concentrated focus on strategic philosophies and concepts that attempts to provide the reader with thought-provoking examples of what can be accomplished and what benefits can be gained by moving from a basic procurement philosophy to that of a strategic supply management philosophy. Examples are used extensively to present various scenarios in which different tools and techniques may be used for value enhancement. There are also two interactive case studies that present situational facts, provide background information, and offer research results. The reader is then asked to make decisions based on all the facts presented. Answers for ideal decisions are then presented in a separate section.

Organizational Alternatives

In any decision-making process there are alternative actions that can be taken in any given situation. Good decision makers do their homework, look at and weigh all of the possibilities, perform research and analysis, and calculate the cost benefit for making a particular decision. *Supply Management and Procurement: From the Basics to Best-In-Class* provides diverse situations and procurement scenarios to allow the reader to see how strategic supply management philosophies and concepts can be applied to bring about better decision making and results. As mentioned, there are always alternatives to be considered in any decision scenario and the examples presented show the reader how to navigate the process of determining alternatives and choosing the decision. Readers may relate the examples to their own operations, with variation, to determine if the processes, tools, and techniques used in the examples can be of benefit to their own particular situation.

About the Author

Robert W. Turner has a BS in business administration and an MBA from the University of Phoenix. He has over 40 years of practical business experience in all facets of business and over 30 years of successful applied supply management and procurement knowledge. The diversity of his experience in a variety of industries has given him a unique business acumen and outlook on what it takes for a business to be successful.

During his long career, Bob has held a number of positions. In the coal industry he was General Manager of Operations at Cumberland Processing and Anker Energy's Cajun Trading, and he was Senior Vice President of Marketing and Operations at Sterling Coal. He has been an independent consultant to several companies, including American Electric Power (AEP), a large electric utility company in the eastern part of the United States, where he performed several consulting projects. Additionally, he was President, CEO, and owner of Pine Ridge Coal and Star Mining, which were mining, processing, and sales companies.

From 1995 to 2009 Bob was a financial analyst and procurement specialist in the Strategic Sourcing department of United Parcel Service Company (UPSCO), the airline of the UPS brand. Bob was responsible for contract development, negotiations, and procurement of several hundred million dollars worth of goods and services to support UPS airline operations globally in 220 countries and territories. He retired early from UPS to pursue his dream of teaching and training individuals in the fundamental and advanced applications of business functions and activities.

Currently, Bob is President and CEO of Business Training Solutions, a company that offers printed, CD-ROM, audio, and web-based training solutions on various business functions and activities such as supply management, negotiating, marketing, process improvement, risk identification, management, and other important business topics. He is also the owner of several web-based marketing sites offering retail goods and services to business and the general public.

Introduction

In good economic times, and even more so in difficult economic times, managers need to understand how the decisions they make affect costs, savings, and profits for their organizations. Managing the supply chain in your organization is a critical tool for adding value to your organization by improving efficiencies, economies of scale, reducing costs, and, thereby, increasing profits.

Supply Management and Procurement: From the Basics to Best-in-Class is a road map for managers and procurement professionals to understand what supply management is and how it can be applied to existing procurement services to improve them. It describes the basics of supply management and offers a benchmark against which you can determine how supply management processes and philosophies are applied and work in organizations.

Benchmarking is a tool that can be used to measure how well an organization is doing and as a goal for how well they want to do. An organization that is considered best-in-class is one that is a leader in their market segment or industry. Achieving best-in-class means that the organization has attained this status by maximizing their efficiencies using best practices to improve their processes of operations for the acquisition and processing of materials and delivery of finished goods or services to its customers.

At J. Ross Publishing we are committed to providing today's professional with practical, hands-on tools that enhance the learning experience and give readers an opportunity to apply what they have learned. That is why we offer free ancillary materials available for download on this book and all participating Web Added Value™ publications. These online resources may include interactive versions of material that appears in the book or supplemental templates, worksheets, models, plans, case studies, proposals, spreadsheets and assessment tools, among other things. Whenever you see the WAV™ symbol in any of our publications, it means bonus materials accompany the book and are available from the Web Added Value Download Resource Center at www.jrosspub .com.

Downloads for *Supply Management and Procurement* include an Incoterm responsibility chart, a sourcing methodology model, a best-in-class sourcing checklist, and a comprehensive listing of supply and procurement terms and definitions.

1

What Is Supply Management?

We have all heard the buzzwords supply management, supply chain management, value chain management, just-in-time, kaizen, lean, and so on. But what is supply management really? I define it as a system or process that supports an organization's total needs for the supply of goods, services, and processes required to accomplish the goals and tasks established by the organization. It is the optimization of material costs, transportation, handling, quality, reliability, and service to internal and external customers. Supply management involves the consolidation of certain business activities such as purchasing, transportation, warehousing, inventory control, quality assurance, and materials distribution into one management department. Strategic supply management, as referred to throughout this book, refers to the various tools, techniques, philosophies, and concepts that can be utilized in striving for a greater level of achievement and efficiency in a supply management and procurement environment.

But do most people really understand what these terms mean from an operational and process standpoint or from a *value opportunity* standpoint? Basic procurement practices of soliciting a minimum of three bids and writing a purchase order for the cheapest price may have the appearance of bringing value to an organization, and in many cases it does. However, there are risks with this type of procurement system, and an organization is most assuredly missing opportunities for increased or maximum value.

Even if your organization incorporates some or all of the concepts and philosophies available through strategic supply management, do you fully understand their implications to the success of your endeavors, the quality of your decisions, and the success of your organization? In this book we discuss supply management from a procurement perspective and focus on two of its key components: (1) supply chain management and (2) value chain management. We look at specific tools, processes, and skill sets that can be used to move individuals and organizations from *basic* procurement and supply activities to *best-in-class* strategic supply management. The concepts demonstrated here will help you achieve improved economies of scale, lower operation costs, higher profit margins, and an advantage over your competition.

Supply management is a concept and philosophy, within and of itself, that uses specialized tools and focuses on specific techniques and processes to maximize effectiveness and add value to an organization's procurement services. These activities produce increased profitability for an organization. Supply management and procurement are both cost centers in an organization's operational hierarchy, but *strategic* supply management and procurement also adds to an organization's profitability by engaging in processes beyond just basic procurement. Every dollar saved through effective procurement and supply management goes directly to the organization's bottom line.

You probably have heard the rule of thumb that the selling price of goods and services would have to be increased by five dollars to equal every dollar saved by procurement. The assumption for this statement is true; the amount would depend on how efficient an organization was and how effectively they practiced strategic supply management. Less efficient organizations would realize less benefit and more efficient organizations would realize more benefit. The beauty of this phenomenon is that less efficient organizations can become more efficient and profitable by changing their philosophies and culture and begin practicing strategic supply management and procurement. As the title suggests—*Supply Management and Procurement: From the Basics to Best-in-Class*—this book describes current basic procurement processes and operations. Additionally, it presents the tools and techniques that can be used to move to a strategic supply management and procurement role that will allow any organization to become best-in-class.

Supply management can be both *tactical* and *strategic*. Tactical procurement is a reaction to a need or requirement. Examples of tactical procurement are buying to replenish inventory or fulfill specific organizational requirements. Strategic procurement goes further by analyzing what the need is, how it fits into the organizational structure, and, most importantly, whether opportunities exist that might add extra value through operational reorganization and process improvement.

There are five main components of supply management and procurement that are the key performance drivers:

1. Cost
2. Quality
3. Time

4. Reliability
5. Technology

For an organization to realize and maximize the greatest value opportunity potential, it must consider *all* key performance drivers before making any decision regarding the selection of activities and processes that will be used in the strategy.

You may be asking 'Isn't supply management and purchasing the same thing?' Not necessarily. Supply management and purchasing are two different concepts although there can be some overlap. Supply management can be a separate business unit or it can be incorporated into the procurement business unit. Supply management encompasses much more than just purchasing. It can also involve logistics. Broadly defined, logistics is the management of the procurement and flow of goods and services along the supply chain from the point of origin to the point of consumption. This includes systems and infrastructure required for movement (transportation and material handling) and storage (inventory) of raw materials. It also includes parts, services, and finished goods that move through an organization and its outside channels to maximize performance and effectiveness. For the purpose of this book we approach supply management from the standpoint of being a function and process of the procurement business unit.

Purchasing—or procurement—is an entity on the organizational chart responsible for buying goods and services that the organization needs to carry out its business. How procurement performs its job determines the effectiveness and value it has to the organization. Basic functions performed by procurement and purchasing are:

- Supplier identification and selection
- Supply market research
- Bidding and buying (creating purchase orders)
- Negotiating and contracting
- Supplier measurement and performance

Supply management is a much broader concept. It manages the supply base in a progressive and aggressive manner. Although procurement frequently has ownership of supply management, it is actually a cross-functional approach and may involve representatives from the following entities, if applicable:

- Purchasing
- Receiving
- Warehousing and shipping
- Transportation
- Production or operations

- Maintenance
- Engineering
- Industrial engineering (IE)
- Marketing

Other pertinent business functions may also be added while others may be eliminated, depending on the type and structure of the business. The purpose of supply management is to identify, evaluate, select, and manage processes, suppliers, and customer relationships (both internal and external) to maximize and improve processes and efficiencies. It is a mandate of supply management to add extra value that will benefit the organization, through their actions, by improving profitability and creating competitive advantage.

As previously noted, two important components of supply management are supply chain management and value chain management. Supply chain management looks at all of the links in the supply chain from the birth of a product until its death—when it is sold or completely used up. It is a primary component of supply management, but it can also be practiced as a stand-alone process. Some companies might not choose to practice supply management as a total business unit, rather they may opt to incorporate supply chain management as part of their purchasing or procurement business unit. This is perfectly acceptable and depends entirely on the structure of the business.

There are many tools and resources used in a successful strategic supply management model and environment, including:

- **Price analysis:** Comparison of prices between suppliers and against external benchmarks with no direct knowledge of supplier costs.
- **Total cost analysis:** Includes additional costs associated with a buy or transaction such as the life of a part (mean time before failure), transportation, tariffs, special packaging (if applicable), warehousing (inventory), and quality control.
- **Total cost of ownership analysis:** The total value of all costs associated with an item over the life of the item. These costs include but are not limited to:
  - Purchase price—amount paid for the item
  - Acquisition costs—all costs incurred to acquire the item
    - Employee time and total compensation
    - Heat, light and power, telephone, building rent or cost, and other overhead
    - Internet and online procurement platforms and services
    - Engineering and/or implementation costs
    - Transportation costs, taxes, tariffs, and so forth
    - End-of-life and disposal costs

- Usage cost analysis—costs associated with converting or using the item or service
  - Receiving, stocking, storage, requisition, picking, and shipping costs
  - Installation (if applicable)
  - Removal and repair costs (if applicable)
- End-of-life cost analysis—costs associated with end-of-life and disposal
  - Removal or disposal costs
  - Shelf life expiration (write off)
  - Beyond economical repair determination (write off)
  - Hazmat costs (if applicable)
- **Financial analysis:** An analysis of suppliers' (bidders') financial capabilities and soundness that includes but is not limited to:
  - Dun & Bradstreet reports—D & B shows credit ratings, credit score, accounts payable, delinquency history, risk of failure by industry, and financial stress, among others
  - Annual reports—published annual reports of publicly held companies show:
    - Income statements
    - Balance sheets
    - Cash flow statements
    - Summary of how the company did the previous fiscal year and plans for forthcoming year(s)
  - Internal financial analysis—calculates financial risks, payback periods, and so forth and is typically performed by an organization's accounting and finance department
- **Technical Analysis:** An analysis of the physical characteristics of the item or service includes but is not limited to:
  - Meets organizational minimum requirements
  - Lead time
  - Reliability (average time before failure or other measure)
  - Repair turnaround time, if applicable

A strategic sourcing model or methodology is a good source for developing procurement project strategy. It is a process road map that helps identify strategy steps and keeps you on course throughout the project. A proven strategic sourcing methodology or model is presented in Chapter 9. Although we discuss this in more depth later, it is important to understand that when using models that cover more than the basics that all tasks listed in the model may not be used in every procurement project. Furthermore, some not listed may need to be added, depending on the needs of the procurement project and your organization. The model does cover most of the basics. There will always be variations since every procurement project is different and each will have its own peculiarities.

2

Managing Supply Management

In Chapter 1 the question of what supply management is was answered and examples of some of the strategic tools and techniques were presented. Now, and throughout this book, we are going to discuss how to specifically manage supply management and the procurement business unit to provide maximum efficiency, process improvement, and profitability to an organization.

There is a substantial distance between *basic* procurement and *best-in-class* strategic supply management. Basic is self-explanatory and is just that, basic. No frills, no extra effort, no real strategy, no extensive research, no in-depth analysis, simply get the job done and buy at the cheapest price. Basic does work for many organizations and it does supply some value. But the big secret is that doing more (strategic supply management) offers substantial benefits in the form of higher cost savings, improved efficiencies, and increased profitability for the organization.

Best-in-class describes an organization that is practicing strategic supply management to its maximum potential and is recognized as a leader in strategic supply management and procurement practices. It also means that a best-in-class organization is using its maximum potential to realize the greatest benefits and achieve a competitive advantage over its competition. They are leaving nothing on the table but rather taking it all. The purpose of this book is to present philosophies and processes that companies can use to become supply management best-in-class organizations.

The first step in managing supply management is to take a look at what you are managing now and how you are managing it. It is helpful to develop an activity and process map to help you understand what you are presently doing and how you are doing it. Activity and process maps are covered in more detail in Chapter 6. It is also beneficial to ask and answer questions about your current activities and processes.

Step 1. Determining current activities and processes:

- What are the current activities and processes that procurement is performing?
- Do we have and use a supply management philosophy and methodology in our present procurement operations?
  - What is it exactly?
- Do we use supply chain management?
  - Would using supply chain management be beneficial to my organization and add extra value and improve efficiencies?
  - What level of supply chain management are we practicing?
  - How efficient is our supply chain management?
- Do we use value chain management?
  - Would using value chain management be beneficial to my organization and add extra value, improve efficiencies, and allow me to recognize opportunities for improvement?
  - What level of value chain management are we practicing?
- Do we know the total costs of goods and services we are buying (price of goods plus other associated costs such as internal costs, procurement activities, transportation, warehousing, distribution, etc.)?
- Do we know the total cost of ownership of the goods and services?
  - Cost of money to purchase or lease
  - Cost in money, time, and resources of owning over the life of the goods or equipment
  - Depreciation
  - Inventory costs (receiving, warehousing, picking, and packaging)
  - Shipping and transportation costs to receive goods and deliver finished products to customers
  - Costs for setup, operation, ongoing maintenance (repairs), and disposal of goods or equipment
- Do we know the cost of raw materials and parts that our suppliers are paying to make the goods we buy from them?

Step 2. Developing a strategic supply management philosophy:

- What is our present organizational culture and will it support philosophical change?

- What level of supply management do we want to practice?
- Will practicing strategic supply management add extra value and improve efficiencies for our organization?
  - Review and learn all of the various tools and techniques that can be used in strategic supply management and determine which ones would have an application in your particular situation.
- What will be the estimated cost of reengineering the business unit and adding strategic supply management processes?
  - Initial costs
  - Ongoing costs

Step 3. Identifying organizational culture:

- What is the current organizational culture?
  - What is the organization's current mission statement?
  - What are the organization's current long-term strategies?
  - What are the organization's current goals?
- Is the current organizational culture compatible or comfortable with change?
- Will there be senior management support for changing practices and processes to add more value and improve efficiencies?

Step 4. Developing strategies for change:

- What is required to change the current organizational culture if needed?
  - What specifics of the organizational culture need to be changed?
- What resources would be required to develop and implement change?
- What is the estimated time line for change implementation?

Step 5. Business unit design:

- Based on what the current supply management or procurement activity and process maps show, what specific activities should be reengineered?
- What specific philosophies, techniques, activities, and processes should be added?
- What would the reengineered procurement business unit look like?
  - Create a redesigned activity and process map.
- Would new job functions and/or responsibilities be added?
  - What new job functions would be added?
  - What new responsibilities would be added?

- Develop and add policy and procedures for new job functions.
- What training will employees need for the new job functions?
- What would the new value targets and goals be for the procurement business unit?

Step 6. New process planning and implementation:

- What is an estimated preliminary time line for implementing the new business unit design?
  - Should the new design be implemented all at one time or phased in?
  - What and how much training will be required?
    - For management
    - For the business unit as a whole
    - For individual job functions and activities
- Will new software need to be added?
  - Identify software functions and types.
    - Is appropriate commercial off-the-shelf software available?
    - Will function-specific software need to be developed?
- Should procurement commodity groups be formed to manage specific families of commodities?

Now assume that you have asked and answered all of these questions. Let us also assume that you have determined a strategic supply management philosophy that would, in fact, add extra value to your organization and that the current organizational culture is compatible with desired changes in supply management and business unit reengineering. Additionally, let us also assume that you have the unconditional support of senior management in making those changes. This is the best case scenario for restructuring a procurement business unit to incorporate strategic supply management. Unfortunately it is not a perfect world and your organization, or portions thereof, might resist change. In this situation strategies should be developed to promote the changes needed. This is discussed in more detail with ideas on how to promote, implement, and manage change in an organization (see Chapter 20).

Back to our scenario where the stars and planets have aligned and you have a perfect situation that will allow you to develop and implement appropriate strategic supply management philosophies that will benefit and add additional value to your organization. In Step 1 you must determine how and why you are performing current procurement activities and processes. To do this you will have to do some research and background work. You should determine the *total* procurement picture of all activities and processes (not just a selected few) if reengineering the procurement business unit is desired.

The key questions are *how*, *what*, and *why*. Developing activity and process maps will tell you *how* and data mining will tell you *what*. To answer why you must determine what the present and past drivers are that led to the current procurement philosophy that you are practicing. To determine what you are presently managing you can run purchase histories from existing databases. The first thing you would want to know is what goods and services you are presently buying and what percentage of the total buy they represent. A hypothetical result of that information is illustrated in Figure 2.1.

Next you would want to know what percentage of the goods and services bought are critical, high usage, and/or high dollar. A hypothetical result of that information is shown in Figure 2.2.

This information (hypothetical) tells you that Pareto's 80–20 Rule applies. Vilfredo Federico Domaso Pareto was an Italian economist and philosopher who developed several economic theories and principles in the field of microeconomics. In essence, as it relates to supply management and procurement, Pareto's 80–20 Rule states that 80% of all goods and services bought

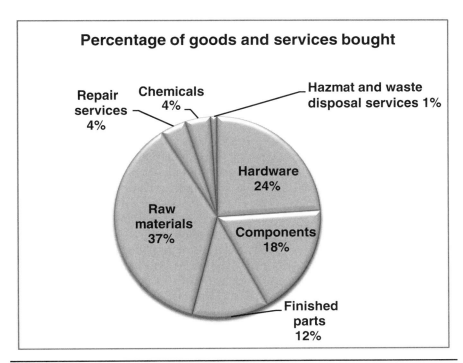

Figure 2.1   Percentage of goods and services purchased

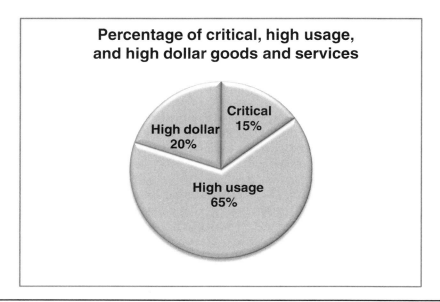

Figure 2.2   Percentage of critical purchases

will constitute 20% of the total cost spent and, conversely, 20% of all goods and services bought will constitute 80% of the total cost spent.

You need to know this information to determine how you will reengineer and strategically manage your procurement business unit. Remember, Rome wasn't built in a day, it was built over time. Some things may not need to be strategically managed or micromanaged initially, or maybe not at all. In the case of the purchase data presented, goods that were easily accessible and available from several suppliers may not be initial targets for strategic supply management. The first thing that you will want to target are items that are critical to your operations. Applying Pareto's Rule, our first main target would probably be the 20% of goods bought that constituted 80% of our costs. Our second target would be those goods critical to our operations that did not fall within the 20/80 parameters but did fall within the 80/20 parameters.

Selling the value and cost-saving benefits to senior management that a strategic supply management philosophy would add to your organization can sometimes be a monumental task. This is especially true if your organization and senior management are resistant to change. That is why you must develop a strategy to sell the change. Be ready to back up your recommendations with facts and justifications for change. Examples are also helpful. Even the most resistant organizations can be persuaded if you have a sound strategy. The key is to *show them the money.* In other words, the best justification is to show management the money that can be saved by practicing strategic supply management. It is hard for someone to say no to something that would reduce your costs, improve efficiencies, and increase profitability.

Management responsibility and structure will vary by organization and is dependent on the type and size of an organization. Locate a current organizational chart of your company. Does your organization have a chief procurement officer (CPO)? If not, what top-level position would be responsible for making strategic decisions regarding procurement and supply management? It is a good idea to know and understand management responsibility flowdown for supply management and procurement. If your organization does not employ some of the supply management strategies and techniques presented in this book it may be necessary to explain their value and justify the reasoning behind proposing new processes or changes to old ones when you present suggestions and models for improvement. In a procurement reengineering scenario, top management support is imperative whether it is the CPO, CFO, vice president, or director of purchasing. These individuals need to know the full impact and implications of practicing strategic supply management. From Mount Olympus (i.e. headquarters), strategic plans and goals are developed and passed along. But it will always be up to supply and procurement professionals to make the strategies and goals a reality.

3

Supply Chain Design and Planning

Supply chain management is a cooperative and systematic process that consists of many different business functions or activities that are combined and managed as one. It is an approach to the planning and control of materials and service flows from suppliers to end users. It attempts to cooperatively manage relationships between external firms and internal business functions in an effort to maximize the efficient use of resources to achieve the service and profit goals of an organization through the supply chain.

Supplies have always been managed in various ways by businesses, but the concept and philosophy of supply chain management as an overseer of the various business functions provides a central point and clearinghouse where the various functions can be managed more effectively and efficiently.

A supply chain consists of all of the groups, companies, and departments that touch or are touched in some way by the acquisition and use of goods and services. Its primary focus is on suppliers, supplier relationships, and the influence and/or impact of intermediaries, third-party service providers, internal business units, and customers.

Intermediaries and Third-party Service Providers

A successful and efficient supply chain management process not only looks at the suppliers that provide goods and services to the organization and get paid for them, but also looks at who supplies the supplier. In other words, identifying a supplier's Tier 1 and Tier 2 vendors enables a supply chain manager to evaluate a supplier's goods or services to better understand their supply and pricing structure (i.e., what they supply and why it is priced as it is). It is beneficial to know who a manufacturer is buying their raw materials or component parts from and what the market is for those materials.

The desire to obtain the lowest price is a driving force in all organizations. However, one must be constantly reminded that the best price does not always equate to best value. Although price will always be a major portion of any best value scenario and carry the highest weight and priority, choosing solely by lowest price can sometimes turn into a disaster and end up being more costly than higher bids. This is where doing due diligence and practicing strategic supply management wins the day. An organization that performs more than the basics of three bids and then taking the best price will always reap higher rewards in the end. A whole litany of strategic supply management tools and processes are available for an organization to use to determine what the best value for the organization might be. These various tools and processes are discussed in detail throughout this book.

A Case in Point

The usefulness of practicing strategic supply chain management can perhaps best be illustrated by using the Chinese drywall fiasco as an example. For several years the United States experienced a boom in construction and home sales. This boom was prompted by the devastation left in the wake of Hurricane Katrina and other storms as well as low interest rates and loose home mortgage requirements. This placed a strain on the usual domestic manufacture of drywall that is a staple in new construction and remodeling. Shortages and prices steadily increased and buyers of construction materials started looking for other, cheaper sources of drywall. They turned to international low-cost suppliers, including China, to fill their needs. Drywall is just drywall, right? Anyway, the prices for Chinese drywall were substantially cheaper than domestic drywall even with the added transportation cost and handling required. Chinese companies could crank it out as fast as distributors and builders could place orders so there was no shortage in the supply. This was a no-brainer. Cheaper prices and abundant supply equaled lower costs and higher profits. So let's pull the trigger and do it. And, they did. Chinese drywall started pouring into the United States from ports in Florida, New Orleans, Texas, New York, and California.

The results were, and are continuing to be, a disaster. Reports have estimated that between 2001 and 2007 over 20 million square feet of Chinese drywall was imported by the United States. Not long after its arrival and use, complaints started surfacing of harmful and pungent sulfur gases being emitted, copper wiring corroding, and damage to air conditioners, appliances, and other electrical apparatus. Everything inside the house was being contaminated. Some estimates have over 300,000 homes being affected. Well, it didn't take long for the finger-pointing and lawsuits to start. Homeowners suing builders, builders suing distributors, and distributors suing the manufacturers (good luck with that one). It will take years to sort everything out and the price tag could well run into the hundreds of millions of dollars.

How Did It Happen?

It happened because of a lack of strategic supply management methodology on the parts of builders and distributors, and perhaps a little greed thrown in. Lower prices and availability were the main drivers in this case example. The rush to obtain an abundant supply and a cheaper price will ultimately result in multiple millions of dollars paid in damages and replacement costs and could result in the ruin of many builders, distributors, and homeowners.

One significant problem is that no national or international standards for drywall composition exist. This is where the burden falls on the purchasing and supply professionals' shoulders. There was no standard by which to perform a comprehensive product comparison study. It therefore falls to the purchasing and supply professional to practice due diligence in conducting research, determining minimum requirements, quality standards, and quality control testing.

Anytime there is a deviation from normal procurement channels, it is even more important to know what you are buying, who you are buying from, and who the supplier is buying from. This is where supply chain design and management comes into play. Buyers should have dug deeper to find out the material and chemical composition of both domestic and foreign drywall and manufacturing processes. That would have given them a basis for comparison, and they would have been able to establish minimum requirements.

Another Supply Chain Management Example

Let's use petroleum as another example of the benefits of supply chain design and planning. A road builder has heavy equipment that uses diesel fuel. Other equipment, including trucks and generators, uses gasoline. The contractor has agreements with a local distributor to supply both diesel fuel and gasoline. The contractor did a good job negotiating the agreements and was able to include an escalator and de-escalator clause that is calculated by quarter to either increase or decrease the price per gallon paid as fuel prices go up or down. This is sound reasoning given the volatility and fluctuations in the petroleum market. It also lets the contractor know in advance what he will be paying each new quarter. But is that good enough? Most highway and road jobs are of long duration, and a miscalculation in fuel prices in the bid could have a major impact on costs and profit.

Petroleum is traded and paid for by the barrel. There is cost for the crude at the well head, transportation to the refinery, refining and processing costs, and transportation to the distributor. If the contractor knew what the price per barrel of oil was trading for, the time it took to process and refine it, and calculated the ratio of cost per barrel verses the cost per gallon, he could then track the costs per barrel and know, within a close percentage, exactly what he will pay per gallon at a future point in time.

As an example let's say that crude oil was trading for $65 per barrel and it took 28 days for a refinery to receive and process it into diesel fuel and gasoline and then deliver it to the distributor. A crack spread can be used to estimate the cost of a petroleum product, including refining. The *crack spread* is the cost of crude delivered to a refinery, inbound transportation, refining costs, and profit margins. Basically it is the difference in the cost of a petroleum future and a refined product's future. The crack spread for diesel fuel ranges from $8 to $12 per barrel. There are 42 gallons of crude per barrel. If crude is selling for $65 per barrel, add the crack spread you determined for what your geological region averages—let's use $12—and you have a cost of $77 per barrel. Divide this by 42 (the number of gallons per barrel) and it equals a wholesale price of $1.83 for a gallon of diesel fuel.

(Cost of petroleum per bbl + crack spread) ÷ 42 gal per bbl = wholesale price per gal

You can then add on other costs such as outbound transportation, handling fees, distributor profit, and so forth. These costs will vary due to several factors such as geographic location, which market the crude is traded on, refinery used, transportation distance and cost, among other factors. With a little work one can determine within a close degree of accuracy what the cost of a petroleum product will be a set number of days after the published market selling price of a barrel of crude. If someone was buying fuel on spot buys or on an as needed basis, they could develop a chart and have a fairly accurate estimate of what their cost would be at any given time. This is a real strategic advantage when bidding jobs of short duration. In the case of the contractor with a job of long duration, by tracking the per barrel price of crude over time and researching what market experts say about the present and future price of crude per barrel, a forecast of what prices might be at a given point in time in the future could be developed that would be beneficial when bidding jobs of long duration.

Keep in mind that all forecasts are just future estimates—or guesses—and not always accurate. Therefore, allowance would need to be made that took this fact into consideration when negotiating a term fuel contract. Price escalators and de-escalators based on market price may be an adequate and sufficient way to manage this risk. Some organizations that use large quantities of fuel may also use *hedging* as a way to mitigate risk. In our petroleum and fuel example, hedging might be used to reduce or eliminate risk of fluctuations in price by purchasing offsetting crude or fuel futures. In other words, if we had a fuel contract for the purchase of diesel fuel based on a price of $2.45 per gallon and we projected that the price for crude was declining and was expected to continue to decline, we might consider buying diesel fuel futures at $2.25 per gallon.

Tracking and knowing the costs of suppliers' raw materials is the first step in designing and planning the supply chain. This is one of the techniques that best-in-class organizations use to obtain best value and competitive advantage. We will get into more specific examples of supply chains that are used in the case studies that follow this chapter. The case studies present facts already known and results of research performed. They also ask questions, present options, and explain ramifications of possible decisions, if made. The case studies are an attempt to help the reader better understand how advanced strategic processes work and show the benefits of using them.

Supply Chain Design

The supply of raw materials, parts, and services is made up of more than a buyer receiving a requisition, bill of goods, or material request and then obtaining three bids and writing a purchase order. It involves identifying everyone and everything that has, might have, or could have an influence on both short- and long-term supply requirements.

The procurement division of a large corporation might have several different purchasing departments within their division such as General Purchasing, Critical Purchasing, Transportation Sourcing, Strategic Sourcing, and Commodity Groups. Each has their own specialty and place in procurement and, even though their functions may be different, their goal is the same—bringing maximum value to the organization. They all should use the same fundamental purchasing concepts and techniques. They each have an opportunity to complement the other in the performance of their individual duties and combined bring greater total value to the organization.

This is referred to as *coordinated supply management*. Coordinated supply management is where individual departments or business units operate independently but share information on prices, new technology, supplier performance, materials or service reliability, and other important and intrinsic information. This allows the supply manager to understand the total picture of what they are buying, what the organization is paying, who they are buying from, and how efficiently they are performing their responsibilities. Some best-in-class organizations maintain a master database. All information is fed into it by the individual departments who also have access to the information from all of the other departments. This concept is usually part of a materials requirement planning or a more advanced enterprise resource planning system. But there are also other methods and ways to manage the sharing of information.

Using commodity groups as an example of how coordinated supply chain management can be used, let us first identify what a purchasing commodity group is and what they do. A purchasing commodity group consists of various personnel with different job functions grouped together to manage a specific family of commodities such as metal, hardware, or plastics. They might consist of inventory planners, expediters, warranty oversight, reliability analysts, or purchase buyers. A purchasing commodity group would include any and all personnel and all job functions in one unit that might pertain to the management of purchased goods and services needed and used by an organization in their operations. A simple example of a commodity group is shown in Figure 3.1.

The function of a purchasing commodity group is to have ownership of their particular commodity family and make sure sufficient inventory of the right parts, materials, and services exists in the right places, are purchased at the right times, and at a price that adds value to the organization. In other words, it is their responsibility to oversee and *manage* their commodity families.

Supply chain management can be useful in managing a commodity more efficiently. They recognize and forecast cost trends, material shortages (and consequently part shortages), inventory control, on-time deliveries, and supplier performance. Let us say that a raw material, such as aluminum, is in short

Figure 3.1 Commodity group personnel

supply. Prices are up and are forecasted to continue to rise. A review of critical, high usage and high dollar parts that are made of aluminum would then be a prudent consideration. Any part or component that is critical, high usage, or high dollar should have a supply chain mapped for that commodity. A supply chain map consists of the identification of external suppliers, internal departments, and external customers that are touched or affected by or that might have an effect or impact on a particular commodity or service. Each entity is a *link*, in succession, in the chain of the supply of a commodity or service. Once a supply chain is identified for a commodity or service, it can then be checked and revised periodically or used regularly to improve processes, reduce cost of purchasing, and reduce carrying excess inventory as well as predict future trends in supply and price.

Later in this book we will be doing several case studies where it will be your responsibility, as part of a procurement project team, to look at a request to buy goods or services that are required by an organization. You will be asked to develop a strategic sourcing methodology to determine the most cost-effective solution that will lend the most value to your organization. Examples of supply chain maps that show various links in the supply chain for the commodity or service looked at will be supplied for each case study. For now we will take a quick peek at a simple supply chain.

Let's look at and discuss a simplified supply chain for metal. We will use the supply chain that was mapped for Case Study 2 to help us understand how the supply chain map was planned and designed, why various links were used, and its importance to supply chain management. Look at Figure 3.2 to get an idea of how a supply chain is constructed and what it looks like.

Procurement is a link in the supply chain and is usually located somewhere in the middle of the chain, although in our example it appears as the next to last link. In a manufacturing organization there would be both inbound and outbound transportation; inbound appearing as a link upstream of procurement and outbound appearing downstream of procurement. Remember, a supply chain starts with the birth of a product and ends with its death (i.e., when it is used up or delivered to its final destination). Every link that precedes procurement is said to be *upstream* and every link that follows procurement is said to be *downstream*. One should always start at the beginning—or the birth—when designing and creating a supply chain map.

The parts that we need to purchase are made of aluminum, therefore we need to look at the source for the raw materials required to make the parts.

Aluminum Ore Mine Link

Aluminum mills and smelters buy aluminum direct from the mine or through brokers, although some of the larger mills may own their own mines. Direct mining costs, transportation, smelting, processing, and milling all add to the

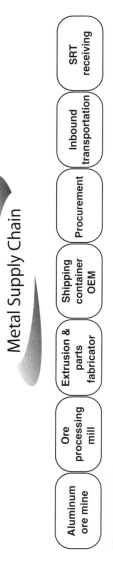

Figure 3.2   Metal supply chain

final costs of processed raw aluminum ingots and pellets. A mill may also perform rolling and extruding processes to produce the final parts we require, or may sell the aluminum ingots or pellets to an extruder. Knowing the costs of raw aluminum ore is important in understanding what makes up the final costs and supply of the parts that make the product we desire. A best-in-class organization will track these costs over time to know what prices have been historically, in what direction (up or down) they are trending, and to forecast what they might be for a specific time frame in the future. Doing this helps identify optimum times to do forward spot buying or negotiate long-term supply contracts. Knowing this information is also important if existing contracts have escalator and de-escalator clauses.

Ore Processing Mill Link

The second link in our supply chain would be the mill where the raw ore is processed, the impurities removed, and any additional metals or chemicals added to make alloys. The cost of the final processed aluminum and extrusions is the price the example shipping container original equipment manufacturer (OEM) in Case Study 2 would pay for the parts needed in the assembly of the shipping containers if the mill also does extruding and/or makes the parts. This scenario would eliminate the third link in the example supply chain map. If the mill or OEM does not make the parts we need, the mill sells the raw aluminum to an extruder or fabricator. Either scenario adds costs to the final price we will pay for our parts. As explained in the first link of the chain, these costs should be tracked over time to build a history of prices and develop forecasts. In the case of aluminum it can be tracked in a number of ways such as aluminum ore, processed raw aluminum (ingots and pellets), roll, sheet, and wire, for example. As in the first link, this information is important for managing and negotiating contracts. As we design and build our supply chain, we now have two links of the supply chain and two cost references.

Extrusion and Parts Fabricator Link

The third link in our supply chain example would be the extrusion and parts fabrication if the mill does not also extrude and make the parts. The cost of the extrusions and parts sold to the shipping container OEM now gives us three links in the supply chain and three cost references.

Shipping Container OEM Link

The fourth link in our example is the shipping container OEM referenced in Case Study 2 from whom we would buy the fully assembled shipping containers. An OEM is the entity that manufactures or makes a finished product, whether it is a single piece item or one made from many different parts and components. This cost is the easiest identifiable cost because it is the one for which we would receive bids. It would include the cost of the aluminum, polycarbonate, hardware (screws, rivets, etc.), labor, and anything required and used for a fully assembled shipping container delivered to our organization. This gives us the fourth link in our example and a fourth cost reference.

Procurement Link

The fifth link in our supply chain example is procurement. The procurement process represents a cost to the organization and affects profitability. For this reason the procurement link of the supply chain should also develop an *activity process map*. Chapter 6, Activity Process and Design, will provide a good illustration of the types of processes and activities required to purchase materials, parts, and services. Procurement of parts, supplies, and materials all have activity costs associated with them and is the fifth cost reference in our supply chain.

Inbound Transportation Link

The sixth link in our supply chain example is inbound transportation to our designated facility. Inbound transportation is a cost ultimately paid by the buyer, whether scheduled and paid directly by the buyer or calculated in, and made part of a suppliers' bid. Even if an organization owns its own transportation equipment, the costs of owning and operating them are usually charged against materials and parts delivered to the organization. If an organization relies on the seller to provide transportation or arranges its own transportation, the delivered free on board (FOB) or delivered duty paid (DDP) price is a cost included as part of the total purchase. FOB designates when the title to goods transfers to the buyer. DDP is an *Incoterm*. Incoterms are a set of internationally agreed to standards governing international shipments, transportation, and title transfer. DDP would apply for shipments coming into or going out of the United States from or to foreign companies. There are several types of FOB designations and Incoterms. A list of FOB designations and Incoterms with definitions are included in the reference portion of this book for your convenience (Appendix B). This gives us the sixth link in our example and a sixth cost reference.

Ship Right Transportation Receiving Link

The seventh and final link in our supply chain example is Ship Right Transportation receiving. This is the point when our example organization receives the delivery of the shipping containers and they are inspected for damages and compliance to specification requirements, and are then accepted or rejected.

This supply chain example is a simple, brief explanation of what comprises supply chains. The links in a supply chain would depend on the activities or functions of the organization, the type of commodity or service that was purchased, and the activities or functions downstream of procurement such as manufacturing and assembly, warehousing, transportation, and so forth.

Let us review what we have discussed so far. The main purpose of designing and mapping a supply chain is to identify the various steps (links) involved in the supply management and procurement processes. The reason we want to know this is to allow the identification of any obstacles, changes, and potential bottlenecks in the process. It also helps us understand the activities and costs that make up the product or service that we are purchasing. Another reason for mapping the supply chain is to aid in looking for opportunities for process efficiency improvement and value increases.

The cost and prices we discovered in the first three links of the supply chain example make up the costs to the shipping container OEM as shown in Figure 3.3.

The price we paid to the shipping container OEM includes his costs for all materials, labor, and his profit plus the cost of inbound transportation. Indirect costs would include the process and activity costs of procurement itself, Ship Right receiving, inventory storage, and outbound transportation to their shipping hubs and facilities. All of these combined would make up the total costs of goods and services purchased as shown in Figure 3.4.

Figure 3.3   Costs to shipping container OEM

Figure 3.4   Total cost of shipping containers

Why Do I Need to Know the Direct and Indirect Costs of a Product or Service?

It is all about adding maximum value to the organization that increases profitability and aids in obtaining competitive advantage. Knowing all of the costs involved in a purchase allows the supply manager to look for opportunities and ways to improve efficiencies and profitability for the organization. Opportunity is the key word here. Understanding and knowing what costs comprise the price an organization pays for goods and services allows the supply manager to identify opportunities for value improvement when they present themselves.

One example of an opportunity would be the identification of possible *linkage* of goods or services. Let us use aluminum as our example again. Aluminum was a key component in the manufacture of the shipping containers the example company bought. The supply manager knows that his organization buys many other parts and equipment made using aluminum. Shells and bracing used in their transportation trailers and customized conveyor and material handling equipment are just two of the items that they buy consistently with aluminum components. They also have repair facilities that buy aluminum parts and components to make repairs to damaged trailers and shipping containers. They buy all of their conveyor and material handling equipment from a small fabricating company.

The supply manager recognizes an opportunity for linkage of all aluminum parts and components. The supply manager performs a value or a value opportunity analysis to determine opportunities for process improvement and additional cost savings. A master purchase agreement could be negotiated with a primary extrusion vendor of aluminum and stainless steel who is a master distributor for Alcoa Aluminum as well as other mills and extruders. This scenario presents several opportunities and options:

- By negotiating a master purchase agreement for a greater supply of aluminum parts with an extrusion vendor, the supply manager could obtain a better pricing structure for a larger amount of parts than the shipping container OEM or equipment fabricator could individually. This cost savings could be made available to both, thereby reducing their costs of manufacture and ultimately reducing the total end cost to the example company. This would be a win-win for all parties.

- A master purchase agreement could also benefit the example company directly by reducing the price paid for repair and replacement parts used internally as well as the cost of the shipping containers.

- Taking it one step further, the example company might also explore the possibility of negotiating a master purchase agreement for polycarbonate required in the shipping containers. Aluminum and polycarbonate make up 98% of a shipping container with polycarbonate having the highest percentage. The supply manager might then consider extending polycarbonate pricing to the shipping container OEM, as in the aluminum scenario, or consider buying both commodity components and then having a third party assemble the shipping containers for them, bypassing the OEM altogether. This would be considered an *outsourcing* strategy.

The point of all of these examples is this—opportunities for process and value improvement do exist but you have to look for them. Knowing *how* to recognize opportunities is the difference between basic supply management and procurement and best-in-class. The commodity group concept may or may not be used in your organization, but there should be a leader or focal group, a department or team that has ownership of supply chain identification, planning, and design. It might be the strategic sourcing department (if one exists), a mid-level individual (usually the supply manager), or someone in senior management who has ownership, but there should be someone or some entity that is in charge and has ownership responsibility.

What Has This Got To Do With Coordinated Supply Chain Management

Everything! For example, the commodity group is comprised of various individuals with different and specific job duties and responsibilities such as planning inventory, buying goods and services, and so on. As a group, they have ownership of specific commodities and it is their combined responsibility to manage them. Other departments or divisions within the organization might buy similar goods and services or buy different items but from the same supplier. If different departments or divisions do not know what each is buying and from whom, they are missing an important opportunity for practicing strategic supply management and procurement. Having a coordinated supply chain management strategy and system allows an organization to take full advantage of the information and resources that exist within the organization. Now you may think a suggestion is being made to move to a centralized supply and procurement system. Not so. A coordinated supply chain management strategy can work in a decentralized supply and procurement system just fine. The key to either system's effectiveness is the sharing of supply and procurement information.

One of the main results of a coordinated supply chain management strategy is having a *full* and complete understanding of what the organization's requirements are and what it buys, *in total*. Knowing this allows better supply chain planning and design. The opportunity for *linkage*, then, presents itself. Linkage is the combining or linking of the purchase of identical goods and services within an organization or, perhaps, different goods and services purchased by an organization from the same or multiple suppliers. Linkage produces *leverage*. By combining all goods and services (linking) purchased by an organization, the strategy and tactic of leveraging the separate buys into one contract or with one supplier is one way to substantially increase gained value. (The example of combining purchases to reduce costs and gain greater value was used in the aluminum scenario.)

One example is a scenario where a department of an organization is buying a part, let's call it a DooJiggy, that has many OEMs and available suppliers. There is competition between suppliers for your business and the bidding is competitive. The organization is also buying a different but distinct part from ABC Company. This part is critical to the organization's operations and is a high dollar item. ABC is the sole source for it. It has been discovered through sharing supply and procurement information and strategic supply chain planning and design mapping that ABC is also one of the suppliers and bidders of the Doojiggy. Knowing this presents the opportunity for linking the two parts and leveraging a total greater value buy from ABC, reducing the cost of the critical part and obtaining better pricing of the DooJiggy. Linkage and leverage are just two of the benefits of a coordinated supply chain management strategy and the supply chain planning and design that best-in-class organizations employ in their supply management and procurement philosophies and processes.

Keep in mind that supply chain planning and design will look different at the various levels of an organization. The supply chain mapped for a single commodity purchased by a single department will look different from one mapped for combined purchases from several departments. This is where a coordinated supply chain management strategy and system can add to effective, productive, and successful supply chain planning and design. Case Studies 1 and 2 follow this chapter and gives the opportunity to apply some of the concepts we have discussed thus far and, further, to think about what strategic supply management tools and techniques can be used by an organization to achieve best-in-class in procurement.

Case Study 1—Made Better Manufacturing

Made Better Manufacturing is a hypothetical company that manufactures a variety of parts that it sells to other suppliers and manufacturers. The mainstay or primary product of the company is DooJiggys. Made Better has been successful as a company and is the recognized leader in DooJiggy manufacture. However, in the past several years competition has been growing to the point that Made Better is now being challenged by two of its competitors.

Due to stiffer competition, market share and revenue have been steadily declining. Prices for raw materials, transportation, and energy have also steadily increased. The combination of these factors is having an effect on the profitability of the company. The purchasing manager of Made Better has been asked if purchasing has any suggestions for improvement. Made Better practices basic procurement—nothing fancy—and it has always worked effectively for them in the past. The present structure of the procurement department consists of a number of buyers and other assorted personnel that support the buyers' function and procurement processes. Some contracts for the supply of goods and services are bid and negotiated, but the majority of purchases are made by the buyers soliciting bids and issuing purchase orders. All purchase orders, even those for contracted items, are written manually by the buyers. Invoices from suppliers are submitted directly to, and paid by, the accounting department. The purchasing manager oversees the overall procurement operation and is involved directly when negotiations of any type are required. A purchasing supervisor runs the actual day-to-day operations and approves all purchases made by the buyers.

The purchasing manager has decided to evaluate Made Better's purchasing procedures to determine, using a basic approach, if any opportunities exist for cost reduction and process improvement that will add additional value to the operation.

DooJiggys are made entirely from rubber, which is a petroleum-based by-product. Although supply chain management is not currently employed by the procurement department, the purchasing manager has decided to look at who and what is involved in the purchase of goods and services used to manufacture DooJiggys. The purchasing manager begins by identifying the DooJiggy supply chain for Made Better. Figure CS1.1 is a descriptive example of what the purchasing manager found.

In most instances, purchasing and procurement services are located in or around the middle of the supply chain. All links prior to or preceding purchasing are said to exist *upstream* of purchasing and all links after purchasing and procurement services are said to be *downstream*. Remember, hypothetically the supply chain begins at the birth of a product or service and flows through the purchasing processes until the product or services death (when it is sold and delivered or consumed).

You will notice that in this example the supply chain starts at the distributor that sells the rubber raw material to Made Better and ends with outbound logistics. It does not define specifics of the individual links. This is considered basic supply chain management. It does work on a limited basis and can add some value to the supply management and procurement process as we will see as we work through this case study.

These are the links of Made Better's supply chain (simplified) that were identified. The purchasing manager is now ready to perform a supply chain analysis. The research performed shows the following facts:

- Made Better does not have a formal transportation department that bids, negotiates, and contracts for transportation.
- Raw rubber is purchased solely from Dexter Distributors. Dexter has been a long time reliable vendor and the purchasing department buys from them on a regular, as needed basis. No contract exists but Dexter guarantees a dedicated, on-hand inventory of the specific requirements needed by Made Better.
- Inbound transportation for raw materials is purchased from ABC Trucking. ABC only has flatbed trailer trucks and their rate is $1.40 per mile. Made Better pays for transportation on an FOB destination basis. Dexter negotiates the rates and pays the freight, which is included in their invoices to Made Better.
- Inbound transportation for maintenance, repair, and operating supplies (MRO) parts and supplies, as well as piece parts, is purchased from DEF Cartage and GHI Transportation. Both have box trailers only and both charge by dimensional weight (DIM weight) which is $0.45 per pound. DIM weight is calculated by multiplying the height of a package by the width and length and dividing by the weight (in pounds). Made Better pays each supplier of parts and supplies on an FOB destination basis. Each supplier bids, negotiates, and contracts for transportation in each situation and includes the rates and details of the freight movement in their invoices to Made Better.

Figure CS1.1   Basic DooJiggy supply chain for Made Better

- Made Better's Industrial Engineering (IE) department has determined that the average cost for receiving, stocking, and warehousing preproduction materials is $1.47 per part.
- Purchasing has a manual purchase order system. All purchase orders are key-entered by buyers, and shipments are tracked manually as well. IE has determined the cost for this process is $165.75 per purchase order. It consists of employee wages and benefits, supplies, associated utilities (heat, light, and power), and other overhead particular to the purchasing department.
- IE has determined that the average per unit cost for picking, packaging, palletizing, warehousing, and preparing assembled DooJiggys for shipment is $1.87.
- Outbound transportation of assembled and packaged for distribution DooJiggys is purchased from XYZ Express and also by Made Better's own fleet of trucks and drivers. XYZ owns both flatbed and box trailers, but since DooJiggys are packaged and palletized, they are only shipped in box trailers. Made Better's own trucks are all box trailers and are used exclusively for the delivery of finished DooJiggys within a defined region. Made Better pays XYZ by DIM weight, which is $0.38 per pound. IE has calculated that Made Better's cost of using its own trucks and drivers is $0.65 per pound.

Based on these facts and findings, identify where purchasing might realize cost savings and process improvement that could bring more value to Made Better's operations by reducing internal and external costs and keeping Made Better competitive in this tightening market. A recap of the different links in the supply chain follows. You may or may not see an opportunity for improvement in each of the links. Answers to this exercise can be found in Appendix A. This is a beneficial exercise to determine if you fully understand the concepts of basic supply chain management and how using it can add value to your organization.

Supply chain links:

- Raw material purchase
- Inbound logistics

- Purchasing
- Production operations
- Inventory and warehousing
- Outbound logistics

Case Study 1—Questions to Consider

1. Based on the findings, which supply chain links and value chain activities did you identify that might be candidates to add more value?
2. List what those opportunities are.
3. Are any of the supply chain links and value chain activities and functions you chose candidates for process improvement or outsourcing?
4. List all opportunities.
5. What links in the supply chain and value chain activities are candidates for process improvement or outsourcing?
6. Explain why they are new opportunities.
7. Give a brief description of your thoughts on how the supply chain links and value chain activities you identified might be candidates for process improvement.

Case Study 2—Ship Right Transportation

Ship Right Transportation is a major air transportation package and cargo shipping and handling company. Ship Right operations has determined that there is a need to buy 100 new unit load devices (ULDs) to fulfill additional requirements generated by the acquisition of new aircraft. ULDs are the metal and plastic containers that packages and nonpalletized cargo are placed in for loading onto aircraft for shipment. They are classified domestically by the Federal Aviation Administration according to size and type. The primary considerations for the purchase would be initial purchase price, weight, reliability (durability and availability), and maintenance (repair) costs.

In a simplistic, basic purchasing environment a material request would be issued with the requirements of the buy project such as type, part number, and description (in this case size). This is a perfect example of *tactical* procurement, a reaction to a need. A buyer would identify three or more qualified suppliers and issue a request for quote (RFQ). When all the bids were received, the supplier with the best price would be issued a purchase order.

In a strategic supply management environment, an analysis of the identified need would be performed. Elements of this analysis are:

- Determination of what is driving the need.
  - Is this a one-time buy or will additional similar or different ULDs be required in the near future?
- Review of existing inventory.
- Research to determine what the ULD component parts and materials are.
  - Industry market research performed to determine.
- Identification of current, historical, and forecasted cost of raw materials and supplies.
- Identification of industry trends, new products, and new technology.
- A purchase history report is run to determine how many ULDs of this particular type have been purchased in the past, from what suppliers, and at what cost. Cost trends are identified and charted.

- Review of historical repair cost is conducted.
  - Analysis of historical repairs is performed by repair type and cost.
- Identification and mapping of the ULD supply chain.
  - Who is affected in some way by the item or service, including companies, internal departments, and customers?
- Identification and mapping of the ULD value chain.
  - Identify primary activities
  - Identify support activities
  - Perform a value opportunity analysis
- Identification of opportunities to improve processes and/or costs.

Ship Right Transportation is a large company that operates and conducts business both domestically and internationally. The procurement department does practice supply management and uses some strategic supply management tools and techniques in its operation. There are several independent purchasing activity departments within the procurement department that do an adequate job of working together and sharing information although there is no formal established procedure. A procurement initiative team has been formed consisting of the stakeholder (project requestor), procurement, finance, and resources from industrial engineering (IE), ULD container control and planning, and the ULD container repair facility. For purposes of this exercise we will assume that procurement has conducted market research on the subject and solicited information from the resources identified. Additionally, they have reviewed presentations of the products and capabilities offered by the qualified bidders. This information is necessary to make an informed *best value* recommendation to the organization. A summary of research results performed by procurement is included with this case study. It contains information and particulars to aid in the decision-making process.

It is now up to the procurement initiative team to review the research, select qualified bidders, issue a RFQ, and perform the necessary analysis to make a decision for the best value recommendation that will be presented to the organization. It is always wise to have a backup. Once you have determined what the best value buy decision is, make sure you have identified what the second best value buy option and decision is. The ideal approach is to list all of the possible buy scenarios from best value to least value after you have performed your evaluation and analysis. A risk analysis to identify potential risks along with risk mitigation recommendations should also be part of your evaluation. Make sure you understand all of the information gathered and be prepared to defend your recommendation.

Biases and favoritism come into play in choosing a supplier. Some people have their favorite suppliers and processes based on past business experiences. Even though a supplier may be an incumbent or current supplier and has supplied excellent goods or services and reliability in the past, it does not mean they should receive any preferential consideration. When any good or service is bid a level and fair playing field and bidding environment should exist so that all bidders will have an equal opportunity to present their proposal for winning the bid. By promoting equality among bidders, you will improve your chances of obtaining a greater value for your organization. This keeps incumbents honest and competitive and allows you to learn new technology advances in other products and services.

Shipping container research discovery results:

- Ship Right developed a procurement model that is used by ULD container control and planning to calculate the projected number and type of shipping containers needed every time increases in the shipping volume reaches a new milestone. The model also projects additional ULD requirements each time a new aircraft is acquired and placed into service. One new aircraft has been acquired by Ship Right and this is the basis for the request by operations to buy 100 new ULD shipping containers.
  - This model does not take into account the number of shipping containers held in existing inventory at transportation hubs and customer locations.
  - A review of the fixed asset books showed that Ship Right owned 35,609 shipping containers at all locations worldwide. These are shipping containers previously purchased by Ship Right over the years.
- Shipping containers are made primarily of aluminum, stainless steel, and polycarbonate plastic.
  - The aluminum and stainless steel are specific extruded shapes of designated alloys and tempers.
  - The polycarbonate plastic's brand name is Lexan and is produced by GE Plastics.
- A purchase history report shows that over the last three years one vendor, ABC Containers, has received 80% of Ship Right's business for new shipping container purchases. The balance of spend went to XYZ.
  - A total of 10,538 shipping containers have been purchased in the preceding two years at a total cost of $45.3M dollars. This is an average cost of $4299 per shipping container.
- A repair history report shows that over the last three years repair costs for ABC Containers totaled $27.6M for 125,471 repairs. This is an average cost of $220 per repair.
- A repair report showed 10 parts constituted 85% of all metal repairs.
- Another repair report showed that six parts constituted 90% of all plastic repairs.
- A supply chain was identified for shipping containers. It is descriptively portrayed from the origin of raw materials to the end user (Ship Right),

and a supply chain was mapped for each specific supply chain as illustrated in Figures CS2.1, CS2.2, and CS2.3. The links in each chain represent the most cost in the manufacturing process and after-market support for the shipping containers.

- Research by IE found that an additional 2000 shipping containers were stored on Ship Right's property that were acquired in an acquisition of another transportation company in the preceding year. These ULDs were not listed in the fixed asset books because they were not the exact same configuration and style number as the standard shipping containers used by Ship Right, although the overall dimensions and other specifications were the same.
  - Ship Right uses a shipping container with a narrow front door opening and a roll up door.
  - The shipping containers acquired in the acquisition have a fully open front and a canvas flap over the door with cargo netting to secure

Figure CS2.1   Shipping container metal supply chain

Figure CS2.2   Shipping container Lexan supply chain

Figure CS2.3   Shipping container repair supply chain

cargo held within the container. All other dimensions are exactly the same as the standard shipping containers used by Ship Right and the specifications of metal and polycarbonate parts are also the same.

- Shipping containers are not retained solely at individual Ship Right locations but travel throughout the world. The ULD tracking system that Ship Right has in place uses a bar code located on the container itself and a scanning system that records when a container reaches and departs specific locations and it is accurate and adequate for their needs.

- A value chain identifying primary and support activities of the procurement and operational processes was developed (see Figure CS2.4).

- A value opportunity analysis was then performed to determine the opportunities for process improvement and additional cost savings. The following were identified as potential opportunities:

  - A master purchase agreement could be negotiated with GE Plastics that would reduce the raw material cost of Lexan sheets by 120%. GE Plastics could also fabricate (cut and drill) the Lexan sheets to the shape and dimension required that would further reduce the costs of fabrication and assembly.

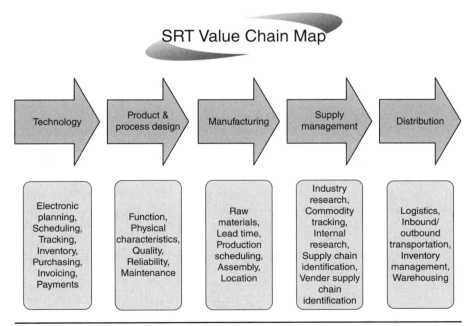

Figure CS2.4 Ship Right value chain map

- o Ship Right could pass these savings on to the ULD vendor that was awarded a contract reducing their material and labor costs and thus should translate to a lower purchase price for Ship Right.
- A master purchase agreement could be negotiated with a primary extrusion vendor of aluminum and stainless steel that is a master distributor for Alcoa Aluminum, as well as other mills and extruders.
  - o Ship Right could pass these savings on to the ULD vendor that was awarded a contract reducing material cost and purchase price to Ship Right.
- Ship Right could purchase prefabricated metal and plastic parts directly from original manufacturers and assemble the ULD containers themselves.
- Ship Right could purchase prefabricated metal and plastic parts from original manufacturers and hire a third-party company (backshop) to assemble shipping containers for them.
- Industry research resulted in the determination that there are seven vendors that can both make and repair shipping containers. After qualification, it was determined that four vendors met all of the criteria required by the operation's stakeholder and all four will be issued an RFQ. These vendors are:
- ABC Containers (incumbent)
- XYZ
- DEF Air
- KLM
- An RFQ was prepared and issued to the four qualified bidders. Responses were received and analyzed. A summary of the bids follows:
- ABC: located in CA, USA—bid $4120 each FOB at Ship Right
- XYZ: located in CA, USA—bid $4096 each FOB at Ship Right
- DEF: located in Holland—bid $4418 each FOB at Ship Right, USA
- KLM: located in Norway and China—bid $2992 each delivery duty paid (DDP) to Ship Right, USA
- KLM owns and operates a mill in Norway and makes aluminum and stainless steel extrusions and sheets that they use to make their shipping containers. Parts are also sold to other shipping container manufacturers.
- KLM has shipping container assembly points in Norway, China, and Texas, USA
  - o Shipping containers assembled in China could be inducted into the Ship Right system at their transportation hub in Japan. This would further reduce their bid price to $1890 DDP each, but it is not included in the decision matrix used to determine best value.
- A capability comparison analysis was developed to compare products, specifications, and price.

Based on the facts presented in the capability comparison analysis, a weighted procurement decision matrix was prepared (see Tables CS2.1 and CS2.2).

What Do I Do Now?

Although Ship Right does practice some strategic supply management techniques, tracking the price of critical and key commodities used in their operations is not performed. However, in this particular procurement buy project, procurement performed research to determine the market stability, supply availability, and price forecast for metal. This was used as background information only and not made a consideration in the decision-making process as the buy requirement was a one-time buy and did not require extended or future buy requirements.

All of the information needed to make an informed decision has been assembled and presented. The procurement initiative team led by procurement has performed all necessary research and analysis and the team is now ready to make a best value decision to present to the organization. There are three viable alternatives to consider in determining the best value decision for Ship Right:

1. Strictly from a purchase standpoint, the research and decision matrix showed that KLM was the best value buy.
2. An alternative approach is to negotiate master purchase agreements with a metal extruder and parts fabricator to manufacture parts to Ship Right specifications and with GE Plastics to have them supply the Lexan cut and drilled to Ship Right specifications. An agreement could then be negotiated with a third-party vendor (outsourced) to receive the parts and pieces and assemble the shipping containers for Ship Right. This offers a lower cost per container than the lowest purchase price.
3. With the discovery of the 2000 shipping containers obtained from the acquisition of another shipping company, another option has become available for Ship Right. Since all dimensions and specifications are the same as its standard shipping containers, with the exception of the fully open front as opposed to a narrow door, Ship Right could use 100 of that particular inventory and not incur any cost. This decision would have to be contingent on IE and operations accepting the new configuration containers. If an agreement was obtained, Ship Right would have the 100 shipping containers that they need now at no cost. Additionally, they would have a reserve inventory supply of 1900 additional containers to draw from for future expansion milestones and for the replacement of existing shipping containers as they become obsolete or damaged beyond economical repair.

Table CS2.1 ULD shipping container RFQ bid product comparison analysis

SRT Minimum Requirements	ABC	XYZ	DEF	KLM
Part Number	4655-215	SC2122	DEF614	K4692
Outside Dims (L × W × H)	130″ × 60″ × 64″	130″ × 60″ × 64″	130″ × 60″ × 63.5″	130″ × 60″ × 64″
Maximum Gross Weight	3175 kg./7000 lbs	3175 kg./7000 lbs	3175 kg./7000 lbs	3175 kg./7000 lbs
Tare Weight	360 lbs	358 lbs	391 lbs	361 lbs
Approximate Internal Volume	252 cu ft	253.8 cu ft	235 cu ft	256 cu ft
Base Material-Alloy/Temper	7075-T6	7075-T6	7075-T6	7003-T6 (weldable)
Base Material Thickness	0.159″	.154 ″	0.157″	0.158″
Base Edge Rail Material	6351-T6	6061-T6	7003-T5	7003-T6 (weldable)
Roof Material	5052H38 Alum	Lexan-0.080″	6082-T6	6082-T6
Frame Extrusion Material	6351-T6	6061-T6	6061-T6	7003-T6 (weldable)
Panel Material	Polycarbonate-.080	Polycarbonate-.080	Polycarbonate-.080	Polycarbonate-.080
Door Dimensions	44″ W × 55″ H	41″ W × 59″ H	40.5″ W × 60″ H	Full Open Front
Lead Time (days)	15	15	16	18
Warranty (years)	5	5	4	4
Repair Lead Time (days)	12	3	8	10
COST COMPARISON-USD	**ABC**	**XYZ**	**DEF**	**KLM**
Metal Cost	$2,824	$2,744	$2,688	$2,226
Panel Material	$402	$485	$395	$287
Miscellaneous Material	$322	$285	$289	$185
Labor	$994	$602	$1,077	$135
Transportation Cost	$205	$216	$160	$159
Total Cost	$4,747	$4,332	$4,609	$2,992
Total Bid Cost (100)	**$474,700 FOB SRT-US**	**$433,200 FOB SRT-US**	**$460,900 DDP SRT-EU**	**$299,200 DDP SRT-US**

Table CS2.2 ULD shipping container purchase decision matrix

	Weight	XYZ Raw	XYZ Score	ABC Raw	ABC Score	DEF Raw	DEF Score	KLM Raw	KLM Score
VENDOR ASSESSMENT	**29.00%**	**19.72**	**0.98**	**22.86**	**1.07**	**16.94**	**0.71**	**18.86**	**0.88**
Company Stability	5.00%	2.72	0.14	4.00	0.20	3.44	0.17	3.38	0.17
Vendor Experience	2.00%	4.00	0.08	4.00	0.08	4.00	0.08	4.00	0.08
Repair Network Coverage	8.00%	4.00	0.32	2.86	0.23	0.00	0.00	2.29	0.18
Repair Lead Time	4.00%	1.00	0.04	4.00	0.16	1.50	0.06	1.20	0.05
Engineering Support	5.00%	4.00	0.20	4.00	0.20	4.00	0.20	4.00	0.20
Documentation Support	5.00%	4.00	0.20	4.00	0.20	4.00	0.20	4.00	0.20
RELIABILITY ASSESSMENT	**17.00%**	**8.00**	**0.68**	**8.00**	**0.68**	**4.55**	**0.58**	**3.80**	**0.47**
Ability to Meet Delivery Schedule	15.00%	4.00	0.60	4.00	0.60	3.75	0.56	3.00	0.45
Warranty	2.00%	4.00	0.08	4.00	0.08	0.80	0.02	0.80	0.02
TECHNICAL ASSESSMENT	**6.00%**	**7.76**	**0.23**	**7.91**	**0.24**	**7.26**	**0.22**	**5.95**	**0.16**
Adherence to SRT Specs	4.00%	3.76	0.15	4.00	0.16	3.76	0.15	2.12	0.08
Weight	2.00%	4.00	0.08	3.91	0.08	3.50	0.07	3.83	0.08
FINANCIAL ASSESSMENT	**48.00%**	**12.42**	**1.23**	**13.24**	**1.42**	**11.75**	**1.10**	**16.00**	**1.92**
Total Cost per Container	35.00%	2.33	0.81	2.74	0.96	2.21	0.77	4.00	1.40
DDP Transportation Costs	2.00%	3.16	0.06	2.94	0.06	4.00	0.08	4.00	0.08
Payment Terms	3.00%	4.00	0.12	4.00	0.12	4.00	0.12	4.00	0.12
Avg Repair Cost	8.00%	2.93	0.23	3.56	0.28	1.53	0.12	4.00	0.32
TOTAL SCORE	**100.00%**	**47.91**	**3.12**	**52.00**	**3.41**	**40.49**	**2.61**	**44.61**	**3.43**

In making the final decision that will be presented to the organization, consider the following questions and be sure to have backup data and information for the decision you recommend:

1. What do you see as the best courses of action for Ship Right?
2. Are there any alternatives to buying more shipping containers?
3. If purchase is chosen, which vendor offers the best overall value to Ship Right?
4. Based on the evaluations and analysis performed, which supply chain links did you identify that might be candidates for change that could add more value?
5. Based on the evaluations and analysis you performed, which value chain activities did you identify that might be candidates for process improvement and/or reengineering that would add more value?
6. Are any of the activities and functions you chose viable candidates for outsourcing?

Try to answer these questions from your personal perspective and experience using the research that was performed and presented. The answers are contained within the information and can also be found summarized in the Case Study 2 answers located in Appendix A. As you work through the exercise, ask yourself how your present organization approaches procurement and supply management. Also ask how your present organization would have handled this buy request. Would you have simply obtained three bids and bought the one with the best price? Or would you have employed any of the tools used in the exercise? Would you have done anything different from or in addition to what Ship Right did?

This case study is a worthwhile exercise that looks at many of the tools and techniques used by best-in-class procurement departments that have a strategic supply management philosophy and process that they follow. Although Ship Right does not currently employ complete and full strategic supply management practices, they do employ some effective supply management practices. This is the category that a majority of procurement departments fall into. They are doing a good job and producing real value for their organizations but they are not realizing their full potential and obtaining the maximum value that may be available. As you progress through the other chapters of this book, the tools presented in this case study will be detailed and many others presented for your consideration. *Supply Management and Procurement: From the Basics to Best-In-Class* was written to present the reader with examples of what tools, techniques, concepts, and philosophies are available to move their procurement departments from a basic procurement process system to a strategic supply management and procurement process system and how to attain and sustain best-in-class in their operation.

4

Value Chain Design and Planning

What Is Value Chain Management?

Value chain management (VCM) looks at all of the sequential primary and support activities that comprise and define an organization's overall activities. The linked set of activities that exist within a value chain closely mirrors the links identified in the supply chain. They include *inputs* and *outputs* that are activities or business functions performed by a company either internally (inputs) or externally (outputs). Primary and support activities add both cost and value to an end product, service, or process. The purpose of a value chain analysis (VCA) is to evaluate and analyze each activity individually and then as a whole. From this analysis the company can determine efficiency and cost and discover any opportunities for process and cost improvement through reengineering. VCA's primary focus is on identifying existing costs and the impact of re-thinking and reengineering those activities and, further, what value it would have to the organization, if any. Actual reengineering of primary and support activities is usually not performed by procurement services but by appropriate departments such as IE or engineering, but value chain mapping and analysis often is handled by procurement.

VCA can get complicated and therefore not many procurement professionals use it. However, it can reap substantial rewards if used and practiced effectively. One of the keys to the effective use of VCM is appropriate departments within an organization working collectively to improve activities and processes. This requires communication between departments and a willingness to strive for higher efficiencies in the activities and processes. Some VCM research can be performed by procurement. You may already be performing a partial VCA and not realize it. As a part of doing due diligence, you may look at a particular process within procurement in an attempt to understand how it works and what effect it has on the supply and procurement process. Doing a process map for procurement is a good example. By identifying each of the activities performed in the existing procurement process, you may also see opportunities to improve a particular activity or the entire process. This is a partial VCA, that is, analyzing the supply management and procurement link in the value chain and determining what the primary and support activities and associated costs are, and then determining what value they bring to the supply management and procurement process.

After a complete value chain has been identified and analyzed and an activity or process is tagged as a possible candidate for reengineering, determine if the preliminary research shows the potential for cost savings, efficiency, or reliability improvement. At this point it is usually passed along to the appropriate department in the form of a recommendation. These recommendations may become projects in and of themselves and procurement may be invited to participate as part of the project team.

Value Chain Management Example

Using a manufacturing organization as an example, primary and support activities are first identified. Within each activity—or link in the chain—the same companies, departments, and customers that have been identified in the supply chain will be found. Additional companies, departments, and activities that are not part of the supply chain will also be identified. A VCA is then performed to determine the cost and impact of selected activities and to recommend those activities as candidates for reengineering. A VCA asks a series of questions pertaining to all activities:

- How are we performing functions and activities now?
- What are the outermost limits of this function or activity?
- Will changes in the external environment affect the way this function or activity is performed?
- Do we have an overall, cross-functional, integrated strategy for the organization?
- How does our competition perform these functions or activities?
- Is our competition's method better than ours?
- Does our competition's method cost less than ours?
- Would our competition's method provide more value to the organization and our customers than we provide now?
- Does what we do in one function or activity complement or affect what we are doing in other functions or activities?

Primary and support activity elements that might be evaluated in an example VCA are:

- Technology (software programs)
    - Databases
    - Inventory planning and control
    - Scheduling
    - Tracking
- Manufacturing (operations)
    - Production scheduling
    - Production
    - Assembly
    - Engineering
    - Quality control
- Procurement
    - Industry research
    - Internal research (history)
        o What is purchased?
        o How it is purchased?
        o Why it is purchased?
        o From whom it is purchased?
        o Cost of the purchase (spend)?
    - Supply chain identification and management
    - Process mapping
    - Bidding, negotiating, and contracting
    - Supplier performance
- Marketing
    - Market research
    - Environmental scans
    - New product development
    - Marketing channels
    - Sales
- Distribution
    - Inbound transportation
    - Outbound transportation
    - Inventory management (receiving, stocking, picking, and packaging)

A value chain map is then created similar to the one used in Case Study 2 and illustrated in Figure 4.1. Value chain maps will vary by organization and industry but most of the basics are incorporated in this sample map. It represents a simplistic example of what might be identified in a VCA. The arrows are primary activities and the boxes below each arrow are broad, general categories of the support activities performed within and as part of a primary activity.

Looking at the procurement link in the chain, you can see that the support activities can be defined further to be more specific to your project. Refer to the descriptive example given previously and note the sub-bullet points.

After the supply chain and value chain are identified for your project, they should also be identified for the supplier(s) you are considering. By doing a value opportunity analysis you will maximize the impact to your procurement project. You will gain an understanding of how different processes work within your organization and learn what effect they have on job functions in other primary and support activities. Process maps should already exist for all departments and be available from IE. If not, you might request that IE develop them for you or ask the specific department of interest for one that they may have developed.

What Is the Benefit of Value Chain Management?

In a free market society it is all about the Benjamin's; in other words, it is all about the money. It is also about competition, market share, and sustained success. To survive, grow, and prosper, an organization must practice strategic management in all of its business functions and activities. To be best-in-class,

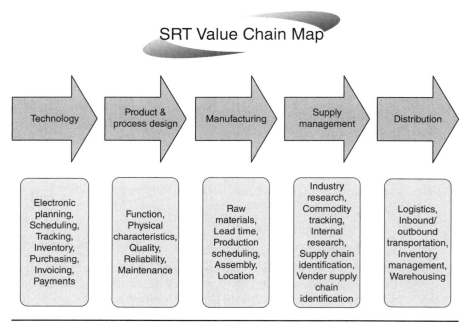

Figure 4.1   Value chain map

an organization must know everything there is to know about its business and how it conducts it, including:

- Who are your trading partners?
- Who are your competitors?
- How do you presently perform procurement and manage supplies?
- What are your benchmarks?
- How do other internal business functions of the organization presently perform activities?
- How do external business functions of the organization presently perform activities?
- Can any internal and external business activities be changed or reengineered to improve efficiencies?

Value chains are used to define what a business does and how they do it. VCA is a process of looking at a business as a series—or chain—of activities and/or processes. All businesses transform, in some way, inputs into outputs that customers value and want to buy. Value to the customer is developed from three basic sources: (1) activities that differentiate the product from other products, (2) activities that reduce cost (internally and externally), and (3) activities that satisfy a customer's need, want, or desire. VCA satisfies this by attempting to understand how a business can create organizational and customer value. In defining the contributions that each of the activities make, an understanding of how the activities contribute to the overall goals can be developed. VCA looks at this through a process point of view. It separates the business process into a series of activities that occur within the business. It starts with the inputs that an organization receives and ends with the products (or services) the organization makes or provides.

VCA analyzes costs incurred in the activities that the organization performs in an attempt to determine where low-cost advantages or cost disadvantages exist. It looks at the attributes of each activity to determine how each activity helps differentiate the company's products or services from other organizations. VCA allows an organization to identify competitive advantages effectively by looking at the business as a process, that is, a chain of events and activities that actually transpire in the business instead of merely looking at historic divisional silos.

Activities within an organization are broken down and divided into two categories: (1) primary activities and (2) support activities. Primary activities are categorized activities that separate one business function from another. They are supposed to be the basic, value adding functions of an organization. Support activities are specific activities that are located within and exist as a part of a primary activity that is required and necessary to make a primary business function operate.

Analyze Cost and Opportunities with a Value Analysis

A VCA can be performed to identify existing costs of business functions and activities to determine the influence and impact to an organization. Consider the following:

- Determine or estimate the cost for each link in both the value chain and the supply chain. This could get involved which is why VCA should be cross-functional. Resources within the organization should be tapped and called on to help provide data and numbers to determine costs for primary and support activities.
- Identify all cost restructuring options. These are opportunities for improvement that we have talked so much about. If you see a situation or opportunity that might add more value by changing the way you presently perform a process or function, explore the possibility for reengineering (changing a process or outsourcing it) to see if it is feasible or makes economic sense.
- Estimate the cost for each option or opportunity in critical links. Doing this allows you to perform what-if scenarios and develop an idea of what the cost of reengineering an opportunity would be and if it would be a justified cost or worthwhile from a value adding standpoint.
- Compare cost restructuring to your competitions' costs. Competitors' costs will most likely be estimates based on best guess evaluations but can be useful for comparison purposes.

Due to the complexities of value chain identification and analysis, not many people or organizations pay much attention to or get involved with this important and useful strategic tool. But the successful ones do, and that is one reason why they are successful. At some level of the organization someone should be looking at VCA, if not on a full time basis then at least periodically. This is an area where supply management and procurement can be helpful to the organization by initiating questions about the value chain associated with procurement projects and seeking qualitative data and information to help them fill in the blanks to determine the best value improvement.

5

The Importance of Benchmarks in Supply Management

Benchmarks are important in analyzing and managing various facets of business activities such as procurement, marketing, operations, and manufacturing. They are particularly important in supply management and procurement. Benchmarks can be set or established for a variety of things, including systems, commodity prices, products, or activities and processes. A benchmark is a goal that an organization wants to attain in a particular business function or activity. The reason we set benchmarks is to establish a point of reference that can be used to make improvements over current levels of efficiencies and against which our success can be measured. A step-by-step model to develop and use benchmarks follows:

- Determine exactly what you want to benchmark and why you want to benchmark it.
- Determine what you will use to set the benchmark.
  - Use goals or achievements that other best-in-class companies have developed.
  - Use goals developed internally for specific purposes or tasks.
  - Use goals recommended by a consultant.
- Determine what the specific benchmark number, point, or goal will be.
- Establish what is critical and what the quality requirements and parameters of the benchmark will be.
- Establish a starting point for what you want to benchmark.

- Determine milestones or achievement levels along a progression line toward the benchmark.
- Develop a process and action plan to achieve your benchmark goal.
- Implement the action plan.
- Monitor the action plan and make adjustments as needed.
- Determine what you will do if/when the benchmark is achieved.
  - Conduct a review of the benchmark process.
    - What went right, what went wrong, and what needs to be changed?
    - Was the benchmark set too low or high?
    - Should the benchmark be reset upward or downward?

Once you have determined exactly what you want to benchmark, you will want to establish a starting point. This will determine how you will establish your benchmark and what the benchmark will be. You will also want to establish when you want to implement the benchmark action plan. This is the beginning point of an implementation final time line that you will establish later in developing what point in time you want to implement the action plan, but for now, you will want a general idea of when to start.

Benchmarks are developed based on information obtained from one of three places:

1. Internally: Benchmarks may have been previously set based on historical achievements. New goals and adjustment targets for improvement may require new benchmarks.
2. Externally: You may look externally to determine a benchmark that you want to use. This could be from a best-in-class company or operation within your organization's industry or an entirely different industry, perhaps a process benchmark. Choosing the type of benchmark that best fits your organization and that you want to use would depend on what you want to achieve from a process and activity improvement standpoint.
3. Hypothetical: Benchmarks may be set based on best guesses and research that has been performed or on recommendations made by an outside consultant.

It is important to now establish what improvement criteria are critical, what the quality requirements are, and what the parameters of the benchmark are. Quality, profitability, efficiency, industry standing, and process activities are a few of the critical criteria to consider. You do this by designing an activity process map starting with the beginning of the activity and/or process and ending when the activity or process is completed. The benchmark may also contain milestones. Milestones are points along the process progression line that indicate important critical points, or decisions that must be made.

Now you are ready to develop a process and action plan to achieve your benchmark goal. I use MS Project software as a model to establish the steps in the process and action plan (tasks) and also as a time line for implementation (Gantt chart). It has proven most useful for me and easily allows the setting of milestones. If you do not have or use MS Project, the process and action plan can actually just be written in MS Word or set up a number of different ways in MS Excel. Excel allows you to make a Gantt chart as well. How the benchmark action plan and time line is established is really a matter of preference for the project designer or team to decide.

The design and draft of a benchmark process and action plan flowchart that shows each step in the process progression line is recommended. When determining and setting benchmarks, it is usually necessary to form a benchmark implementation team and assemble resource personnel to research, brainstorm, and establish criteria, milestones, and goals for the benchmark.

For example, we will assume that an organization's supply management division wants to change how it makes purchases to improve efficiency, reduce internal operating and purchase costs, and increase profitability to the organization. A benchmark implementation team has been formed and has developed, quantified, and answered the following questions:

- What do we want to benchmark?
  - Purchase cost reduction
  - Purchase order creation cost reduction
  - Inventory level reduction
  - Time-to-purchase improvement
  - Overall purchase process improvement
- What is our benchmark starting point?
  - We will use best-in-class supply management criteria and processes for developing benchmark goals.
    - We will use as our base model Robert W. Turner's *Supply Management and Procurement: From the Basics to Best-in-Class.*
- We will develop critical criteria, quality requirements, and parameters of the benchmarks.
- We will design a benchmark process and action plan flowchart.
- We will design a benchmark process implementation time line.
- We will monitor the process and action plan and make adjustments as needed.

Specifics of the Benchmark Process and Action Plan

Based on the recommendations of the benchmark implementation team, the supply management division of our organization has chosen the following benchmarks as goals for supply management:

- Reduce purchase costs of one-offs and spot buys by 25% and reduce cost of contract purchases by 35%.
- Reduce on-hand inventory levels by 40%.
    - Institute an electronic (computerized) minimum/maximum inventory variation of the inventory system.
    - Institute a warehouse bar code scanning system for receiving and shipping to automatically adjust received, stocked, picked, and shipped inventory levels electronically.
- Reduce time-to-purchase and internal cost by 20% minimum, that is:
    - Inventory minimum level reached
    - Requisition to buy generated
    - Supply chain identified
    - Required research performed
    - Qualified bidders selected
    - Minimum requirements established
    - Request for quote (RFQ) or request for proposal (RFP) prepared and issued
    - Bids received and analyzed
    - Negotiations conducted
    - Award made
- Purchase process improvements implemented to facilitate successful achievement of the preceding goals.

After critical criteria, quality requirements, and parameters of benchmark goals are set, a benchmark process and action plan flowchart is designed. A simplified example for spot buy processes is illustrated in Figure 5.1. Process maps for contract buys are basically the same but with additional steps added that may be applicable and appropriate for a particular contract or buy project. One example might be adding steps where accounting performed the financial analysis, procurement performed the technical analysis, and a weighted decision matrix was developed that incorporates all of the key elements required to make an educated decision and used as criterion to make an unbiased best value decision.

You might say that many tasks and substantial work must be completed to reach a benchmark. The example used in Figure 5.1 is a simple one, but to

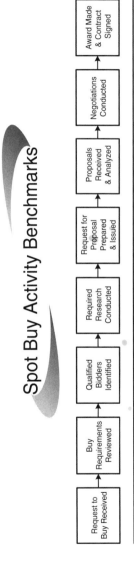

Figure 2.1 Percentage of goods and services purchased

show some of the things that transpired in achieving the various benchmarks in our example, we will discuss each one briefly.

Request to Buy Received

Before the first benchmark is reached several things must occur so that a request to buy can be generated. In both manual and automated inventory scheduling systems, something has to trigger the reorder or resupply of inventory. This can be an individual tasked with the responsibility of notifying procurement or it can be automatically generated by an electronic inventory scheduling system.

One example is a Kanban inventory scheduling system. Kanban is Japanese that, loosely translated, means card, sign, or visible record. Kanban is a pull inventory scheduling system that uses a single- or double-card method of recording inventory as it is used (pulled). It then alerts appropriate personnel when an inventory minimum is reached and that information is passed to procurement to reorder or resupply the inventory. Kanban is also an important process in an electronic materials requirement planning inventory system. Because of the effectiveness of the Kanban system, it is incorporated in most Lean and just-in-time (JIT) philosophies and processes.

Buy Requirements Reviewed

Regardless of what inventory supply system used, the next benchmark in our example occurs when purchasing receives notification or a requisition to buy. The benchmark is that buy requirements are reviewed by purchasing. What results in the culmination and achievement of this benchmark is the due diligence that purchasing performs in evaluating the size, scope, time requirement, and cost of the buy. These activities can range anywhere from requesting quotes for price and lead times from a minimum of three known and established suppliers to a more strategic approach. Evaluating inventory minimum and maximum levels, researching industry trends, evaluating forecasted commodity price and supply information, tightening quality and delivery requirements, as well as other applicable activities are all strategic supply management and procurement functions employed in reviewing buy requirements.

Qualified Bidders Identified

The next benchmark in our example is achieved when a list of qualified bidders is identified to whom an RFQ or RFP will be issued. Activities performed to make this determination may be:

- Deciding to expand the number of bidders beyond three

- Qualifying new supplier sources
- Reviewing supplier score cards to determine supplier performance
- Determining the financial soundness of suppliers

Required Research Conducted

The next benchmark in our example includes not only those mentioned and performed in previous benchmarks but additional items as well. Evaluation of the buy itself in relationship to the overall inventory and procurement strategy is in order. A series of questions should be asked about the buy to determine if there are any value opportunities that might reduce costs, improve efficiencies, streamline processes, and increase profitability:

- Is the buy a candidate for electronic data interchange (EDI)?
- Is the buy a candidate for inclusion in an existing contract?
- Can the buy be leveraged with other buys to reduce costs?
- What does commodity tracking of price and supply show?
  - In what direction are prices, supply, and demand trending?
    - If trending up and forecasted to continue to rise then forward buying might be an option as well as placement on contract to protect from future price increases and/or supply shortages.
- Can inventory levels be reduced?
  - Is the buy a candidate for JIT?
- Can inventory minimum and maximum levels be adjusted to maximize cost efficiencies?
- Are there any industry trends that might affect the buy?
- Do quality and/or delivery requirements need to be tightened?
  - Are the acceptance/rejection levels of current buys within parameters?
  - Are current lead times acceptable?

Request for Proposal Prepared and Issued

The next benchmark in our example requires the assembly and evaluation of the research and work that has been performed in all of the preceding benchmarks. Considerations are given to any changes proposed in the status quo of existing buy requirements such as inventory levels, price reduction goals, contract consideration, supplier qualifications, and bidder selection. These will be used along with minimum requirements and scope of work to build and prepare an RFQ or RFP that will allow for maximum value to the buyer.

Once the RFQ or RFP is prepared, it is then issued to the bidders chosen. This benchmark has now been reached.

Proposals Received and Analyzed

At the end of the proposal or bid period, all of the bids are submitted to the buyer for consideration and evaluation. This starts work on the next benchmark in our example. Various analyses will need to be performed for the buyer to make the best value decision. Some additional research may also be required. Once all of these tasks have been completed and a decision is pending, this benchmark has been achieved.

Negotiations Conducted

The next benchmark in our example takes the work performed in the previous benchmark and uses it to draft goals and the strategy for negotiating a final award. Even if the buy was a spot, or one-time buy, there should still be a minimum of negotiation. The same philosophy and reasoning used in designing and preparing negotiations for a contract can also be applied on a smaller scale to spot buys. Even in one-time and spot buy situations, extra value may be gained by going that extra step with the winner. Asking for additional discounts, shorter lead times, discounted payment terms, or other value considerations presents an opportunity for additional value to the buyer. You will never know until you ask.

Of course contract negotiations require much more thought, planning, work, and preparation. Whether it is a spot buy or contract buy, once all of these tasks are performed the benchmark will have been achieved. The importance of negotiating the right agreement will be discussed in Chapter 15 and includes guidance on preparing and tracking effective negotiation strategy.

Award Made, Contract Signed, and Purchase Order Issued

This is the final benchmark and the culmination of all of the work performed and other benchmarks achieved in our example. In the case of a spot buy, a purchase order is issued. If it is a contract purchase, the legal department works with procurement and the awarded bidder to prepare an acceptable contract. When these tasks are completed, the final benchmark is achieved.

The benchmark examples we use are for purchases but benchmarks may be set and used for a wide variety of things in numerous business activities, including production, marketing, accounting, and the list goes on. You can set benchmarks for virtually anything you want because they represent goals that you wish to attain and can be monetary, numerical, or physical. One example of a monetary benchmark is a cash figure wanted to buy a particular item. A numerical benchmark might be reducing the overall departmental procurement costs by 16%. Reducing the amount of time required to evaluate, research, bid, and award purchases is considered a physical benchmark. Setting benchmarks is a strategic way of defining what goal you want to achieve and the tasks that are required to achieve them.

Budgets, schedules, processes, and procedures are cost drivers and key success factors that are essential to operational control and evaluation because they dictate how operations will be implemented and managed. They are actually benchmarks that are used to evaluate and measure success or failure. For example, budgets state how much money has been authorized to pay for the operational plan. The budget is the benchmark for what the operational plan should cost, and, additionally, it is a way of controlling what is spent. Meeting or coming in below budget means the budget that was established was accurate and that the operational plan was successful. Exceeding the budget means that there were unplanned for surprises that occurred or that the operational plan contained flaws, indicating it was not well planned and designed.

Schedules are benchmarks for how a particular plan is to operate and what it is supposed to do. Schedules also contain benchmarks for how a particular plan is to operate, what it is supposed to do, and when it is supposed to do it. For example, the marketing plan calls for 10,000 widgets to be sold per month. Based on the marketing plan, the operational plan may call for 8,000 widgets to be made each month (based on previous sales history) with a reserve capacity to make 15,000 widgets per month total. Marketing may or may not make changes to the existing plans, but as long as they are in the 8,000 to 15,000 range of widgets sold per month, the operational plan would still be successful and would be within budget. If marketing decided to do a special promotion and offer a sales incentive for widgets that would exceed the existing operational plan, then the existing plan would need to be revised to accommodate the increase in production involved. This then becomes a collaborative process between marketing and operations with procurement having a vital role in facilitating the changes that will be required in the acquisition of new and existing raw materials, parts, and components needed to increase the production of widgets. These types of opportunities are chances for supply management and procurement professionals to show their stuff. A situation like the one described for increasing the supply of widgets might be seen as an inconvenience to some, but it offers the procurement professional who is practicing best-in-class supply management the chance to take advantage of the opportunities that increase in the supply requirements offer.

Monitoring and evaluating benchmarks are important because they inform management whether or not goals are being met. If goals are not being met, they will help in identifying why goals are not being met and help in the redesign to institute remedies. Further, if marketing consistently sold 12,000 widgets per month then management would want to adjust the production schedule higher because doing so would lower overall production costs and increase profits. This is a simplistic answer to the question posed and there is substantially more involved than what is presented here. However, this is a good example of how cross-functionality between departments works (or should work) to achieve the overall goals and strategies of the organization.

The reason an organization should monitor and track performance standards is so that they will know how well they are performing and can determine what can be done to improve performance and efficiency. If it is determined that performance does not meet the standards and requirements that have been set and is below what is expected, it allows adjustments to be made to correct nonconforming areas and bring performance back into balance. If it is determined that the standards themselves are the problem, it allows the standards to be reevaluated and changed.

There are several things that may cause deviations from performance standards:

- The effect of unforeseen circumstances and events
  - Situations that might occur in the economy
  - Changes in competition
  - Process inefficiencies
  - Disruption of supplies
  - Work stoppages (strikes)
- Bottlenecks in activity flow
- Increase in rejects due to out-of-spec items, quality problems, or performance problems
- Changes in the performance plan or strategy itself

Monitoring performance due to unforeseen events alerts the organization that adjustments need to be made to realign performance. If performance declines it creates problems in other areas as well and can even have a ripple effect on other activities downstream. Monitoring performance helps to identify problems early so that steps can then be taken to assure they will not recur. Bottlenecks sometimes occur in a process's activity flow that disrupts or stops activity progress. Monitoring process performance allows for the identification of bottlenecks and the analysis of why they occurred and what can be done to resolve the situation and to keep it from happening in the future. Quality or performance problems can also be monitored in the process control system and action can be taken when quality processes reach the outer limits of acceptability. There are several types of accepted process control methods:

- Statistical process control is a procedural process that involves the inspection and testing of manufactured parts to assure quality and adherence to required specifications and/or tolerances. It can involve random or predetermined quantities of samples.

- Statistical quality control is a procedural process that inspects and/or tests incoming parts and materials to assure they are conforming to the standards, specifications, and requirements established in a purchase order or contract.
- Six Sigma is a strategy for managing processes to identify, correct, or improve quality defects. A defect in Six Sigma is defined as any output that does not meet required standards or customer satisfaction. It is most often identified with manufacturing processes but can have other applications in nonmanufacturing activities as well.

Changes in organizational strategies and philosophies may require a rethinking of performance criteria and standards and can involve creating or changing current performance standards to reflect new processes, strategies, or changes in fundamental philosophies. Examples would be an organization wanting to change from a basic procurement philosophy to a strategic supply management philosophy, changes in an organization's standard operating procedures to comply with new laws, regulations, requirements, or needs, and changes in certification and/or compliance such as ISO level attainment.

After benchmark criteria, goals, and milestones are established, a time line for the implementation of processes required to reach the benchmarks should be established. This can be accomplished in several ways as previously mentioned. In our example we chose the following five procurement activities to benchmark in an effort to reduce operating and purchase costs as well as to improve process efficiency.

1. Purchase cost reduction—Goals were set for the reduction of purchase costs of one-offs and spot buys by 25% and the reduction of contract purchases by 35%.
2. Purchase order creation cost reduction—Current cost for generating purchase orders manually is $150 per purchase order. A goal has been set to switch all contract and recurring buys from the same vendor to an EDI platform. The cost of this purchase order generation is calculated at $0.15 per purchase order.
3. Inventory level reduction—A goal of the reduction of inventory levels by 40% will be set. All critical and noncritical items will be reviewed to determine if existing minimum and maximum inventory levels can be revised. This will reduce the buy cycle time and the number of purchase orders required. Additionally, a new system of inventory management will be instituted using a bar code and scanner system to automatically adjust inventory levels when goods are received, stocked, picked, packaged, and shipped.

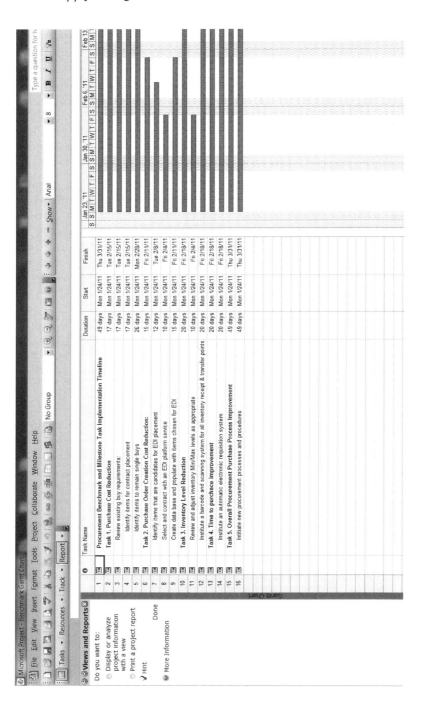

Figure 5.2

4. Time to purchase improvement—A goal of 20% in the reduction of time required to purchase goods is set to improve procurement process efficiencies.

5. Overall procurement purchase process improvement—A goal of 25% improvement in overall procurement processes is set. This includes activities and processes involved in the previous four benchmark targets as well as the consolidation of some procurement activities and jobs. An example of this would be the formation of commodity groups to oversee and manage specific commodities, goods, and services required by the organization.

An implementation plan and time line should now be established. As previously stated, there are many ways this can be accomplished. Each of the category goals and benchmarks can be portrayed individually or combined as a whole. Figure 5.2 shows these benchmarks using MS Project.

Benchmarks are used by organizations on several levels and in multiple departments to set goals and measure performance and the success that is achieved against those goals. Within each benchmark tasks must be performed to attain the benchmark. A milestone is a significant point that is reached within the benchmark process or task that has been performed. Milestones are the signposts along the benchmark highway that tell us we are on the right route, how far we have come, and how far we have to go to reach our destination. This chapter has described why benchmarking is important to an organization and its processes from a supply management and procurement point of view. It also described why and how using benchmarks allows an organization to set goals and monitor their success in achieving those goals. The use of benchmarks is an important function and ingredient in achieving best-in-class supply management and procurement.

6

Activity Process and Design

Whether you are beginning a new procurement project, developing a strategy to do a specific project, want to change a process or business activity, or want to understand how you are presently doing a process or activity, it is important to know how to identify the way an activity or process works. You can do this by mapping it. This is most commonly referred to as creating a process flowchart. Process mapping can be used in all aspects of an organization's operation, including procurement, marketing, accounting, and manufacturing. Anywhere there is a business function, activity, or process, a process map can be developed. But since this book is about supply management and procurement, let us look at activity process and design from a supply management and procurement standpoint.

There are examples of supply chain and value chain maps illustrated in other portions of this book. Both supply and value chains are activity processes and their maps are actually process flowcharts. A process map starts with the onset of an activity or process and progresses step-by-step to the end of the activity or process, that is, when the activity or process is complete. In the case of supply management and procurement, everything that occurs prior to the procurement link of the supply chain map is commonly referred to as upstream and everything that occurs after procurement is said to be downstream.

So let us break this down into activity processes. How many activity process maps one would create depends on the desired outcomes. Mapping all activity processes associated with a project may not be necessary. However, many are and can lend a better understanding of what is involved in a particular business function, activity, or process. The number of processes or activities mapped would, then, also depend on the size, cost, complexity, and value of the project. Using the metal parts scenario in Case Study 2 as our example, let us first review the supply chain map for metal in Figure 6.1.

Figure 6.1   Metal supply chain

Procurement might be a good place to begin mapping. We would need to determine exactly what activities make up the procurement process, what work is required in each activity, and how the work is performed. Figure 6.2 is a simplified example of an activity process map for a basic procurement department.

This is a basic activity process map that might be used for procurement and it represents the major individual activities—or links—in the procurement process. One could expand the map to include other activities or actually map the individual activities. As an example, you might find mapping the steps required in issuing a purchase order beneficial. Mapping the purchase order generation process does several things:

- Used to bring clarity and visibility to the process
- Used as standard operating procedures once identified and mapped
- Used for training new employees
- Used to calculate the time and cost involved in purchase order generation

Mapping identifies what steps are actually required in issuing a purchase order for anyone involved in procurement. An example of a process map for basic procurement purchase order generation is illustrated in Figure 6.3, but it only shows a minimum of basic procurement activities. A strategic supply management process model would be much more involved as we note later in this chapter. But, whether it is a basic or detailed procurement process map or something in between, the reasons for process mapping are based on sound business principles that promote greater efficiency in the procurement process.

A greatly expanded process map that includes recommended steps to select for use on a project is contained in Chapter 9. Although we discuss this process map in detail later, there are a few basic points worth mentioning here. Considering its comprehensive nature, on review of this model you might say that this is too much work to do every time you have a project to buy something and you would be right. You usually only need to do it one time. You may modify the map to include a unique requirement for a specific buy project,

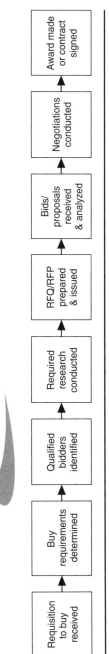

Figure 6.2 Activity process map

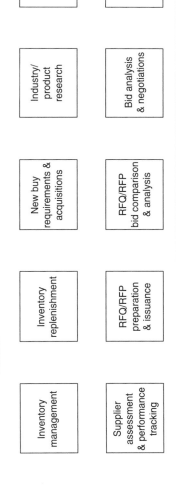

Figure 6.3 Basic procurement process map

but basically the process map is an illustration of what the actual processes are. After the initial map you only need to update or revise the map as changes in standard operating procedures or circumstances warrant. The main purpose of doing the map is to fully understand what business functions and activities are required and performed. An activity process map should be developed and included in the procurement department's process and procedures manual. It becomes a part of official policy and standard operating procedure. It then can be referred to and updated as needed. It can also be used as a guide to train new employees and used to calculate the internal costs of issuing a purchase order or contract.

Time and resources are costs that impact the procurement budget and the profitability of the organization. They are important considerations that should be taken into account when looking at opportunities to improve value to the organization through process improvement. An example of this is identifying activities that would be candidates for technology improvement such as new software implementation that would simplify activities and reduce the time of operation. One consideration might be implementing a material requirements planning software system such as MRP II or the more advanced Enterprise Resource Planning. Both would allow an organization to control inventory, automatically generate requests to buy when inventory reached minimum levels, plan production or other requirements, receive and ship goods, issue purchase orders, and pay invoices electronically.

Another example is the identification of activities that would be candidates for electronic data interchange (EDI). Any process activity that can be designed or reengineered to add more value by reducing costs should be researched and considered. EDI is an electronic platform that allows the transfer and receipt of data electronically such as issuing purchase orders, issuing and receiving invoices, receiving shipping or order status notices, and paying invoices. There are several independent companies that offer these services for a fee. As an example of how much money might be saved, you could use the process activity map for procurement to assign cost values for each activity performed for manual purchase order generation along with other associated costs such as pay and benefits, office supplies, utility costs, and so forth. The average cost of writing a single purchase order averages about $150, but whatever an organization's cost, it will increase as time goes on. If an organization issued a large number of purchase orders, after the fee for an EDI service, their cost for issuing purchase orders automatically and electronically could be as low as $0.04 to $0.08 per purchase order. If your organization has an industrial engineering department, they can help with assigning costs to individual activities (they may already have established those costs).

In practicing best-in-class supply chain management, it is also useful to know what the activity process maps of the other links in the supply chain are. Since you probably do not have visibility into the companies that make up your supply chain, how can you find this information? One way is to request a copy from the companies of interest. More efficient and progressive companies will have activity process maps and most do not object to sharing. But you will be surprised at the number of companies that do not have current activity process maps and have never completed one. You could also make the supply of activity process maps a requirement when request for proposals (RFPs) are written and issued. This technique also keeps suppliers honest because they know that due diligence is being practiced.

You may ask why you would need activity process maps from companies other than your own. It allows you to look for efficiencies or deficiencies in the companies with which you do business. Activity process maps with bidders as part of the supplier assessment were used in the decision matrix illustrated in Case Study 2 to qualify their efficiency, capabilities, and reliability. Activity process maps from supply chain partners may also give an indication of how well they are practicing supply chain management.

A certain purchasing professional bought large quantities of metal for the manufacture of their product. They were on contract with a supplier who had been the low bidder and the supplier had given them excellent service over many years. This particular individual started practicing advanced, strategic supply chain management techniques by tracking the cost of metals that were used in the parts they purchased. He discovered that the cost his company was paying for metal parts was disproportionate to the cost of the raw metal market. The purchasing professional invited the supplier in for discussions and showed the supplier the results of his research. The supplier was shocked. The supplier stated that they had historically purchased from one mill and had accepted the prices that they were quoted. Together they developed an activity process chart for the supplier's company and found other areas that could be improved as well. The supplier went back and issued a bid to several different mills for the metals that they required. Ultimately they received and accepted a bid for 24% less from another reputable mill and passed the savings on to the example company and to all their other customers. They were able to generate even more business for the companies they normally supplied and picked up additional business from new companies as well. It pays to do your homework (research), and if you do not know the answer to something, ask. Because this individual went the extra step, it turned out to be a win/win for both his company and his supplier.

Now we are going to look at a more advanced procurement process model and map. Earlier in this chapter we saw what a basic procurement activity process map looked like. We now map and discuss what a strategic supply management and procurement activity process map might look like. Figure 6.4 shows an activity process map for an advanced procurement department that practices strategic supply management and procurement. You will notice that the activity process elements roughly resemble an upside down pyramid.

The first, or top row of elements, is the foundation of the strategic supply management activity process and each subsequent descending row constitutes additional elements that build on themselves. This creates and develops opportunities for substantial process and activity improvement as well as reducing costs, improving efficiencies, and increasing profitability for the organization.

Now let us explore the business functions and processes individually that are displayed in Figure 6.4. In each function, activity and process design plays a crucial role. Mapping can sometimes be used to improve effectiveness, efficiency, cost reduction, and profitability.

Supply Chain Management

Effective and extended supply chain management is the cornerstone of strategic supply management and procurement philosophy and processes. Without *effective* supply chain management there is little use of practicing many of the other elements listed. However, even practicing supply chain management less efficiently is better than not practicing it at all, because some value can still be gained. But the greatest value to an organization comes from a maximized effort in practicing strategic supply chain management and will always produce greater rewards for an organization.

Commodity Tracking and Forecasting

Commodity tracking and forecasting is an ultra-rewarding strategic tool and activity. No organization will ever gain their maximum potential if they do not employ this valuable activity. Knowing historical prices and supply availability of commodities that make up the goods and services an organization requires allows the prediction of what they might be in the future and promotes more effective and profitable strategic plans and decision making. Many companies and procurement departments do not practice commodity tracking and forecasting. Their reasoning is that it takes too much time and resources or that they do not have anyone qualified. The reality of this is that they are dependent on information that suppliers tell them and through bids that they receive. Remember, if you don't know where you have been you will never know where you are going. If you do not have anyone qualified, then train somebody, and if you do not have time and resources, reorganize to create more. How can a procurement department expect to be effective and avoid risks and surprises if they do not know and understand what effects a commodity or service that they depend on will have on their operations if unforeseen events happen? Commodity tracking and forecasting is a core ingredient of strategic supply chain management.

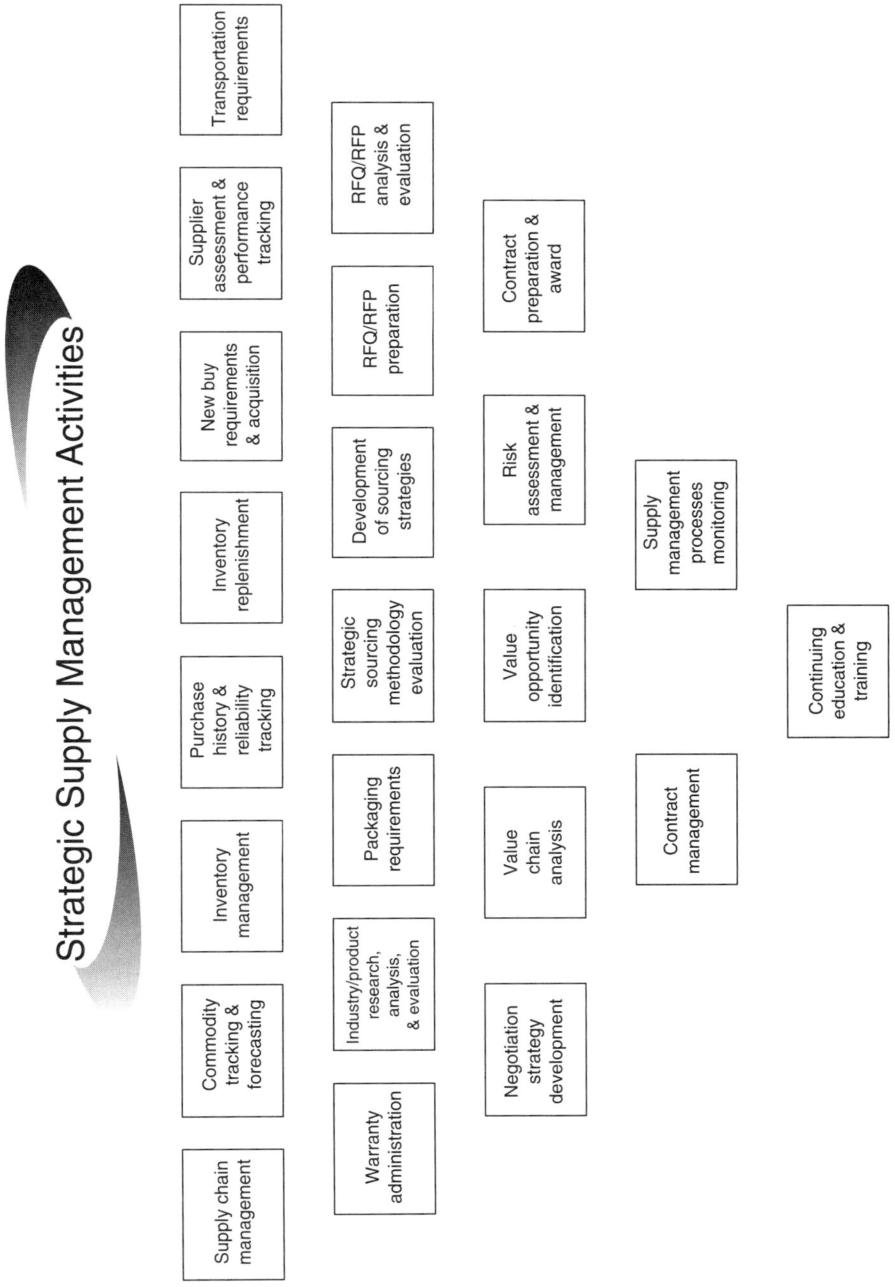

Figure 6.4   Strategic supply management and procurement process map

Inventory Management

Manipulation and management of inventory can generate significant cost savings from a purchase and inventory level standpoint. Strategic supply management and procurement looks at and evaluates ever changing requirements and demands and seeks opportunities and ways to improve efficiency through innovative ways of managing inventory. Some examples of strategic inventory management are:

- Reviewing and adjusting inventory minimum and maximum levels regularly to maximize efficiency and reduce cost. Buying in smaller quantities too often adds costs on the procurement end and runs the risk of interruption of supplies. Buying too much at a time adds costs on the financial end by reducing available cash and producing increased carrying costs.
- Commodity family grouping and contract placement is a way to realize and assure guaranteed supply and price concessions.
- Just-in-time inventory supply is not for everyone or every situation but should be evaluated for potential process improvement and cost reduction.
- Vendor managed inventory (VMI) also may not be applicable to everyone or every situation but can produce rewards through cost reductions in certain instances.
- Electronic inventory management is a process I recommend. A bar coding and scanning system that electronically records and adjusts inventory on receipt and at each transfer point allows maximum visibility and the effective management of inventories and stocks. Some VMI arrangements are also conducted electronically, sending inventory data (usually at designated times daily) to a remote vendor where replenishment stocks are automatically generated and shipped to the customer. Another electronic inventory management system is radio frequency identification and can also be an effective inventory management and tracking system.

Purchase History and Reliability Tracking

If an organization practices any type of effective procurement, at a minimum they will run purchase histories queries for any large or significant buy projects. Organizations that practice strategic supply management and procurement make the tracking of purchase price, quantity, supplier, lead time, and reliability a part of the standard operating procedures, not just at buy time. Reliability tracking is often overlooked as being important, but it is a necessary function that identifies poor product quality and performance. A software system that monitors purchase history and reliability information and then generates reports (both at regular intervals and on-demand) allows for better management of the supply chain and identification of opportunities for process and financial improvement.

Inventory Replenishment

Inventory replenishment is the meat and potatoes of the procurement process. It is the regular fulfillment of required parts and services needed for an organization to perform the tasks and processes required to attain their goals and be successful. How well a procurement department executes this activity will determine the degree of success and profitability of the organization. Using the basic three bids and then writing a purchase order using best-in-class strategic supply management and procurement techniques and philosophies, the level of effective participation by a procurement department will dictate the level of efficiency and cost reduction in an organization.

New Buy Requirements and Acquisition

In addition to regular or scheduled stock replenishment, procurement is also responsible for new buy requirements, one-offs, and spot purchases such as new product development requirements, equipment, and machinery. Some of the strategic supply management and procurement activity elements used for regular or scheduled stock replenishment might not be used in these situations, but most are still applicable.

Supplier Assessment and Performance Tracking

Tracking how well a supplier performs is an important aspect of practicing effective supply management and procurement. To avoid surprises and problems resulting from poor supplier performance, procurement departments should practice proactive and aggressive supplier performance due diligence. This consists of a supplier management program that tracks supplier performance in several categories such as capabilities, financial stability and strength, delivery performance (on-time deliveries, lead times, backorders, etc.), quality, and reject rates. Some organizations use a supplier scorecard system to rate supplier performance, but whatever system they use, all have the same goal— to determine the dependability, efficiency, and cost effectiveness of suppliers. If an organization does not currently practice comprehensive supplier management, they should strongly consider instituting a program as part of their standard operating procedures.

Transportation Requirements

Transportation is a necessary evil required in all procurement transactions. Determining transportation rates and costs can be a real headache and also time consuming. Determining at what point title and/or responsibility transfers from the seller to the buyer is a financial and legal consideration that should not be taken lightly, especially in international transportation and movement. That is why some organizations only practice basic procurement and choose to pay for transportation of goods through the supplier by bidding and buying on a delivered basis only. Organizations that practice strategic supply management and procurement recognize the importance and cost effect that transportation has on the total cost of goods. Some organizations have independent departments within procurement that do nothing but purchase and schedule transportation while others require the buyers to obtain the best deals.

Warranty Administration

Believe it or not, warranty administration is one element that some companies do not track or manage effectively. Tracking the amount of warranty claims and warranty repair relates closely to reliability tracking and supplier performance, although it is usually a separate business function within procurement. Interdepartmental communication between working groups and functions is essential to identifying problem parts, components, and suppliers, and then having a procedure to address and correct them.

Industry/Product Research, Analysis, and Evaluation

Industry and/or product research, analysis, and evaluation of materials, parts, components, suppliers, and financial/economic conditions and projections all fall on procurement's shoulders, usually the buyer's unless specific individuals have been designated for that responsibility. The degree of importance and the level of requirement that procurement places on these elements will determine the amount of success that procurement and the organization will have. There are many types of research on various topics and at different levels that can be performed to provide data and information useful in decision making and strategic planning. Likewise, there are numerous analytical tools available that enhance the evaluation process. The degree of emphasis an organization puts on these elements and the amount of support is one thing that separates basic from best-in-class.

Packaging Requirements

Packaging is another function of procurement that is occasionally neglected. Many procurement departments arbitrarily accept pack, carton, skid, or container quantities offered by suppliers. Sometimes a little extra research will produce higher dividends. Here are two quick examples that illustrate this point. At a company I previously worked for, one of the high-volume items that they bought were rivets. They used several different types of rivets in their operations of varying lengths, diameter, and purpose. They bought hundreds of thousands of each type of rivets (at least 25 different types) each year. Rivets are historically sold by the box with a certain quantity per box, depending on size and type. They run between 900 and 1700 per box. When a box of rivets was received, with a few exceptions, it was placed in central inventory and the rivets were dispensed or picked piecemeal from the box as requisitions came in. Because of the difference in piece count for each part number and box, every box of rivets received in inventory was recorded as one (box). But they were being issued in multiple quantities. This wrecked havoc with the inventory and ordering system and resulted in more rivets being purchased than were needed and used. Rivets are cheap, even if bought by the box, and this particular company decided it was not worth the time and effort to look at changing packaging requirements. Suppliers only sold them by the box anyway. Wrong! It is never a wasted effort to practice strategic supply management and procurement, even if an exercise proves unworthy of changing. The procedural processes that you go through may bring something else to your attention that you never saw or thought of before and might prove to have value. One of the material planners decided to investigate and, after contacting suppliers to get their input, presented a plan to the organization to change packaging requirements from purchasing boxes of rivets to purchasing packs of 100 each. The supplier was required to provide a bar code on the package identifying part number and quantity. With justification data presented for the change, the plan was accepted. This may sound like a minor, insignificant change from a purchasing standpoint but it dramatically improved overall efficiencies. The price breakdown remained the same on a per piece basis, but the rewards came on the back-end. Inventory count was finally accurate and a substantial amount of money was saved by allowing faster pick times, eliminating spillage, loss, and excessive ordering.

The second example was at the same company. Several types of specialized grease were required. Each type, or grade, was purchased in 35-gallon and 50-gallon drums and pumped into grease guns. Even though usage requirements did not justify that volume of purchase, it was the only way it could be purchased. The same inventory planner began working with a distributor of these materials to determine a solution that would reduce cost overall. The grease being purchased in drums had a shelf-life that was being exceeded and excess grease had to be disposed of as hazardous material. The solution that was arrived at was for the distributor to repackage grease from the barrel to disposable tubes and label them for use in individual grease guns. Bingo, problem solved. Through repackaging and only having to purchase actual quantities needed, significant cost savings were realized from over purchasing and disposal costs, and a convenience factor was added. It actually worked out to be less expensive because the distributor took the same concept and sold it to his other customers and that allowed him to keep our costs low. Process and activity maps that were developed for both examples allowed visibility into the actual processes instead of relying on perceived notions. Both examples also illustrate another strategic supply management and procurement tool that is available. Sometimes involving a supplier in the procurement decision process upfront can produce some nice rewards and it is known as early supplier involvement.

Strategic Sourcing Methodology Evaluation

As one saying suggests, there is a method in the madness. This can also hold true for supply management and procurement strategies and processes. When sourcing buy requirements, a plan should be developed that lends itself to achieving the highest degree of success possible. That means that the plan should be well thought out and include any and all functions and activities required for the buy project to be successful. The need and benefit of sourcing models is discussed in Chapter 9. The model presented there basically lists every possible requirement that might be used in a procurement buy project. Since all buy projects are essentially different, each will have specific requirements and peculiarities associated with the circumstances of the project. Not all examples listed in the model will have usefulness or value in every buy project, but they are all presented so that at the beginning of a project they can be evaluated for usefulness in planning a strategy for the project. Developing process and activity maps will help define which steps or tasks are actually required in a project and will keep the project on course until it is completed.

Development of Sourcing Strategies

It is the responsibility of procurement and supply managers to develop and plan what strategies should be used in accomplishing the goals set by the organization. This is not something that is required in day-to-day operations, but it should always be a strategy tool that can be activated whenever opportunities are recognized or when changes in the business environment and structure warrant it. Best-in-class supply management and procurement departments recognize this and make developing new sourcing strategies a regular part of their strategic review process. Developing new sample process and/or activity maps can be a significant aid in understanding what new strategies might entail.

Request for Quote and Request for Proposal Preparation

Another primary responsibility of procurement is preparing and issuing request for quotes (RFQs) and RFPs. Much thought, strategy, planning, and research should be applied in their preparation. This important supply management and procurement activity is discussed in more detail in Chapter 14.

Request for Quote and Request for Proposal Analysis and Evaluation

RFQ and RFP analysis and evaluation in supply management and procurement requires a great deal of detail in its performance. There are several types of analysis available that can be used to evaluate different portions and aspects of RFQs and RFPs. Some are as simple as basic product and price comparisons; others are more detailed and require research or even other analysis to be performed to supply certain data before the desired analysis can be performed. A variety of these along with applications to supply management and procurement are exampled and discussed throughout this book. An evaluation process map allows you to determine what analysis, tasks, and decisions should be made at what point in the process.

Negotiation Strategy and Development

Whenever negotiations are required, planning a strategy for the negotiations is required. Information gathered from RFP responses, analysis, as well as other sources of information, are used in the development of primary and alternative strategies for negotiating. A negotiating plan that includes reasonable beginning and final requirements should be developed prior to the opening of any negotiation. If a team is to be used, team members and resources that might be called on should be chosen, roles assigned, and a leader chosen. After a strategy is developed, team members should meet to discuss the strategy and understand their role in the negotiation process. It is a good idea to develop a written negotiation strategy plan for review with the negotiating team in advance of pre-negotiation meetings. This way changes in strategy can be made and discussed. Some of the key elements identified and incorporated in a negotiation strategy plan are:

- What is the most desired outcome
- What is the least acceptable agreement
- What is the best alternative to a negotiated agreement
- What assumptions are you making (all things you think you know)
- All things you do not know
- All things you must have that are not negotiable
- What you might ask for by way of probing
- What concessions you are willing to make in the form of trade-offs

- What options there might be for mutual gain (creative trade-offs)
- What obstacles might exist for reaching an agreement
- What risks might exist after reaching an agreement

It is always wise to create a negotiating planning sheet with the elements described before beginning any negotiations. The author uses this strategy in all types of negotiations, both in business and in personal life when appropriate. Chapter 15 discusses negotiating strategies in more detail and displays an example of the negotiating planning sheet mentioned here as well as how to use a negotiation tracking log.

Value Chain Analysis

Value chain analysis (VCA) is an ultra-strategic tool that is not used all that often, but when it is used it can have a dramatic impact on major buy projects. What a VCA does, and the reason for doing one, is to look at all of the primary and secondary activities required and performed both internally and externally for an organization to determine cost and value for each activity. Once identification of all primary and secondary activities is made, an analysis and evaluation is performed to identify efficiencies and deficiencies in each activity, their volatility and importance, what they cost, what value they bring, and, most important of all, what opportunities exist for cost reduction and efficiency improvement.

Value Opportunity Identification

Identifying opportunities for adding additional value to a project, activity, processes, and the organization as a whole is a significant strategic supply management activity. A value opportunity analysis may be performed at any time and may even be performed several times during a specific buy project to adjust for new discoveries or changes in what was previously known or assumed. A value opportunity analysis usually requires research and information gathering, as well as the findings from other analyses, to determine if changes are possible and warranted. Additionally, it reveals what the cost and impact of changes might be, what value might be gained from making a change, and whether they are worth making a recommendation to change.

Risk Assessment and Management

Risks are always present in everything we do or attempt. They are especially significant and relevant in new buy projects and changes of any type that may be considered. Even continuing with a present process or direction may pose some risk. Risk identification and assessment, as well as risk management, is a top priority in strategic supply management activity. Beginning with SWOT analysis to identify strengths, weaknesses, opportunities, and threats and then performing a risk analysis for things identified in SWOT is a key strategic supply management activity. Without identifying potential risks and designing a plan to deal with and manage them, we leave ourselves open for bad things to happen. It is really not worth taking a chance by not considering risks and developing a risk mitigation plan to overcome possibilities if they materialize. Chapter 11 discusses risk analysis and management in detail and looks at some examples of how to perform them.

Contract Preparation and Award

Another primary strategic supply management and procurement duty is overseeing contract preparation and award. After proposals are received, analysis performed, negotiations conducted, and agreements reached, it is then time to prepare a contract that will be acceptable to both parties. Procurement professionals are not lawyers. They are good at what they do and should play a role in contract preparation, but they should never prepare an offer or sign a contract without a qualified business law attorney first reviewing it. Ideally, procurement personnel should work with the organization's legal representatives to draft a contract to present to the apparent bid winner. There will always be standard boilerplate language and requirements specific to the organization that must be inserted, but the primary purpose of writing the contract is to define and explain the responsibilities and requirements of each party that were agreed to. To avoid any misunderstanding, confusion, or ambiguity, it is always a good idea to record what was discussed and agreed to during negotiations. To aid in both negotiations and contract preparation, a negotiation log of events and agreements that transpired during the meetings should be kept. To make negotiation planning and contract preparation easier, it is a good practice to structure RFPs to reflect the terms and requirements that would ultimately be included in a final contract. This makes contract preparation so much easier and saves time and confusion that could result in the necessity to reopen negotiations.

Contract Management

After contract preparation comes the contract signing and, after that, contract management is implemented. Comprehensive contract management is a pivotal strategic supply management activity. Logically, the responsibility for monitoring and managing contracts should fall to supply management and procurement since they are the entity that was involved in setting the terms and are the most familiar with them. How well contracts are managed determines the amount of true value they produce for an organization. One can negotiate the best terms in the world but if they are not monitored, managed correctly, or taken advantage of it will result in just so much wasted effort. Chapter 16 discusses the value advantages of practicing strategic contract management. It presents good examples of how effectively managing contracts can bring extra value to an organization.

Supply Management Process Monitoring

Procurement departments that practice strategic supply management and procurement have a philosophy of continuous improvement. To continuously improve, three things must be in place and then utilized:

1. A process and procedure should be developed to monitor current activities, processes, and procedures for efficiency and effectiveness. Results should be recorded and tracked. A periodic review of results should be conducted.
2. An awareness that business is continuously changing and new concepts and techniques may become available at any time that might have value in application should be noted. Suppliers are a great source for learning about new technologies that they have to offer or use themselves. Keeping up (staying informed) on changes to your industry, profession, and business in general through trade and industry journals and periodicals should be a habit sustained.
3. Comprehensive education and training programs for both management and employees allow the discovery of new concepts, processes, and applications. Many readers of this book may find themselves discovering new concepts and ideas previously not known or new ways to apply previously known concepts. A conscience attempt is made in this book to present proven supply management and procurement tools and techniques in real world examples, scenarios, and exercises.

Continuing Education and Training

You will notice that this is the tip of the strategic supply management activity pyramid portrayed in Figure 6.4. It could be said that no other supply management and procurement activity has any greater long-term benefit for an organization. Other activities may produce significant savings or improvements in specific or even ongoing situations but continuing education and training increases the specific and overall knowledge base and understanding of the employees involved in the supply management and procurement process. Sadly, training is one of the first things eliminated with budget cuts in economic hard times. Some organizations do not realize the importance of and reliance on education and training to sustain success.

Companies that practice best-in-class supply management and procurement include activity process design and mapping as part of their core processes and procedures. The rewards for them doing so equate to lower operating costs and higher profit margins. Another benefit is that they are able to gain competitive advantage over their competition and sustain their success. In the case of activity process and design (process and activity mapping), a little work goes a long way in understanding how your company, your supply partners, and your competition operates. It also helps you identify opportunities for improvement.

7

Organizing and Prioritizing Projects

To maximize your efforts so that you realize the most efficient and effective strategic supply management and procurement, you must learn to organize and prioritize your supply and procurement projects. What this means is that you select projects that will result in the highest reduction in costs and that have the greatest financial impact (increased profits) for the organization. These two goals can be realized by implementing a strategic supply management methodology that includes such techniques as supply chain management, value chain management, and other techniques discussed in this book and by process and activity improvements that increase efficiencies and effectiveness.

We know there is never enough time or resources to do everything that should or could be done. This fact is even more evident in today's business world where economic pressures are forcing organizations to try to do more with less in order to contain costs. That is why it is important to organize and prioritize procurement projects to determine their importance and to discover what and how much value each project will mean for the organization. This allows you to provide better, more efficient use of your time and budget dollars.

Let us assume that your procurement department has three existing long-term purchase contracts that will expire soon and you have identified two new opportunities that could be candidates for long-term contracts. This is in addition to the regular, daily spot purchases your department must make to maintain established inventory levels and satisfy the organization's requirements. How do you identify which projects will yield the highest return for the work required, which projects will require the most time, effort, and resources to accomplish, and which projects should be assigned the highest priority? To help you make these determinations you can:

- Calculate the savings each project will realize (this will have to be a best guess initially).
- Calculate the cost that each project will demand (employee time, etc.).
- Calculate the time and resources that will be required for each project (how long the project will take, etc.).

Sounds easy, doesn't it. But how do you make these calculations? In the case of how much savings a project will realize, initially you will only be able to make an estimate. You will not know exact savings for sure until all of the bids are in and analyzed. If you set a goal, such as a certain percentage of savings you want to attain, that is a good place to start and gives you something to work toward. The rule of thumb is that you should save an average of 30 to 35% when you move purchases from a spot buy to a contract buy. However, this depends largely on how efficient your existing procurement techniques are and how well your buyers are buying. But contracts can also offer additional value adds other than a reduced purchase price such as increased reliability, reduced on-hand inventory, and guaranteed on-time delivery just to mention a few.

Calculating the cost for a project is also an estimation, but you can get fairly close if you have a project completion history of similar projects or tools such as Microsoft Project to plan or schedule the project tasks in advance. Knowing how much employee time and resources is allocated to the project can then be calculated. Do not forget to include costs of vendor visits and any peripheral expenses anticipated.

Calculating how long a project will take is done in tandem with calculating the cost of the project. I use MS Project to plan in advance how long a project will take. This type of planning methodology is also an excellent way to control costs and keep the project on track. Most procurement projects have defined end dates, but more complex projects might require substantial preliminary research and may have open end dates. Whether you use MS Project, some other type of planning software, or nothing at all, you can assign daily or weekly time requirements for each task of the project to be performed. By nature I am a planner, which I consider a good thing but it drives my wife crazy. I call her Annie Oakley because she prefers to shoot from the hip and make decisions as she goes. This works for many people for most things but not for project planning. You must have a general plan and time frame to follow that facilitates your efforts and allows you to stay on course.

The benefits of prioritizing are many, but the main benefit is adding maximum value to the organization. You have probably heard the phrase *low-hanging fruit* before. In project planning this axiom refers to projects that are easy to accomplish and that can be accomplished quickly, mainly from a time standpoint. But these projects may not always be the ones that should carry the highest priority. The priority of the project will have to be a decision you make based on need, time, cost, and resources.

Now back to our scenario. Your procurement department has three existing long-term purchase contracts that will expire soon and you have identified two new opportunities that could be candidates for long-term contracts. You also have to continue to issue the daily bids and issue spot purchases orders to maintain established inventory levels and meet internal customer demands. Here is a little background and some fast facts to consider:

- All existing contract buys are done automatically and electronically through an electronic data interchange (EDI) platform.
- You have three buyers and it takes them approximately 30 minutes per spot buy item to research, issue bids, evaluate them, and write and issue a purchase order (PO). At eight hours per day and 30 minutes per PO times three buyers yields a potential of 16 POs per day and 80 per week. Remember, these numbers represent a perfect situation that generally does not hold true.
  - Researching (finding suppliers), issuing bids, and writing POs are not continuous processes. It takes time to receive direct bids and quotes from suppliers. Consequently, the buyers are working several buys simultaneously. Less time is required for retrieving a price from an online catalog or bid request.
- Your department issues approximately 347 POs per month based on the numbers we have noted.
- You have identified 180 items that can be considered candidates for two new contracts.
- You have three existing contracts covering 896 items that will be expiring over the next two to six months.
- All of the 896 items presently on contract and 128 items identified as candidates for new contracts are considered critical items to your operation.

How do you identify which projects will yield the highest return for the work required, which projects will require the most time, effort, and resources to accomplish, and which projects should be assigned the highest priority? To answer these questions we will make some assumptions:

- The spend on Contract 1 that will expire in two months is $875,000 per year.
- The spend on Contract 2 that will expire in four months is $1,215,000 per year.

- The spend on Contract 3 that will expire in six months is $746,000 per year.
- After projected savings, the spend on one opportunity (proposed Contract 1) identified for possible contract and covering 128 critical items was estimated to be $578,000 per year.
- After projected savings, the spend on the other opportunity (proposed Contract 2) identified for possible contract and covering 52 noncritical items is estimated to be $125,000 per year.
- Approximate time to bid, analyze, negotiate, and award items on the existing contracts is 30 days per contract, based on previous experience.
- Approximate time to research, bid, analyze, negotiate, and award items on the proposed contracts is 50 days per contract.

At first glance you may be able to see some obvious decisions that can be made with regard to prioritization. Keep those in mind to see if you are correct as we do the next exercise. Oftentimes what we think is the obvious and most valuable decision may not be. To aid in our decision making for which procurement project offers the greatest opportunities for cost savings and the greatest value to the organization, and therefore should have the higher priority, we can develop a matrix of all of our knowns and assumptions. A matrix has been prepared using the information and assumptions supplied for this exercise that is reflected in Table 7.1.

Take a moment to review this table. Did you make the same priority decisions as the matrix reflects? Do you agree with the matrix data and priority decisions? Developing a project priority matrix to visually define and portray the parameter objectives desired, as well as the known and assumed criteria, is a tremendous help in making the most value decisions and assigning their priority. Each organization will have criteria specific to their organization and its needs. Other columns of criteria may be required to evaluate value such as whether or not items and contracts might be candidates for just-in-time, vendor managed inventory, or other criteria that is required.

We will now break down the matrix presented in Table 7.1 and discuss the reasoning behind the decisions made. The matrix lists the five contract opportunities, the three existing contracts that will be expiring in the next six months, and the two new contract opportunities. The matrix lists criteria that are known and also that which is assumed. Known criteria are based on absolute facts such as the number of items that will be bid, whether or not the items are considered critical to the operation, and what the current annual spend is. Assumed criteria are based on the estimated days it will take to bid, analyze, negotiate, and award a new contract. The estimates used for all of the existing contracts are based on historical times it took to bid and award the previous contracts. The two new contracts will require additional time

Table 7.1 Project priority matrix

Contract opportunity	Items	Annual # of POs issued	Critical items	Current estimated annual spend	Days to award	Estimated savings contract vs. spot	Estimated savings (EDI vs. Manual)	Total estimated annual savings	Value rank	Priority assigned
		Knowns				**Assumptions**				
Existing No. 1	278	1,132	Yes	$875,000	30	$350,000	$169,630	$519,630	3	1
Existing No. 2	380	1,620	Yes	$1,215,000	30	$420,000	$242,757	$662,757	2	3
Existing No. 3	258	1,089	Yes	$746,000	30	$245,000	$163,187	$408,187	5	4
Proposed No. 1	478	1,923	Yes	$948,000	50	$185,000	$288,162	$473,162	4	5
Proposed No. 2	312	4,468	No	$201,000	50	$76,000	$669,530	$745,530	1	2

Assumption No. 1: Average cost of issuing a manual purchase order is $150.00 per PO.
Assumption No. 2: Average cost of issuing a purchase order via EDI is $.15 per PO.

for research and negotiations so allowance was made for those points. The cost differential of savings from buying on contract from one supplier versus noncontract, spot buying from several buyers is calculated and used as an estimated buy savings projection.

There is additional savings to be had from buying on contract and using an EDI platform that automatically issues POs and makes invoice payments electronically as opposed to a manual bid and PO system. The cost of a manual system is calculated at $150 per PO. This calculation includes the time of the buyer, including salary and benefits. It also includes all other associated costs such as heat, light, and power. The cost of using an EDI program that automatically identifies inventory minimum levels and issues a PO automatically and electronically is calculated at $0.15 per PO. The estimated savings from the contract buys are combined with the estimated savings from using an EDI system to show a total estimated savings. Each of the five contracts is then assigned a value ranking based on their total cost savings to the organization. After reviewing all of the information and criteria, a priority ranking is assigned.

Existing Contract 1 covers 278 critical items and has an annual spend of $875,000. It has an estimated annual cost savings of $350,000 for contract buy versus spot buys. Each of the 278 items is bought multiple times throughout the year, depending on usage requirements. In the case of Contract 1, it has been determined that there will be an estimated total of 1,132 POs issued each year. This will represent a potential cost savings of $169,630 for issuing POs via EDI versus doing so manually. This makes the estimated total annual cost savings potential of $519,630. The total number of critical items and the total annual cost savings earns Contract 1 a value rank of two, but because this contract is set to expire within two months it is assigned the top priority of number one.

Existing Contract 2 covers 380 critical items and has an annual spend of $1,215,000. The estimated annual cost savings for contract versus spot buy is $420,000. Each of the 380 items is bought multiple times throughout the year and it is estimated that there will be a total of 1,620 POs issued each year. This represents a potential cost savings of $242,757 for issuing POs via EDI versus doing so manually. The total estimated annual cost savings is projected at $662,757. Because of the highest number of critical items, total annual spend, and highest total potential cost savings, Contract 2 earns a value rank of one but is assigned a priority of two because the contract does not expire for four months. If time and resources are available, Contracts 1 and 2 could be considered to be worked simultaneously with the greater emphasis placed on Contract 1.

Referring to the table again, existing Contract 3 has a high number of critical items, a high annual spend, and cost savings that earns it a value rank of four, but it is assigned a priority of five because this contract still has six months to run before it is set to expire. Proposed Contract 1 currently has the second highest annual spend that covers 478 critical, high-dollar items that are bought approximately 1,923 times a year. Substantial cost savings can be realized by moving the buy of these items from noncontract spot buys to contract buys and using EDI to purchase. Additional time to bid and award will need to be allowed for in order to cover research, identifying, and qualifying bidders. Because of the number of critical items and the potential cost savings, proposed Contract 1 earned a value rank of four and a priority rank of five. Proposed Contract 2 is interesting. It covers office and miscellaneous supplies that include computers, printers, scanners, and software. These are noncritical items that are being purchased with no standardization or consistency and are purchased more often than they should be. In fact, if you look at Table 7.1 again, you will see that the cost of issuing POs for these items is actually two-thirds the actual cost of the supplies themselves. This opportunity is what is referred to as low-hanging fruit and is a no-brainer where inventory control and costs are involved. It has been assigned a value rank of one and a priority of two due to the amount of money that can be saved by moving to an EDI system, and it will be easy to bid and award before existing Contract 2.

Before this exercise, how many of you picked the same priority schedule as the exercise? The old saying *time is money* is certainly true. Some procurement departments take work as it comes without little, if any, planning or looking for opportunities to gain more value for their organizations. The items included in proposed Contract 2 were being purchased indiscriminately without any inventory control. It really does not take too much extra time to think through situations and effectively prioritize procurement projects. Developing a prioritizing matrix will help in the decision making. It only took about 15 minutes to prepare Table 7.1, but it really aided in making the best value priority decisions in the example.

8

Creating Competitive Advantage with Supply Management

Organizations continually strive to obtain and sustain competitive advantage over their competition. Competitive advantage is one of the driving forces in business, and organizations are continually looking for strategies to become more efficient and cost competitive. Additionally, they look for ways they can bring more value to their customers than their competitors. One might think first of marketing as having sole ownership and responsibility for achieving competitive advantage. Although marketing does play a primary role, the reality is that every business function and activity within an organization also has an important part to play in the organization achieving and sustaining competitive advantage. For an organization to obtain competitive advantage it must understand what benefits will be created by achieving competitive advantage. They can do that through developing greater efficiencies that equates to increased profitability. An organization must also understand what it takes to achieve competitive advantage and how to get there. The topmost level of management sets the goals and strategies for an organization. Those goals and strategies then become the game plan, so to speak, of what the organization wants to accomplish. An important ingredient of this plan should address the achievement and sustainability of success in the organization's individual industry market segment, in other words, competitive advantage. There are many tools that can be used by upper management in developing goals and strategies to help determine what can be done to obtain competitive advantage. Data received from internal and external environmental scans is one good example. Information from internal scans helps upper management understand how the organization is currently operating and how efficient each department is individually and overall as an organization. It allows upper management to identify inefficiencies and determine steps that should be taken for improvement. External environmental scans provide information to upper management about crucial areas such as:

- How well the organization is performing overall and in their market segment
- Who their customer base is
- How the organization is perceived by their customer base
- What their market share is (the percentage of sales in their market segment)
- Other information deemed important to the organization's strategies

Internal and external environmental scans are discussed in more detail in Chapter 10. One key way to obtain competitive advantage is by practicing successful strategic supply management. It offers ways to reduce costs and improve processes and efficiencies. Many believe that supply management is the single most important business function in an organization and offers the greatest opportunities to improve an organization's market position and profits. Other business functions such as new product development and marketing are important, but because supply management supports and touches so many other business functions and activities, it allows an organization to improve what they already have without costly expenditures to develop something new and unproven.

How Can Supply Management Help Achieve Competitive Advantage?

To discover how supply management can aid in achieving competitive advantage, let's first review some of the things we have already discussed. By implementing strategic supply management techniques, tools, and processes that add extra value to the organization and by improving efficiencies and increasing profitability, supply management supports the organizations overall and specific goals that allow the organization to attain and sustain competitive advantage. Key performance drivers for supply management include:

- Cost
- Extended value
- Quality
- Time
- Efficiency

- Reliability
- Technology

Each of these points are of equal importance. Cost is often looked at by some in procurement as the only—or main—driver. Although cost (what it cost an organization to buy goods and services) is crucial, without value it can actually be detrimental. This is where some organizations miss the boat because they fail to realize the importance of things other than buying at the cheapest price. Procurement should make the best value buy, not just the cheapest buy. What makes up a best value buy? It is a combination of price, availability, lead time, vendor and materials reliability, and adherence to quality standards set by the organization. This is what extended value means; all of the things over and above the cost of a product purchased that adds reductions in operating costs and improvements in operating efficiencies. It is up to the supply management and procurement professional to find out what those things are and act on them. To do so, they need to develop a philosophy and a tool kit to help them obtain it.

Quality describes how good a product is when it is received. Zero defects and rejects should be the ultimate goal. Rigid quality standards and specifications should always be addressed in purchase orders and negotiated into contracts and have consequences for nonconformance. Procurement can, and should, include in their purchase contracts provisions for allowable defects and then address rejects. This would include how rejects and warranty claims are handled such as returns and credit procedures, replacements, and penalties (monetary or otherwise).

Time includes several considerations and also determines a part of the overall cost to an organization. Dedicated and on-hand product inventory at the supplier's facilities, lead time for product delivery, repair lead time, the length of time it takes to purchase, bid, and negotiate purchase orders and contracts, to name a few. Anything that requires time to accomplish an objective carries an associated cost.

Efficiency denotes how successful individual tasks and processes are being performed. The more efficient individual tasks and processes are performed, the lower the cost to the organization. Efficiency optimization should be at the top of the list of process improvement and be one of the first things looked for in any and all procurement buy projects and, indeed, in all day-to-day operations. Efficiency equates to degree of profitability and therefore is an important cost control component. If you can do something better and faster, you then, in effect, reduce the cost of doing it. Best-in-class supply management and procurement continually asks the question 'Can we do this business function, activity, or process better and if we can, how can we do it?'

Reliability of products purchased is the degree, or amount of time, to which parts and components last before failure. This is an important factor in determining what parts and components to buy and from whom to buy them. Obviously the longer a part or component lasts, the fewer you need to buy. One should look at the manufacturer's guaranteed mean time between failure (MTBF) to determine availability of parts and components, that is, how long a part or component could be expected to last when installed before it was expected to fail and must be removed and replaced or repaired. Another aspect of reliability is how much a part or component costs to repair and how long it takes to repair it. This allows determination of how many spare parts should be kept on hand and what inventory levels should be.

Technology is one item often overlooked. It is constantly changing and improving. Technology is an important factor because it allows us to work faster, handle more information, increase efficiencies, and reduce costs. Don't forget, technology also comes with a cost and the addition of new technology should be analyzed to determine the cost benefit, that is, the cost to purchase and implement a new technology versus the cost savings and efficiency it might provide going forward.

Some of the tools, techniques, and philosophies of supply management include:

- Supply management
  - Price analysis—Straight line comparison of bid prices
  - Total cost analysis—Total cost of the purchase
  - Total cost of ownership—Total cost of an item through its life
  - Purchase history analysis
    - Usage analysis—Types of items and quantities purchased and used
    - Prices historically paid for individual products and services
    - Who products and services were purchased from and when
  - Financial analysis—Financial details and credit ratings of suppliers and bidders
  - Technical analysis—Technical aspects and attributes of an item
  - Weighted decision matrix—An unbiased tool to determine the best value buy decision
  - Value opportunity analysis—Determines what opportunities for cost and process improvement are available
  - SWOT analysis—Identifies strengths, weaknesses, opportunities, and threats to a procurement project
  - Risk analysis and risk management plan development—identification of potential risks and mitigation plans determined for procurement projects
- Supply chain management
  - Supply chain link identification
  - Supply chain management plan developed

- Value chain management
  - Primary and support activity identification
  - Value analysis
  - Opportunities for increased value identification
- Data management
  - Databases created to manage and track supply management information
    - Purchase history
    - Vendor performance
    - Purchased goods and services reliability
    - Raw materials, purchased goods, and services market prices
- Quality management
  - Inspection, testing, and quality control
- Reliability management
  - MTBF determined
  - Repair costs and lead times established
- Vendor management
  - Vender performance
    - Vendor report cards
    - Vendor audits, site visits, and inspections
- Contract management
  - Monitoring of price increases, materials and parts shortages, on-time deliveries, warranty work and failure rates, product reliability, vendor performance, indices covering escalator and de-escalator clauses, and monetary milestone rebates
- Technology management
  - Continuous technology identification and improvement management

To attain competitive advantage an organization must distinguish itself from its competition. This is achieved by being innovative, more efficient, quality-driven, and by offering more value to the customers. An organization must be bold and, at times, be willing to take some calculated risks. Sometimes an organization's culture needs to be revised or changed. Business is fluid and constantly changing. A culture that helped make an organization a success originally may not be sufficient for the present day realities of business. In this instance, change in organizational culture and philosophy must occur or an organization runs the risk of being overtaken by its competition or even failing altogether. From a competition standpoint, the statement 'if you are not doing it, somebody else will' is true. You then need to ask the questions why we are not doing it, why should we do it, and how can we do it. Every strategic tool and technique may not be the right fit or best process for every situation or for your operation. Keep in mind that every situation is different and has its own set of circumstances and requirements that will dictate what tools and techniques best fit your industry, processes, and situation.

Throughout this book many broad statements are made. This is done because many of the subjects are topics within themselves and you cannot cram every detail into one book and expect people to read and comprehend it all. Specifics and details of many of the topics presented here are left for subsequent books and discussions.

9

Strategic Sourcing Methodology Models

Whether your organization is practicing basic, best-in-class supply management and procurement or something in between, you should be employing some kind of sourcing methodology. This may simply be your departmental standard operating procedures or something more extensive. Whatever you are practicing, you should develop a formal model(s) to use as a guide in your sourcing initiatives. Well-developed models serve as road maps that can be followed to arrive at a desired destination. Consider the strategic sourcing methodology model as a procurement GPS that gives directions and tells you when to make the next turn or which step of the process to perform. Process models keep everyone on track as they work through it step-by-step to a successful purchase.

The model presented in this chapter is a combination of requirements, tools, and techniques that have consistently produced successful results in real-world practice over the years. They are taken from many different supply management situations in various industries and companies. Basically, the following model is a collection of just about everything one could employ in practicing strategic supply management. But remember, every supply management or procurement project is different. Each situation will have requirements and specifications that will be specific to that particular industry and project and any outline of strategies developed should take this into consideration. You do not want to do any additional work that is not necessary or beneficial and, by the same token, you do not want to leave anything out that would promote creating added value to your project.

Request for Proposal: Procurement Buy Project
An Advanced Strategic Sourcing Model Example

Define the opportunity

- Obtain all project information
- Identify the stakeholders
- Select project team members and resources
- Review all project support documentation
- Evaluate the size of the buy
- Evaluate the amount of inventory on hand (if applicable)
- Evaluate the term of the buy
- Analyze historic usage demands (if applicable)
- Project team then brainstorms preliminary project strategy

Define the supply chain and create a map

- Identify demand drivers
- Review specifications
- Standardize the review
- Identify and map the supply chain
- Identify all related costs to buy
- Map the current process being used
- Determine the total cost of the current process
- Evaluate current process effectiveness
- Benchmark current costs and milestones
- Determine if opportunities exist to improve efficiencies

Define the value chain and create a map

- Identify primary activities
- Identify secondary activities
- Map the value chain
- Perform a value analysis
- Identify opportunities for improvement or reengineering

Analyze the supply market

- Identify all potential supply sources
- Identify any diversity suppliers
- Evaluate your industry
  - Research industry trends, what others are doing, new technology available, and so forth

- Perform environmental scans, both internal and external
- Perform supplier performance assessments
- Perform supplier comparisons and financials
  - Qualify suppliers
    - ◦ Eliminate unqualified suppliers as potential bidders
- Determine current and historical spend with potential suppliers
- Draft and issue a request for information (RFI) if necessary
- Receive and analyze the RFI
- Identify qualified suppliers with an RFI review
- Report results, findings, and recommendations to project requestor (primary stakeholder)

Develop a sourcing strategy

- Develop minimum requirements and specifications for the request for proposal (RFP)
- Standardize requirements where possible
- Identify what the desired outcomes should be
  - Term and quantity of buy
  - Other desired conditions of buy
- Brainstorm supply strategies to use
  - Inventory evaluation
    - ◦ Determine cost to receive, carry, and distribute inventory
    - ◦ Increase/decrease inventory minimum/maximum levels
      - Time between buys
    - ◦ Determine if a just-in-time delivery candidate or not
    - ◦ Determine if a vendor-managed inventory candidate or not
    - ◦ Determine if an EDI candidate or not
- Identify all decision matrix elements and assign weights according to importance and value
- Develop bidding/negotiating strategies for the RFP
  - Establish number of bidders
  - Establish a time line for bidding, analyzing, negotiating, decision-making, and award
- Draft and issue an RFP
- Start a bid tracking log
- Receive and analyze the RFP
  - Perform a bid specification analysis
    - ◦ Technical analysis
  - Perform a bid comparison analysis
    - ◦ Perform appropriate analysis (when applicable)
      - Straight-line price analysis

- Total cost analysis
- Total cost of ownership
- Usage cost analysis
- End-of-life analysis
- Financial analysis of bidders
- Develop a short list of bidders
- Draft and issue a revised RFP if necessary
- Receive and analyze the revised RFP
- Develop a bidder finalist list

Implement sourcing strategy

- Develop a negotiating plan and strategies for negotiations
- Select the negotiating team and assign roles
- Conduct negotiations
- Use the weighted decision matrix to make unbiased best value decision
- Procurement evaluates the RFP and negotiations
- Finance evaluates the RFP and negotiations
- Project team makes recommendations for award
- Obtain final approvals for award
- Select, notify, and award contract
- Finalize contract

End-of-project strategy

- Contract turned over to contract manager
- Conduct an end-of-project review meeting
  - Determine what went right, what went wrong
  - Identify improvements that might be made to the process
- Issue a project summary report for management and stakeholders

Monitoring

- Periodically review the contract to determine compliance
- Determine any problems or changes that should be made
  - Tweak for improvement
- Report any changes in conditions or price to the contract manager or person of responsibility

Several types of requests, or bids, may be required and used in the strategic procurement process. The type of buy, requirements of the buy, and specifics of the buy will dictate what is necessary. If new technology has been developed, new suppliers considered, or changes made to internal processes, then an

RFI may be required preceding issuance of any type of bid. It is used to obtain information about:

- A supplier
    - Who they are and their capabilities
    - Financial stability
    - Standard products offered
    - Other pertinent information
- New technology
    - What new technology is currently available
    - What new technology is being developed
    - What companies offer new technology

10

The Importance of Critical Thinking and Strategy Development in Supply Management

Critical thinking, or thinking outside of the box, like most buzzwords and catch phrases, become passé over time and lose some of their meaning and importance. They are taken for granted and not practiced aggressively or at all. About 14 years of my career was spent at UPS airlines in strategic sourcing. This was a department within procurement services that negotiated all of the purchases and contracts for the supply of parts, materials, and services (maintenance, repair, and overhaul procurement) to support the maintenance of the 220 heavy jets that UPS owned and operated worldwide. During that time I stressed thinking outside the brown box. UPS has a unique culture that has driven its amazing success in the package delivery and transportation industry, but its success has also affected its ability to embrace some needed changes internally. This phenomenon is not unique to UPS but is prevalent with most large organizations as well as many midsize and smaller companies. Why? Because if you are successful doing what you are doing, why do you need to change? The reason is because the business world, business models, and, most importantly, your competition is changing. Business and economies are fluid and customers demand more value for the dollars they spend. Businesses need to understand this important concept if they are to survive, obtain, or sustain success. Best-in-class organizations understand the importance of change and make staying ahead of the change curve a priority.

Critical thinking is absolutely necessary in the development of both long- and short-term goals and strategies. It is one thing to set a goal but quite another to develop a strategy to successfully attain that goal. A major part of critical thinking is creativity. Being creative in your critical thinking cannot be stressed enough. An atmosphere and endorsement of creativity is conducive to successful strategy development. A strategy is a plan of action that is developed to achieve or obtain a specific vision or goal, and it requires evaluation of any and all specifics that may affect or have an impact on the vision or goal. A few of the initial questions that should be asked in the preliminary stages of strategy development are:

- What do we want to accomplish?
- Why do we want to accomplish it?
- When do we want to accomplish it?
- How can we accomplish it?
- What will it cost to accomplish it?
- Who will have the responsibility to accomplish it?

Strategies are developed and implemented at various organizational levels such as corporate, divisional, and departmental. Strategies may be developed by an individual person (smaller or single-owner companies) or by a group of individuals (larger organizations) operating as a team. In both situations brainstorming ideas is important in identifying and developing a list of possibilities and alternatives that can be explored. Some of the questions that might be asked in a brainstorming session are:

- Corporate strategy
  - What is the present direction and goals of the organization?
  - What new direction or goals does the organization want to develop?
  - What markets are the organization presently in?
  - What new markets does the organization want to develop?
  - Who is the organization's present competition?
  - How is the competition performing (what is their market share)?
  - Who might the future competition be?
  - How can the organization perform better than the competition in those markets?
  - How can the organization develop competitive advantage?
  - What external and internal environmental factors affect the ability of the organization to be competitive?
  - What resources will be required to allow the organization to compete successfully?
    - Personnel
    - Skills
    - Technology

- ○ Finances
- ○ Assets
- • Who are the stakeholders in the organization who would have the responsibility of implementing strategies?
- • Divisional or business unit strategy
  - • What strategies and processes are required to meet organizational goals?
    - ○ Resources
    - ○ Personnel
    - ○ Skills
    - ○ Equipment
    - ○ Processes
      - • Activity
      - • Procedural
    - ○ Markets
      - • Products
      - • Services
    - ○ Opportunities for improvement
  - • How can existing processes and procedures be restructured to accommodate changes required?

After the goals and strategies are developed and implemented they then have to be managed. This is referred to as strategic management. Strategic management is an ongoing process. Processes and procedures must be continually monitored or tracked to determine how successfully the strategy or plan is working, and then steps need to be taken to correct or improve processes and procedures when it is not.

Strategic Management

In its broadest sense, strategic management is about making strategic decisions, that is, decisions based on research performed and questions asked such as the questions just presented. The strategic management process consists of three main components: (1) analysis, (2) choice, and (3) implementation as shown in Figure 10.1.

Strategic analysis is concerned with establishing the conditional aspects of the business such as:

- • Financial status
- • Profitability
- • Operational effectiveness
- • Market share
- • Competition

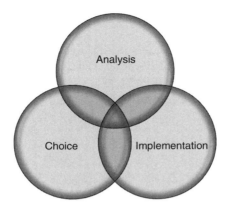

Figure 10.1   Strategic management process

- Process improvement

Strategic analysis is also concerned with any factor that might affect the success of the organization, now or in the future. A few of the tools and techniques used in strategic analysis are listed but many more are available:

- Environmental scanning—One of the primary ways of discovering information about the present conditions of an organization is through internal and external environmental scanning. It produces information and data on organizational financial status, operations, industry standing and rank, customer satisfaction, and competition, to name a few. A more in-depth look at environmental scanning is covered later in this chapter.

- PEST analysis—PEST stands for political, economic, social, and technological and is an analysis that addresses the different aspects of the environment in which the organization operates. PEST analysis is used to identify and understand the environment the organization operates in and usually is only used in the development of corporate strategy.

- SWOT analysis—SWOT analysis identifies the strengths, weaknesses, opportunities, and threats in a particular situation. SWOT analysis can be performed on the corporate, divisional, and departmental levels to aid in development of strategies for organizational direction. It can be used on the divisional and departmental levels to determine how to effectively meet organizational goals set and how to complete individual projects successfully.

- Risk analysis—Risk analysis is a continuation of SWOT. Weaknesses and threats identified in SWOT are usually general in nature. Risk analysis takes a more detailed and analytical approach. Specific risks are identified and detailed and an action plan is developed to overcome any risk that might manifest.

- Five forces analysis—This analysis was developed by Michael E. Porter in 1979 for business development. Five forces analysis would only be used on the corporate strategy level. They are:
  - Threat of new competition
  - Degree of competitive rivalry
  - Threat of alternative products or services
  - Bargaining power of buyers (customers)
  - Bargaining power of vendors and suppliers
- Sensitivity analysis—Sensitivity analyses are basically what-if scenarios. It looks at a potential scenario and then thinks it through to a possible conclusion. Sensitivity analyses are not often used or are called by a different name. They can be useful in any business activity but are extremely beneficial in supply management and procurement activities. I have used sensitivity analyses extensively and found them helpful in determining best courses of action. A graphic representation of what is involved in a sensitivity analysis is shown in Figure 10.2.

Choice is involved with identifying and understanding what the expectations of options are, evaluating them, and testing them against benchmarks, and then selecting the strategic option that offers the organization the most value. Setting benchmarks is important as these are goals set that the organization wishes to attain. They might also be called milestones but milestones are usually points along a progression line that are achieved in the pursuit of meeting a benchmark.

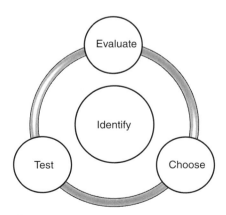

Figure 10.2   Sensitivity analysis components

Implementation of strategies is the final step in strategy management. Once strategies have been identified, analyzed, and tested, they are then ready to be implemented. A plan for how the strategy will be implemented, an implementation plan, and time line for implementation is then developed and the strategy initiated.

What are environmental scans and how can they be helpful? Environmental scanning is an analytical technique used to gather and analyze data both internally and externally to determine factors that might affect the organization and how it conducts its business. Findings of the scan and analysis can then be used to perform a SWOT analysis to determine strengths, weaknesses, opportunities, and threats, and a risk analysis to formulate goals of both tactical and strategic plans for the organization. An example of an external environmental scan might be determining the percentage of potential customers for a particular product by demographics, consumer trends, or new technology that is available. When Apple's iPhone was being developed, you can be assured that environmental scans were performed to test and determine if a market for the iPhone might exist and what degree of success might be expected for the product as well as identification of who the target customers might be. Likewise, an organization might perform an external environmental scan to determine their level of performance against competition to discover their industry rank in effectiveness. From this they could establish benchmarks, set goals, and develop strategies.

Environmental scanning is most often used externally but can also be used internally as well to analyze specifics of the organization's business processes and procedures. This allows determination of the capabilities of the organization as they exist today and determine if they will be adequate to fulfill the needs of the organization in the future. It can be used to perform a variety of procurement duties. Internal environmental scans might be used when gathering information on internal processes of user departments to aid in the development of process maps to help understand how user departments depend on procurement to operate successfully. External environmental scans might be used in identifying supply chains to determine how suppliers conduct their business, who their Tier 1 and Tier 2 suppliers are, and how they conduct their business. And, both internal and external environmental scans might be used in identifying and understanding the value chains of an organization, who and what is/are involved, their financial impact on the organization, and potential cost reduction alternatives.

Any and all data obtained from environmental scanning must be analyzed in order to be useful to an organization. This requires screening of the data to eliminate unnecessary data or data that is not useful. Questions asked when analyzing will aid in fine tuning the data to maximize its usefulness. Value chain management's purpose is to determine the efficiency of primary and secondary business activities of an organization and to determine if any opportunities exist for improvement. Therefore an environmental scan is done (in this case, both internally and externally) to gather data about how business activities are performed, who performs them, what factors affect how they are performed, and how the competition performs the same activities. A few of the questions that might be asked in an environmental scan are:

- How is our organization performing each of the business functions and activities identified in our value chain?
- What are the outer limits to what we can do?
- Will (or should) changes to the external environment affect the way various functions are performed?
- How does our competitor(s) perform these functions?
- Are our competitors' methods better than ours?
- Does it cost less?
- Does it provide more value to my company and customers?
- Does what we are doing in one activity affect and fit with what we are doing in other activities?
- Do we really have an integrated strategy? If so, what is it?
- What are the overall cost drivers?
- What is the cost for each link of the chain?
- What are the cost-restructuring opportunity options?
- What is the estimated cost for each opportunity option?
- What are the different reengineering configuration opportunity options at critical links?
- What is the cost-restructuring compared to competitors' costs?
- What are the economies of scale?
- What is the capacity utilization?
- Is there any linkage between activities and/or functions?
- What is the relationship between business units?
- What is the degree of vertical integration?
- What is the time to market of our product or service?
- Are there any institutional factors (regulations, union activity, taxes, etc.) to consider?

Answering these questions go a long way in determining how an organization currently conducts its business activities and how they compare to the competition. From this an organization can develop strategies that will help them obtain or maintain competitive advantage.

Pretty involved and heady stuff isn't it? You may think that this and many of the examples and recommendations made in this book would create significantly more work for you and your department. You are right, it will, but the extra effort will result in huge dividends in the form of improved efficiencies, lower costs, and higher profits for your organization. It is understood that you don't have enough time to do the work required of you now, so how can you expect to take on more work? This is partially true. Best-in-class organizations realize the importance and value that the techniques represented here have for their operations. Other organizations may not have the resources available to practice many of the techniques or they may believe that they are unnecessary. But here is the secret to including these techniques in your supply management and procurement processes. There is connectivity with many of the techniques. There is also duplicity in many of the techniques performed that lay a foundation for other techniques that helps reduce the workload. As an example, results of environmental scanning can be used in developing supply chains and value chains. If your organization does not want to dedicate the resources and support to implement any of the techniques presented here, or is adverse to change, there is a chapter included in this book that addresses this and shows ways to gain support for change.

You do not have to do everything presented in this book every time you do a procurement project. Many are one-time events. Environmental scanning is one such technique that falls into this category. The data and information you learn from doing generic or project-specific internal environmental scan yields information that applies all across the supply and procurement spectrum, for all products or services you buy. Simply put, what an internal environmental scan entails is finding out what other internal departments do, how they do it, what the interaction or dependency is with procurement, and all of the associated costs. Then opportunities can be identified to improve efficiencies and reduce costs. Environmental scans can be used in just this way with great success. They not only provide information you may not have previously known, but also allow you to create process maps for the internal departments you deal with or are responsible for supporting to determine how you can service their needs better and improve the organization as a whole. As stated, environmental scans are something you may only do once but a good recommended practice would be to do them annually, semi-annually, or on an as needed basis.

So what does this information have to do with supply management? Everything. Some people do not fully understand the interconnectivity of business functions and activities. This is primarily due to the fact that they have not performed other business activities and are limited through experience to the specific job they are presently performing. They do not realize the dependence each activity has on the success of other activities and to the overall success of the organization. It is important that an organization share as much information with its employees as possible. The more information employees have about why and how other departments in an organization operates, the better understanding of the importance and effect of what they do has on the organization as a whole. Everyone should be encouraged to look past what they do and learn more about how other departments, and the organization overall, operate. This information will serve both you and the organization well.

An example of how all of this plays out is that upper management sets the overall strategy of the organization, that is, the direction the organization wants to go and how to get there. Divisional management develops plans and processes to achieve the strategies and goals that upper management has set and departmental management develops plans and processes to achieve the goals set by divisional management. So, let us say that one of the upper management strategies is that the organization wants to become best-in-class in their market segment. Divisional management sets goals and develops plans of how to achieve this. You, as supply manager or department procurement manager, and yes, even buyers and other employees, have a major role to play in achieving these goals.

Best-in-class means being the best in what you do. Being the best-in-class in business means being recognized as an organization that maximizes its efficiencies and strives to maintain competitive advantage. Everyone in the organization has a role to play and a contribution to make.

11

Risk Identification and Risk Management

Business is fluid and ever changing as noted earlier. Additionally, circumstances for the unforeseen are always changing. If an organization is practicing strategic supply management that includes good risk management and is monitoring its operations effectively, adjustments can be initiated to control circumstances and changes that might occur. If you are not proactive, you can expect bad things to happen.

Risk Analysis

There are risks associated with everything we do, therefore it is important to identify what things pose a real or potential risk to supply management and procurement initiatives that you contemplate and then develop a plan of action to mitigate or eliminate those risks. Risk management plans sometimes fall short for several reasons. The primary reason is that the people performing the risk analysis and the people who have the responsibility of managing the determined risks don't fully understand what they are doing or they simply don't place the degree of focus and importance on risk as they should.

Not enough research and analysis on the front end is oftentimes the culprit. It limits the development of comprehensive alternative solutions upon which a viable risk analysis can be performed. Another problem area is that once a risk analysis is performed and the risks are identified, there is little or no attention given to developing effective and executable plans to mitigate them. Identifying risks, developing plans (primary and contingency), tracking plan performance, and making decisions as they are warranted to resolve issues that might develop does not seem like rocket science, in fact, it is pretty basic stuff.

It is just common sense and sound business practice. Yet so many people make it more difficult than it should be.

It has always amazed me just how little importance many organizations and some individuals in management PEST place on risk identification and management. Plans just don't happen, you have to make them happen and that's where risk management plays a major role. What could happen to affect the completion of the task? If one of those possibilities (risks) does occur, what can you do to accomplish the task anyway? How will you know if something (risk) is going to affect what you want to do (monitoring)? These are questions that should be asked whenever you attempt a procurement project, are changing processes, or are developing strategies. The reasons for having a comprehensive risk mitigation and management plan are many, and the construction of any plan will be based on the variables that exist for the situation. A risk management plan should be concerned with the possibility that if any identified risk does in fact manifest, the risk mitigation plan previously developed will show the alternatives and include instructions on how to deal with and eliminate (mitigate) the risk.

Risk identification and management should be an integrated part of all supply management and procurement decision-making processes. It should be transparent and inclusive, involving anyone who is affected by a risk or can contribute to the resolution of the risk. You will see risk analysis mentioned in many of the chapters, exercises, and examples throughout this book, because risk analysis and management is one of the core tools utilized in strategic supply management and procurement.

There are three types of analysis that can help identify potential risks and threats:

1. PEST
2. SWOT
3. Risk

PEST is an acronym that stands for political, economic, social, and technological. These four categories are used to identify factors that might affect an organization's operations to some degree. PEST analysis can be used effectively by an organization's senior management to develop strategic and long-term plans and goals for the organization. It is an absolute necessity prior to an organization contemplating operations or doing business in a foreign country and has significance for domestic operations as well. PEST analysis uses tools such as research and external environmental scans to gather information and data useful and necessary in allowing an organization to formulate plans and strategies and identify potential risks.

The political portion of PEST analysis identifies such things as tax, labor, and environmental laws, trade restrictions between countries, tariffs, duties, as well as political and economic stability. These are all important factors that influence the degree of success or failure of an organization and its endeavors. Compliance with all applicable laws, domestic and foreign, is mandatory and must be identified and considered when organizations develop operational plans and strategies.

The economic portion of PEST analysis pertains to economic activity, inflation rates, interest rates, and monetary exchange rates in relation to international commerce. All of these factors have a major impact on how an organization might operate, formulate plans, and make decisions. Interest and inflation rates determine an organization's cost of capital that in turn determines growth and expansion. International monetary exchange rates affect the costs of doing business in or with other countries. Overall economic activity indicates strength or weakness of an economy and its ability to support goals and objectives of an organization. This can be determined by analyzing GDP and other economic indices such as producer and consumer price indexes, unemployment rates, and other recognized economic indicators.

The social and cultural portion of PEST analysis involves cultural aspects. This includes the demographics of population, age, income, and other factors that affect or influence an organization's operations or product offerings.

The technological portion of PEST analysis involves factors such as changing and new technology, research and development, automation, and other factors pertaining to technology that might affect quality, cost, and lead time.

PEST analyses are fairly easy to analyze once data is obtained, and it can be portrayed visually by listing the findings of each of the four categories in a matrix. Figure 11.1 shows a generalized and simplistic example for international and domestic package delivery. The economic section of the analysis in the figure lists several acronyms. GDP stands for Gross Domestic Product and is the market value of any and all final goods and services produced within a country during a given period of time. GDP is a good indicator of a country's level of standard of living. GDP can be calculated in any of three ways by using different approaches. One is by using products (outputs), another is by using income, and the third by using expenditures. In theory, all three approaches to calculating GDP should yield the same results. GDP is tracked, calculated and released by individual country governments. In the United States, the GDP report is published on the last day of each calendar quarter for results of the previous quarter.

PPI is an acronym that stands for Producer Price Index. It reflects the average change in the price of a market basket of goods and services manufactured by producers and sold to consumers in a wholesale market. The PPI is published monthly and is a good indicator of the rate of inflation and deflation. For this reason, the PPI is used as a basis for determining price adjustments in contracts that include escalator and de-escalator clauses.

CPI is an acronym that stands for Consumer Price Index. It reflects the average change in the prices paid for a market basket of goods and services

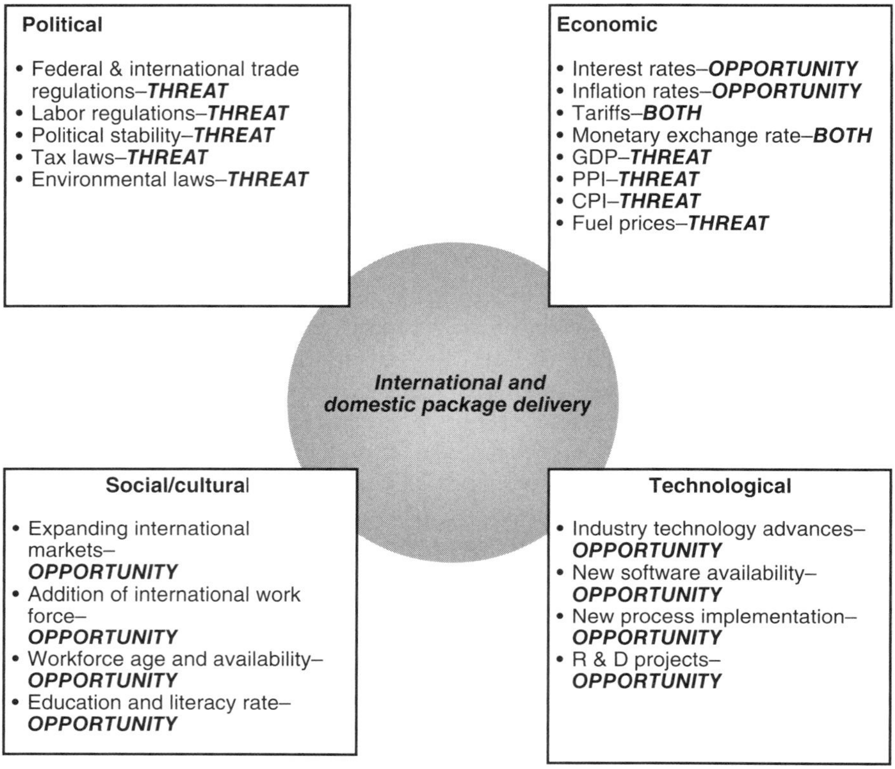

Political		Economic
• Federal & international trade regulations–*THREAT* • Labor regulations–*THREAT* • Political stability–*THREAT* • Tax laws–*THREAT* • Environmental laws–*THREAT*		• Interest rates–*OPPORTUNITY* • Inflation rates–*OPPORTUNITY* • Tariffs–*BOTH* • Monetary exchange rate–*BOTH* • GDP–*THREAT* • PPI–*THREAT* • CPI–*THREAT* • Fuel prices–*THREAT*

International and domestic package delivery

Social/cultural		Technological
• Expanding international markets–*OPPORTUNITY* • Addition of international work force–*OPPORTUNITY* • Workforce age and availability–*OPPORTUNITY* • Education and literacy rate–*OPPORTUNITY*		• Industry technology advances–*OPPORTUNITY* • New software availability–*OPPORTUNITY* • New process implementation–*OPPORTUNITY* • R & D projects–*OPPORTUNITY*

CONCLUSIONS

The organization has the opportunity to increase sales and revenues by expanding into more international markets and taking advantage of local labor and management forces at less than domestic rates. The organization also has the opportunity of reducing operating costs both domestically and internationally by evaluating current operating procedures, refining the supply chain, and making adjustments. Another opportunity is to implement new technology available to reduce operating requirements. There has been a decrease in shipping volume due to the recession worldwide. Other threats would exist if the recession deepens further, recovery slows, fuel prices continue to rise, or labor unrest grows and there is a strike. Analysis of all the things mentioned should be performed and forecasts formulated. A plan should then be developed to compensate by taking advantage of opportunities and mitigating risks or threats.

Figure 11.1   International and domestic package delivery PEST analysis—2010

purchased by consumers in a retail market for specified periods of time. In the United States, the CPI is released and published monthly and is sometimes referred to as a cost of living index because it reflects inflationary trends and consumer confidence.

In a real PEST analysis the data would be specific and more detailed. Once an explanation of the specific data is placed in the appropriate category, one can state whether it is determined if it is a threat, opportunity, or both. Conclusions can then be stated and recommendations made. A more in-depth and detailed analysis can be performed by assigning a weight to each piece of data and using a decision matrix to determine the overall best course of action. Weighted decision matrixes can be used in any business function or activity where a decision has to be made and are covered in more detail in Case Study 2.

SWOT (strengths, weaknesses, opportunities, and threats) analysis is a cousin to PEST and can be performed similarly; except that SWOT is used to identify more defined factors for specific categories. SWOT analysis can—and should—be used on the divisional and business unit level to analyze specifics such as implementing a new project, changing existing work processes or activities, and marketing a new product developed. In the specific case of supply management, SWOT can be used to analyze changing procurement processes, doing business with a new supplier, looking at linkage of different commodities with the same supplier, or consolidating spot buys of several commodities into a term contract.

Figures 11.2 and 11.3 show two simple examples of SWOT analysis. Figure 11.2 is an example of a small, individually owned gourmet food and specialty store. The SWOT analysis is for the development of an overall strategy for the company. This example is included to show how SWOT can be used for many types of decisions and to illustrate the importance of supply management to a business overall.

Figure 11.3 is procurement-specific and is an example of a decision whether or not to contract with a new supplier. The strengths and opportunities outweigh the weaknesses and threats so the decision to enter into the supply of goods on a term contract with this supplier is probably a sound one.

Keep in mind though that all decisions are a roll of the dice and unforeseen circumstances can affect any decision. That is why specific risks should be identified and alternatives developed in advance to mitigate any risk that manifests itself. Further, a risk mitigation plan should be developed to manage the identified risks. Developing a risk management plan is being proactive and allows a supply manager to be prepared to act should the circumstance warrant it. Having a risk management plan keeps a supply manager from being unprepared and getting blindsided if something unexpected happens. Risk analysis should be comprehensive and address any and all uncertainty. It needs to be systematic in its approach and structured. Additionally, it should be based on

Strengths	Weaknesses
• Small company – can react quickly to changing conditions • Employee loyalty • Non-Union • Brand loyalty in market niche • Good supplier relationships • No direct competition	• Limited financial resources • Limited expansion opportunities because of specialty nature of business • Deal with perishable foods and shelf life products • Susceptibility to market whims & fads
Opportunities	**Threats**
• Potential for increasing sales through new innovative products and services • Potential to expand markets and sales domestically and internationally through Web based catalog and promotions • Reduced costs and increased profit margins through supply management and process improvements • Negotiated cost and supply contracts that replace daily spot purchases • Potential to sell operations	• Potential for competition • Financial – increased interest rates and credit restrictions • Increase in labor costs • Sluggish economy and deepening recession

Figure 11.2   SWOT analysis for new strategic plan

Strengths	Weaknesses
• Small company – can react quickly to our changing requirements • Non-Union • On-hand inventories adequate • Good on-time delivery record • Honors warranties • Extended & discounted payment terms • Internal QC testing before shipment	• Limited financial resources • Limited number of stock items • No desire to expand • Only been in business 5 years
Opportunities	**Threats**
• Willing to sign term contract • Lowest bidder • Willing to guarantee dedicated inventory • Willing to guarantee lead times & on-time delivery	• Limited financial resources • Increase in material costs

Figure 11.3   SWOT analysis for a procurement decision

the best available information. If it is felt that not enough data is available to make the best decision, then additional research should be conducted.

Risk Identification and Assessment

The following examples of risk management identification and planning are a continuation of the weaknesses and threats discovered in the SWOT analysis example. An effective sequence is to complete a SWOT analysis and then a risk identification analysis, followed by risk mitigation and a risk management plan. Threats are identified in SWOT but are usually general in nature. The risk analysis allows for more details and definition of the specific risks.

Once a risk has been identified, it should be assessed to determine the potential negative impact and, if possible, the likelihood or probability of its occurrence. Determining the probability of risk will not have supporting data available that can be statistically calculated so it can be difficult. In most instances risk assessments are simply best guesses based on general information and assumptions. The examples of risk identification, mitigation, and management used in this chapter are simplistic and basic, aimed at giving a general idea of the risk analysis process. However, there are several risk formulas available that can be applied to evaluating and assigning a risk rating (value). Our example uses the simplest assessment rating of low, medium, and high. This assessment can also be expressed by assigning values on a numerical scale to represent the possible minimum and maximum potential of occurrence and/or impact. This is known as an index. If this concept was applied to our example, we would have used a scale of one to three with one having the lowest impact and three having the highest impact, or a variation thereof. Numerical value assessments would be made for both the potential of occurrence and the degree of severity or impact the occurrence might produce. This is referred to as a risk composite index and can be written:

Composite Risk Index = Impact of Risk × Probability of Occurrence

The range chosen in a numerical index approach is the choice of the preparer. The lower the difficulty, or number of variables, the lower the index scale can be as in the example used in this chapter. If the difficulty factor was higher, an index of zero to ten might be used and so on. If a potential risk was identified but it was determined that it would have no real discernable impact, then a zero would be used. If the top number of the index would represent an absolute probability (100%), then that number would be used. Whatever the index scale or approach chosen, the development of a risk analysis to identify and manage risks is one of the best decision tools you can use.

Another formula that can be used to calculate risk is taking the rate of occurrence (value assigned) and multiplying by the impact (another value assigned) to determine the risk rating. This formula is written:

$$\text{Risk} = \text{Rate of Occurrence} \times \text{Impact}$$

There are several risk management software programs available with templates, wizards, and calculators that can be purchased, but the degree of difficulty is low and most people prefer to do all of the assessment evaluation, calculations, tables, and charts themselves. A matrix is used to display the specific risks that are identified and described as illustrated in Table 11.1. Next, the individual risks are assigned a risk factor of low, medium, or high. This risk factor relates to the likelihood of the risk materializing. The next step is to estimate the impact each risk might have. Then, the priority of each risk is assigned. Finally, a recommendation of who should have ownership of the risk is made.

Risk Mitigation Plans

Risks can be dealt with in several different ways. Risk mitigation might include:

- **Avoidance**—One way to mitigate risk is to avoid it altogether. If there is a high degree of risk occurrence probability or certainty, the best decision might be not to attempt whatever is being contemplated in the first place.
- **Reduction**—Develop a workable plan to deal with risk occurrence if it materializes. Make sure there are alternatives that can be triggered if an identified risk actually manifests itself.
- **Transfer**—Transfer the risk to another entity. Transferring a potential risk to a supplier, contractor, or back-shop mitigates the risk.
- **Sharing**—A risk can be shared by delegating responsibilities, asking for guarantees, and/or imposing penalties of some type.
- **Acceptance**—If a risk occurrence is low, it can simply be accepted. It would be wise, however, to make budgetary allowances if the risk occurrence actually materialized.

A matrix is also used to describe and display the specific risks that were identified and described in Table 11.1, as well as details and instructions of how the risk should be mitigated. This is our risk mitigation plan and is illustrated in Table 11.2.

Risk Management Planning

When developing a risk management plan, several factors should be considered:

- Identify what, when, how, and who. That is, what the risk is, when it might occur, how it might occur, and who is responsible for mitigating it.

Table 11.1 Risk identification analysis

Risk type	Risk description	Risk chance	Risk impact	Risk priority	Risk owner
Interruption of supply of raw materials to supplier	Supplier has difficulty maintaining inventory	Low	Medium	Medium	Supply manager
Supplier has cash flow problems	Credit limitations and high interest rates keep supplier from expanding operating line of credit	Medium	High	High	Accounting manager
Supplier goes out of business	Supplier can no longer operate its business or honor commitments	Low	High	High	Supply manager

Table 11.2 Risk mitigation plan

Risk description	Mitigation plan
Interruption of supply of raw materials to supplier	Supply manager works with supplier to identify other sources of raw materials. Prepares to exercise clause in contract that allows acquisition of goods from other sources if supplier fails to fulfill requirements.
Supplier has cash flow problems	Finance and accounting manager works with supplier to expedite payment of invoices. May also work with supplier to increase supplier's line of credit; will monitor supplier for indications of more severe financial and credit problems. D&Bs regularly run.
Supplier goes out of business	Supply manager replaces supplier with second-choice supplier and negotiates a new contract with new supplier. Reviews on-hand inventory received from supplier and determines severity of shortages. Finance and accounting manager audits supplier's account. Legal department reviews contract and looks for legal remedies.

- Prepare a risk mitigation plan prior to developing a risk management plan. This will give clarity to the identification and alternative solutions as well as facilitate determining who should have ownership of the risks and the individuals responsible for overseeing the risk on an operational level.
- Assign a risk manager. This is an individual with the authority to make decisions and has the overall responsibility and ownership of the risk.

- Include individual tasks, activities, responsibilities, and budgetary considerations. They should be examined and evaluated when developing the risk management plan.
- Initiate and maintain a risk database that tracks and reports risk status.
- Develop appropriate mitigation measures and controls to measure the risk.

Once a risk identification analysis has been performed a risk mitigation plan should be developed. A proposed time line for implementing solutions to risks should also be developed in advance.

Risk Development and Occurrence Communication

After the development of a risk analysis that includes risk identification, mitigation, and management plans, make sure that all parties involved with or that might be affected by the risk are notified of the plan's details. It is also wise to keep people informed on a continuous basis as events unfold. In other words, communicate the risk status. Communication goes a long way and keeping people informed on a timely basis can avoid confusion or mistakes.

This sequence of threat and risk identification, mitigation and management planning is used by many people. It can be adopted for various types of business functions or activities. Of course, not all organizations and types of businesses have the same requirements, and any risk management plan should be structured to fit the organization or business unit's individual requirements. The bottom line is to make sure you practice risk management, in whatever form you may choose.

12

Forecasting for Future Success

Successful strategic goals and plans are based on forecasts developed from data that is well-researched, analyzed, and thought out. If markets, economies, and competition never changed there would probably not be a need to forecast future events, but since business is constantly changing, a need does exist to try and determine what those changes and their effects will be. Forecasts are predictions of situations, events, or outcomes at certain points in time, both short- and long-term, that might occur in the future. No one has a crystal ball and can accurately predict what will happen in the future, so forecasts are actually best guesses that are based on available information and data that has been researched and analyzed at the time of the forecast. Forecasts are essential in helping set goals and strategies. Goals are objectives you wish to attain and strategies are the plans for attaining those goals. If the economy, markets, industries, prices, and availability of goods were always constant, there would not be a need to consider forecasting. This is far from the case, however, because business is fluid and constantly changing which necessitates the need for organizations to employ techniques and tactics to counteract and overcome market conditions that affect cost, profitability, and competition. Forecasting is one of the strategic tools that supply management and procurement can use to remain cost effective, profitable, and competitive.

There are several different types of forecasts. Some forecasts are considered fact-based and use hard information to identify trends and develop best guesses for the future such as historical information on prices and supply availability at specific points in time. Other forecasts are opinion-based and use forecast information that is supplied by recognized experts to predict future market conditions. Still other forecasts are change indexes that gather information on a variety of economic and market topics and statistics that are presented individually and considered in total to produce a forecast based on data for a specific defined period, for future growth, or discipline. The Institute for Supply Management (ISM) *Report on Business* is one such index and there are others available from various financial organizations, investment groups, and government publications or agencies. Whenever a forecast is developed, information and data from all three examples presented should be used to make the most informed, and hopefully best, forecast on which strategies can be developed and decisions made.

Not all forecasts will produce positive results. Some forecasts can have negative ramifications for projections if they do not hold true and can have severe consequences that could be catastrophic. Therefore, forecasts should be challenged before inclusion in a strategic plan. Challenges to forecasts can be anything from questioning and verifying specific data used to develop the forecast to getting second opinions and seeking independent evaluations. The effect of any decision made based on a forecast should be evaluated for the impact on other business activities and functions within the organization.

When a forecast is proven wrong it can affect the strategic plan and compromise or hurt the organization's efforts. Therefore, the forecast needs to be as accurate as possible. Unexpected and unforeseen events that might have an impact on a forecast can and do occur. It is therefore prudent to look at all of the possible situations that might affect the forecast and develop contingency plans to deal with them. This is done by performing a strengths, weaknesses, opportunities, and threat (SWOT) analysis, completing a risk analysis, and then developing a mitigation and management plan to deal with the identified risks. Then you can perform a series of what if scenarios based on the various risks and alternative actions (mitigation plan) and determine what courses of action offer the least amount of risk with the best opportunity to overcome problems.

In many industries, price and supply requirements tend to run in cycles. You either have access and opportunity to more business than you can provide or are starving to death. Therefore, making mandatory tracking and forecasting requirements part of the standard processes and procedures will improve the opportunity for success. For specific and significant buy projects, a forecast of industry trends, future materials requirements, and costs of those materials and parts is wise. These are all core pieces of practicing successful and best-in-class supply chain management and procurement.

To forecast potential future material requirements and price increases as well as decreases in materials and parts, it is necessary to track historical information. Queries ran using an organization's database to identify purchase histories (quantities purchased, at what price, when purchased, and from what supplier) are necessary. To determine potential future prices with some degree of accuracy, it is necessary to track historical prices of raw materials and commodities used in the manufacture of those parts and materials. Armed with this information one can develop a fairly dependable forecast (within a defined range) of what prices might be at specific points in the future. Knowing this information, one can then develop contingency plans to cope with surprises and unplanned events. There are seven basic areas that are candidates for forecasting:

1. Price or cost—What raw materials, goods, and services might cost to purchase in the future and, from an operations standpoint, what it might cost to produce goods and services in the future.
2. Supply availability—What both short- and long-term availability might be in the future based on supply and demand tracking and analysis.
3. Industry capacity—What the capacity to produce or supply in the future might be based on economic and other factors all of which might be tracked and forecasted. Industry and market saturation points are two of the components of industry capacity forecasting.
4. Technology—What certain technology research and development might be or mean in the future. This could apply to system software development, process, or ideology technology application and philosophy.
5. Quantity requirements—Goods and services purchased are based on usage and sales data forecasts. Markets that are considered seasonal and/or cyclical in nature are particularly sensitive to such things as price, availability, and time of requirement.
6. Supply assurance—This is different from supply availability, but can be tied closely to, and be dependent on, availability of supply. Supply assurance forecasts are the schedules of supply (delivered and received goods and services). The supply of critical parts must be consistent to keep and maintain production schedules, especially in a just-in-time supply arrangement.
7. Requirements planning—The flow of credible and accurate information and data is crucial to strategic and tactical planning in several segments and departments of an organization. Forecasts of price and availability as well as other forecasted elements supply the information required to develop plans and strategies for the future.

Every business activity in an organization can be forecasted and used in the development of both tactical and strategic plans. In the case of a strategic plan (three to five years), an organization might develop both financial and nonfinancial forecasts for use in developing strategic plans. Financial forecasts specific to an organization that might be used include:

- Marketing and sales
  - Domestic markets
  - International markets

- Accounts receivables
- Debt retirement and notes payable
- Overhead increase/decrease
- Payroll and benefits
- Depreciation
- Parts, supplies, raw materials, and new equipment purchases
- Taxes
- Costs of future expansion (as calculated and included in other financial forecasts)
- Commodity price and supply availability (more specific to supply management and procurement)

Nonfinancial forecasts specific to an organization that might be used include:

- Industry
- Production
- Expansion requirements
- Buildings and space (office, plant, parking, and warehousing)
  - Transportation
  - Equipment
  - Software/Hardware
  - Personnel

Depending on the type of requirements, other forecasts might be developed and used as well. External financial forecasts that might be used are:

- Economic (local, national, and international, as applicable)
- Business cycle (may include price elasticity forecasts)
- Economic indicators (both leading and lagging)
  - Money supply
  - Inflation rates
  - Interest rates
  - Employment/unemployment rates
  - Gross National Product and Gross Domestic Product

Different types of analyses can be used independently of one another or collectively to achieve a desired projection. A forecasting model and methodology should always be developed and followed to maintain a consistency in data acquisition, application, and interpretation. A comprehensive forecasting model may employ various methods of forecasting. Some of the more important methods are:

- Short- and/or long-term—Both methods may be used independently or in conjunction. Short-term forecasting is usually used for developing best buy plans and activities for terms up to a year. Long-term forecasting involves multiple year terms and is used for more strategic decisions such as negotiating long-term contracts.

- Trend analysis—Trends indicate changes in data over extended periods of time. Elements that may affect trends are changes in price, supply, demand, productivity, and technology.
- Time-series analysis—This is a statistical method of analyzing a variety of data. From a procurement perspective, this can include purchase price, total costs, and inventory usage, for example, that has been accumulated within specific, regular intervals of time and can be analyzed.

We will concentrate on forecasting from an applied strategic supply management and procurement point of view. Forecasts are important to the development of plans and strategies, and they are only as good as the forecasts they are based on. Any forecast is a best guess of a future situation. Unforeseen circumstances may affect forecasts, therefore, it is always a good idea to have contingency and backup plans available to negate or minimize any negative effects.

Historical price information and data for various commodities can be obtained from many different sources. There are several services available for a fee that will track and chart commodity prices for you, or you may choose to check and track prices regularly. These can be completed either on a daily, weekly, or monthly basis and charted. This is time-consuming, however, and paying for a service to do this for you may make more sense, and the fees for subscription prices are reasonable and can easily be justified in a budget. The rewards of tracking commodity prices will more than offset any costs associated with it.

Aluminum has been used in examples in several chapters in this book, so let us use it once again for tracking commodity prices to use in developing a forecast for what the price of aluminum might be for points in the future. Figure 12.1 shows a graph of aluminum spot prices for a five-year period from 2003 through 2008. The left side of the graph represents the price in U.S. dollars per pound that aluminum sold for over the course of that five-year period. The timeline is portrayed in six-month intervals. You can see from the graph that the price steadily increased from October 2003 through April 2005. After that, there was a modest decline until July 2005 when prices started increasing sharply until they peaked in June of 2006. From July 2006 through January 2008, prices were moderately stable (within a range) when they again rose sharply to their highest point since the beginning of the historical study period. Then, in June 2008, prices started a sharp and drastic decline.

This is a useful and worthwhile exercise and many things can be learned from looking at the five-year historical price data. For those of you supply management and procurement professionals who track and chart historical commodity price data, please bear with me. For those of you who may have

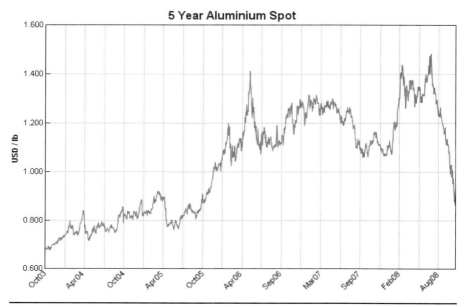

Figure 12.1   Five-year historical aluminum spot prices (www.kitco.com)

not used this useful and beneficial tool, let's determine what this information tells us.

Before we go on, look at the chart in Figure 12.1 again and jot down what you think the chart is portraying. Then answer the following questions:

- What conclusions can be drawn from the data?
- How could this information be used in supply management and procurement duties and activities?
- How would you use the information in developing short-term goals for the procurement department?
- How would you use the information in developing long-term strategies and plans for the department?

The chart shows that the market for aluminum is volatile and subject to extreme increases and decreases in price. This is good information to know, but we need to do additional research to determine why this is the case. The short answer for the period studied is simple—supply and demand. But we need to go even further and determine what affected supply and demand to cause the extreme increases and decreases in price.

These questions lead to the first reason why you should make tracking commodity prices a regular part of the supply management and procurement process. It allows you to practice supply chain management more intelligently and successfully. If you are buying parts and components made of aluminum, it only makes sense that the aluminum supply costs of those items will directly affect the cost you will pay for them and also their availability (supply). The chart roughly shows that from May 2005 until May 2006 aluminum prices increased from $.80 to $1.40 a pound. That's a 57% increase over a twelve-month period. This would have a negative and undesirable effect on the price you pay your supplier if you are making noncontracted or spot buys. Even if you are buying on contract it could still affect the price you pay if there is an escalator clause in the contract. Either way, it is going to cost you more, which also means the profit margin is going to decrease to some degree unless the sales price of your product is increased. This is an undesirable course of action as it may decrease an organization's competitiveness. How can it decrease competitiveness? Because an organization can lose market share if their competition is practicing strategic supply management and procurement techniques such as commodity price tracking and negotiating better, more valuable supply contracts. Get the picture now? Commodity tracking is a prime example of why an organization should move from basic procurement to strategic supply management philosophies. It results in higher efficiencies, lower costs, and increased profitability. Knowing what commodity prices are and how they are trending helps to prepare an organization for what might be coming and taking steps to adjust to or compensate for adversity. It also allows an organization to take advantage of positive opportunities that might present themselves for future purchasing.

Aluminum prices peaked at $1.50 per pound in July of 2008, then started a dramatic and drastic decline until November 2008 where it dropped to about $.90 a pound—a 60% decrease. In this situation an organization might want to take advantage of decreases in prices to stock up on inventory if it felt that aluminum was going to bottom-out price wise. This is called forward buying, that is, buying in advance of a need in spot or noncontract buy situations. If there were de-escalator clauses written into a contract that involved parts and components made of aluminum, and the organization was practicing effective contract management, they would want to take advantage of the decreases in price and apply the de-escalator clause to reduce purchase prices. Of course there is a lag period in price fluctuations in all of this. Prices for a current day, month, or period do not instantly translate into price increases or decreases. There is a trickle, flow-through period involved for prices paid for raw materials to work their way through the supply and demand chain before they manifest in parts and finished goods prices. Another key factor that affects prices of commodities is supply. An overly available supply of raw or base materials or excessive inventory can produce decreases in price. On the other hand, a shortage of raw or base materials or low inventory levels can produce increases in price. To illustrate what effect this has on prices look at Figure 12.2 and compare it to Figure 12.1.

Figure 12.2   Five-year historical aluminum stock levels (www.kitco.com)

You can see a direct correlation between spot prices and inventory levels. High inventory levels directly correspond to low spot prices and low inventory levels directly correspond to high spot prices. In other words, manufacturers are buying fewer raw and base materials when spot prices are high and more when spot prices are lower. This directly affects inventory levels. The fewer raw and base materials purchased results in fewer products being made. Manufacturers sell existing inventory in the interim and reduces inventory levels. This holds true for the reverse as well. A good source for this type of data and information is the ISM *Report on Business* assimilated and published monthly and there are other sources as well. If you decide to subscribe to a commodity tracking service, I would advise that you do so with a subscription service that provides more tracking services than just tracking the price and that also does the charting for you. Is tracking prices and inventory all I have to do? No, although tracking price and inventory are the two main ingredients of successful strategic supply management and procurement forecasting, other factors enter into it as well.

Economic issues have an important influence and impact on markets, industries, and organizations. The price of an item is primarily based on principles of supply and demand in a free-market economy but other factors can have an influence as well. Some of the basic supply and demand principles are:

• Supply elasticity—Elasticity is the ratio of the percentage of change in one variable to that of the percentage of change in other variables. How elastic supply is overall might be based on the availability of raw materials and other factors such as the global and individual supply of a particular country. Economic conditions, political and economic stability, transportation shortages, etc., also are considerations in supply elasticity.

- Price elasticity—Products and materials all behave differently. Changes in economic conditions may produce changes in price. A change in the price of something may, in turn, produce a change in demand. In this scenario prices are said to be elastic. Conversely, little or no change in prices may not produce a change in demand. These are simplistic definitions and elasticity can be based on more than these two concepts.

- Transportation conditions and trends—Transportation equipment shortages and work stoppages (such as strikes or labor disputes) can impact forecasts. The shortage of barges and towing equipment (boats that push the barges) and damage to the locks on rivers, for example, could impact inland waterway transportation. In the mid-70s and -80s, the inland waterway transportation business was booming and that eventually led to shortages of equipment. Barges are not produced on regular production schedules but rather are made-to-order. There are approximately 20 locks and dams on the 981 miles of the Ohio River running from Pittsburgh, Pennsylvania to Cairo, Illinois. Barges would occasionally ram locks when passing through to the next pool or level of the river. Damage sometimes was extensive and took extended periods of time to repair. This delayed delivery of already-loaded barges and the loading of new barges. Shortage of physical equipment for the industry could have been tracked and availability forecasted knowing the tonnage being moved yearly and existing or planned equipment availability. Damage to locks and downtime for repair is a good example of how unforeseen events can affect and impact a forecast.

- Expanding global markets—The addition and inclusion of goods and services from new or expanded businesses in other countries has an effect on supply availability and market price. Both are opportunities for the organization that practices strategic supply management and procurement to add additional qualified suppliers. Increasing the supplier base increases available supply options and, in most cases, offers additional opportunities for price reductions. From a tracking and forecasting standpoint, expanding global markets can be handled two ways: (1) individually track markets, industries, or individual companies of interest, or (2) combine and include those items of interest in current tracking of already-established models.

- Political stability—Tracking and forecasting the economic and business stability of countries can prove a worthwhile endeavor, especially if an organization is dependent on critical raw materials, goods, or services supplied by the country of interest. The world can be a dangerous place and, if an organization is invested in a country, either directly or by proxy through supply contracts, it is wise to keep abreast of economic and political developments. Being able to forecast, with some degree of probability, future potential problems allows an organization to plan for or activate contingencies.

- Business cycle trends—Markets and economies do not remain static. In fact they are continually fluctuating by expanding or contracting. Business cycles are not measured in defined increments of time as each business cycle varies in duration. But a business cycle that is being tracked can identify trends that are developing and a forecast of probable milestones and outcomes can be predicted. An example of a business cycle would be the time between when a recession begins and when it ends. Some of the benefits of tracking and forecasting business cycle trends are such things as interest rates, money availability, unemployment, and consumer confidence.

Best-in-class supply management professionals not only track and chart commodity prices and inventory levels but are also aware of the market, economy, and other factors. Keeping up with industry and economic trends and paying attention to what experts say is important. A supply management and procurement department may not actually track and forecast everything themselves but instead use forecasts published or furnished by reputable economists, government agencies, or other trusted sources. The point is that they are smart enough to use available data and forecasts to develop strategic future plans. You might think that it sounds like an awful lot of extra work. It can be initially but with practice it really does not take that much more time. Some best-in-class supply management and procurement departments have a dedicated department such as strategic sourcing that is responsible for tracking and reporting information to all of the other procurement departments (commodity groups, etc.) as well as management and other stakeholder groups within the organization. This is usually done in conjunction with their other duties and responsibilities. There may be a single dedicated person responsible for tracking and charting commodities or other areas of importance and interest or it may be a group of individuals tasked with those responsibilities. Whoever might do it, it does require extra time but it pays huge dividends in the end. Contract bidding and negotiations, contract management, supply chain management, and strategy development and the organization overall are the beneficiaries of comprehensive commodity tracking and successful forecasting.

13

Sensitivity Analysis

This is actually a continuation of Chapter 11, but has applications in other situations as well so a separate chapter has been dedicated to it. We have talked about several best-in-class techniques and processes and discussed several types of analysis available for use in practicing best-in-class supply management and procurement. Now we are going to present another one for you to consider. It is called *sensitivity analysis* (SA). Many functions and activities of business are sensitive to internal and external forces that can have either a positive or negative effect on procurement, other departments within the organization, or the organization as a whole. In the author's estimation, SAs are an absolute necessity when developing strategic or contingency plans to deal with unforeseen forces. They are part of the what-if scenarios one would run to determine what the best options and alternatives are for doing something. By taking a set of circumstances and applying different scenarios that might have an effect on the outcome, one can predict (or forecast) to some degree what the eventual result might be. Knowing the projections and alternatives allows for planning of reactions to a certain set of circumstances or events, that is, contingency plans. There are many ways you can do an SA. Each way may be defined by the need you have or a combination of analyses used to make a determination of something. These combinations will be describe and outlined in detail later in this chapter.

SA is a process and technique used to determine the possible outcome of a situation on which a decision and/or plan is made or will be made in the event that a key ingredient such as a prediction, forecast, or other results turn out to be in error. SA can then be implemented to determine the outcome of a situation given a set of different events or variables. Variables exist in everything we do. In one approach to SA you can mathematically assign values to variables. An example of this type of SA would be a production department wanting to know the effect of varying prices on the cost of finished goods. Marketing would also be interested in this information to determine what price to set for selling the finished goods. Some people find it useful to plot and graph the results of their analysis to report their findings and make recommendations to present to management. To illustrate this approach, here are two simplistic examples:

1. Operations department: What effect will varying prices of a raw material have on the cost of the finished goods? Assumption: Y = cost of raw material and Z = all other production costs (assumed constant). What is X (cost of finished goods)?

2. The easiest and quickest way to perform this SA is to set up an Excel spreadsheet. The formula for this example is $Y + Z = X$. Column A is Y, the cost of the raw material. Column B is Z, the combined total cost of all other production costs. Column C is X, the cost of the finished goods. Fill in the variable prices of the raw material in Column A and the other production costs in Column B. Place a formula in Column C of A + B or simply highlight all of columns A, B, and C and hit Auto-Sum. Bingo, now you know what the price of a finished good would be at a specific raw material price—it's just that simple.

3. Marketing: What impact would varying costs of finished goods at varying percentages of profit have on profit margins? Assumptions: A = sales price per piece, B = cost of finished goods, C = total of all other associated costs such as warehousing, packing, and shipping. X = profit per piece.

$$A - B + C = X.$$

In this scenario marketing can test the result of applying different sale prices to the products to determine and establish desired profit margins. It can also be used as a marketing tool to establish special promotions and sales pricing. A variation of this SA can also be used as a breakeven analysis to determine the point at which costs and sales price equal zero. Once the breakeven point is established, the analysis can continue to determine the optimum selling price and profit margin. Example 2 used a set total of all other combined costs but in a real world situation costs can be divided into several categories, all of which may contain different cost variables and all used within the analysis. This type of analysis is helpful to new companies just starting business and established companies desiring to add a new product.

In a given set of circumstances or assumptions, independent variables will affect dependent variables in various ways that will change predicted outcomes. In other words, SA identifies the impact of an outcome for a particular variable if it differs from what was assumed. By creating a given set of scenarios, one can determine how changes in assumptions, forecasts, and predictions will be impacted by different sets of changes (variables). It is a systematic evaluation and analysis of what the effects might be to predicted outcomes and assumptions. It is also the determination of what the degree of sensitivity might be to outcomes based on predictions, forecasts, and assumptions. In other words, an expanded SA shows us what effects might be expected if a forecast turns out to be wrong, how severe the effects might be, and how likely (the degree of sensitivity) it is that something might happen. In Chapter 12 we used aluminum to historically track prices as well as on-hand inventory levels to develop a forecast for what prices might be in the future. As discussed previously, the purpose for doing this was to enable better management of the supply chain. Let us now assume that we are also beginning a request for proposal bid process for a three-year contract to supply critical parts for our operation. We need an idea of what the price and availability for the primary raw material (aluminum) used to make the critical parts will be over the contract period. We also need to know what the anticipated or forecasted stability of the industry as well as the market will be and which direction aluminum prices will be trending—up, down, or holding steady.

Using our historical tracking of prices and inventory levels from Chapter 12, Figures 13.1 and 13.2 show us prices, availability, and trends over a specific time period. From this information we can begin to develop a forecast for future aluminum prices and availability, but we also need to know how sensitive

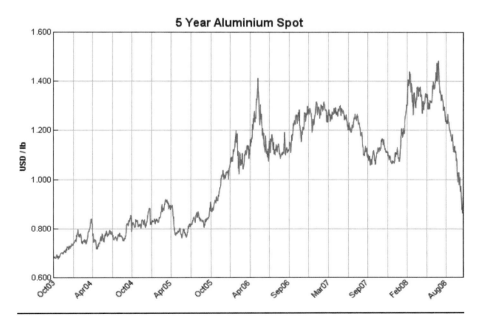

Figure 13.1 Historical aluminum spot prices (www.kitco.com)

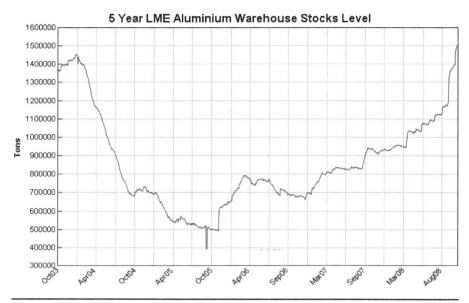

Figure 13.2   Historical aluminum stock levels (www.kitco.com)

the aluminum market might be for this period. In the case of commodity price, availability, and stability, we would also need additional information to understand and evaluate the status of the aluminum market and of the industry overall for at least the next three years. We do this by an in-depth research of the aluminum market. Articles in trade magazines and publications, white papers, news reports, and advice and forecasts of industry and financial experts should all be considered and evaluated. Armed with all of this information we can then begin to formulate a forecast.

We have previously discussed SWOT and risk analysis and the important roles they play in developing appropriate supply management and procurement strategies and decisions. Both are also part of a best-in-class operating philosophy and process. They are required prerequisites to a comprehensive and successful SA for developing a forecast of a commodity. The reason for doing SWOT and risk analysis first is to identify potential areas that might be sensitive to internal and external changes or factors that might affect normal processes and have a negative impact. It will give you direction for what you will want to concentrate on and research in-depth. If this is unclear, review the examples of SWOT and risk analysis presented in Chapter 11 again. The requirements involved in doing an SA are dependent on what is being analyzed and measured, and it will vary according to what you are trying to accomplish. Do not be misled, SAs can be involved depending on the situation and what you are trying to measure. Examples 1 and 2 used earlier in this chapter were simple examples of SA. Some SAs can be involved. An example of a complex SA would be the outcome of a scientific experiment exposed to many different sets of variables. But most SA requirements, including supply management and procurement, can be limited in scope and somewhat basic in nature.

We will now do an exercise involving an SA for the example in Chapter 12 using aluminum. We will utilize a basic and simplistic approach to our SA. First we need to ask a few fundamental questions and make some assumptions.

- Do we really need to do an SA for aluminum? Yes. Due to the volatility and extreme fluctuations of the aluminum industry and market over an extended period, we need a better understanding of what the industry and market forces are as well as what is affecting and driving this market. This is necessary to manage the supply chain more effectively. A three-year contract to supply aluminum-based parts is being contemplated and a forecast of market prices, stability, and trends is needed to develop a comprehensive bidding and negotiating strategy.
- What do we need to measure?
  - Price
  - Availability (supply and demand)
  - Industry stability
  - Market stability
- What information do we need to develop our SA?
  - Historical prices
  - Historical inventory levels
  - Industry reports and articles
  - Financial and economic reports and articles
  - Identification of risks and opportunities
- What analysis will we need to perform prior to developing our SA?
  - SWOT
  - Risk
  - Market forecasts

Let us begin our exercise by doing a SWOT analysis. We will list the strengths, weaknesses, opportunities, and threats based on the information we know at this point. Now refer to Figure 13.3 for a representation of SWOT analysis for the aluminum market.

The statements made in the SWOT analysis are based partially on known facts but also on perceptions and assumptions we made from the knowledge we have at this point. The next step would be to perform a risk analysis like the one presented in Table 13.1. The information presented in the SWOT analysis is used to identify potential risks and their potential impact on our supply chain. Additionally, it aids in developing bidding and negotiating strategies for a term contract for critical parts made of aluminum.

Strengths	Weaknesses
• Based on five year tracking, prices have dropped continuously over the last six months. • Suppliers have good on-time delivery records. • Suppliers practice comprehensive internal quality control testing before shipment. • Suppliers honor warranties. • Extended & discounted payment terms are available.	• On-hand inventories are low. • Economy is weak and in recession. • Market has proven volatile over a five year period. • Extreme fluctuations in price over extended periods.
Opportunities	**Threats**
• Market prices may continue to fall. • Suppliers receptive to term contracts with locked in pricing. • Suppliers receptive to escalator/de-escalator clause to compensate for drastic fluctuations in market price.	• Pending strike at largest ore producing mine could produce shortages in supplies. • Continued low inventories at mills could produce higher spot prices.

Figure 13.3   SWOT analysis example

Now we have a better understanding of what areas we need to concentrate on and research in order to develop a comprehensive forecast and make strategy decisions. After the completion of a risk identification analysis, one should always develop a risk mitigation and management plan.

After talking to our suppliers about the future of the aluminum market, reading related articles, white papers, and forecasts/predictions made by market and industry financial experts as well as commodity trading sites, we found the following information (summarized):

- The aluminum market historically has been one of extremes and continues to be volatile, both from a supply and demand standpoint.
    - This volatility is marked by dramatic fluctuations in price and availability.
- The market price of aluminum has declined drastically over the last six months and is the lowest in the five-year period studied.
    - This is credited in large part to the state of the economy as a whole and a deepening recession.
- A labor contract at the world's largest aluminum ore mine has expired. Labor and management are in negotiations but the possibility exists of a potential work stoppage that would disrupt supply to some degree.

Table 13.1 Aluminum risk analysis example

Risk type	Risk description	Risk chance	Risk impact	Risk priority	Risk owner
Interruption of supply of raw materials to mills	Pending strike at largest ore producing mine	Medium	Medium	High	Supply manager
Low inventories at mills	Low inventories may produce higher spot prices	Medium	Medium	Medium	Supply manager
Economy in recession	Recession effecting economy creating lower demand for products	High	High	High	Accounting manager

- The mine in question is located in a third-world country. The suppliers that will be considered for supply of parts are all U.S. owned domestic suppliers.
  - After a canvas of all qualified potential suppliers to be considered for a three-year purchase contract, it was determined that none of the suppliers bought their processed aluminum from mills supplied by the mine facing a potential labor stoppage.
- The mine in question makes up only 2% of the world's supply of aluminum ore.
  - Although a work stoppage would have some impact on world supply, suppliers that will be considered for a term purchase contract all buy from domestic mills that only buy aluminum ore from domestic mines.
- The recession has had a dramatic impact on all markets. Fewer goods are being purchased and made.
  - Market analysts and industry experts have projected prices for aluminum will continue to decline over the next 12 months with supplies holding steady.
    - This could change if the recession lessens and the economy improves or if there is an interruption in the supply of aluminum ore to the mills.

The results of our research presented here are basic. If this was an actual project we would have more detailed information backed up with excerpts of written statements, graphs, and charts. Backup and support information is always beneficial when presenting reports and making recommendations to management and the organization. Support information is a validation and basis for the assumptions, forecasts, and recommendations that you make. But we do have enough information to proceed with our exercise. The value in conducting this type of research is plainly evident. For example, if all we knew was that the world's largest aluminum ore producing mine may have a strike and disrupt the supply of aluminum ore causing a shortage that might lead to higher prices, we would not have all of the pertinent facts. This could lead us to make erroneous assumptions and develop flawed forecasts that would result in developing incorrect strategies. We might also agree to pay more for parts made of aluminum than we would have to if we did not know and understand the true condition of the aluminum market.

A risk identification analysis, in and of itself, is actually an SA. The risk analysis we initially performed in this exercise was done to identify areas where we needed more facts and information. Armed with the new information we obtained from our research we would now want to perform a new SA, or revised risk identification analysis if you will. This analysis can be presented solely as an SA or as a revised risk identification analysis.

Now you have a true, representative picture of the aluminum market and can proceed with developing forecasts and making recommendations to upper management and the organization. To support our supply chain management efforts, we can do a separate SA, like the one illustrated in this chapter, to establish projected impact to procurement's noncontract spot buy efforts and requirements. We can also use it to establish a target price, or target price range, to use in developing bidding and negotiating strategies as well as parameters for a term purchase contract. Examples of this would be establishing a most desirable outcome (MDO) and least acceptable agreement (LAA) used in developing a negotiating plan as well as determining the optimum term, escalator/de-escalator clauses, and so forth. MDO and LAA along with other negotiating strategies are discussed in more detail in Chapter 15.

SA can be an important tool and resource in identifying situations and conditions that present threats, opportunities, and risks to a procurement project, and it also has applications for other business activities and functions within an organization. The use of SA is one part of a best-in-class methodology and process. In the examples and exercises presented in this chapter we used SWOT, risk identification, and SA to identify, analyze, and understand the aluminum market. This information will allow the supply manager to make informed recommendations and decisions and add extra value to the organization that will allow the organization to compete successfully, and profitably.

14

Writing Appropriate and Successful RFPs

There are several key points to remember in writing and issuing requests for proposals (RFPs). First, determine if a request for proposal is appropriate for what you want to accomplish. Sometimes a simpler request for quote (RFQ) may suffice. The differentiator between an RFP and an RFQ is the complexity of the solicitation. You are asking the bidder to meet certain criteria and asking them for a proposal of how they intend to satisfy your requirements. For a basic solicitation of a specific quantity of product or services for a one-time buy or for a short duration with limited or simple requirements an RFQ would probably suffice. An RFQ is a less complicated solicitation with fewer requirements. It is usually used for a one-time buy although, some one-time purchases may be complicated, have tight requirements, or may require a more in-depth approach because of the variability or technical aspects of the purchase.

One of the many high dollar items purchased by major airlines is heavy jet, Class D, full flight simulators (FFS). They are used by airlines to train pilots, flight crews, and mechanics on a specific aircraft fleet type such as a Boeing 747 or Airbus A-380. They are hydraulically and electronically driven with a full-scale enclosed cockpit, actual or replicated aircraft controls and instrumentation, and virtual visual/audio displays of different airports and flying conditions as well as actual satellite imagery of the terrain. They are state-of-the-art, computer software-driven, and also very expensive. A single Class D FFS costs between $10 and $14 million dollars new, depending on the fleet type and equipment configuration. There are a limited number of qualified and recognized Class D FFS manufacturers that are located in Great Britain, Canada, and the United States. Each FFS is usually a one-time buy but, because of the technical nature of the product and the variations of the separate offerings, an RFP to present minimum requirements and specifics of the purchase parameters is usually issued. Dealing with products from three different countries requires an approach that should take into account the uniqueness of product, currency conversion, and the approach and philosophies of the individual companies regarding FFSs. It is sometimes difficult to compare apples to apples in the individual offerings and more often an apples to oranges comparison will have to be made. This makes it difficult to perform price analysis, cost analysis, and total cost of ownership. Use of an RFP to define and narrow the offerings and to facilitate analysis and decision making is often warranted.

Factors to consider in deciding whether to issue an RFP or an RFQ are:

- The duration of the agreement
  - Term the agreement will cover
    - One-time buy or multiple years
- Composition of the product or service
  - What a product is made of or what a service provides
- Guarantees required
  - Adherence to minimum requirements and specifications, lead time, inventories, and warranties.

There are several types of RFPs. Each may differ in content, format, and intent, but they all have the same desired objective, to solicit price, terms, and specifics for the purchase of goods and services that are desirable, necessary, and acceptable for the issuing organization or entity. One example of a difference would be an RFP issued by a governmental organization as compared to one issued by a public or private organization. Governmental bids and proposals have tight and specific requirements and guidelines. They are required to incorporate explicit requirements regarding bidder qualifications, minority quotas, set-asides, timeline, and other specific information. Nongovernmental organizations have much more flexibility in the bid process, although good business practices should always be followed and be the foundation of any RFP. This book primarily deals with topics regarding the private sector.

When writing and issuing RFPs, there are several things that should be taken into consideration. Fully understand what you are trying to accomplish with the issuance of the RFP. Is it to supply existing inventory levels, procure never before used parts or services, satisfy a unique or special requirement, or some other qualification requirement? Understanding the true need will determine how detailed and comprehensive the RFP should be.

Understand the priority that the procurement project has within the overall supply management strategy. This is important. As the old saying goes, time is money, and the time it takes to do something is valuable so you will want to prioritize your projects. The projects that are the most necessary or have the greatest value should be assigned the highest priority.

Make sure you have a comprehensive and complete statement of work, engineering orders, bill of materials, and so forth and make sure they are incorporated into the RFP. It should be complete before the RFP is issued. Having to amend an RFP because of omissions upsets and delays the timeline, and it may cause confusion on the part of bidders and reflects poorly on an organization's image of preparedness and professionalism.

Determine a suitable and doable timeline for response, evaluation, analysis, negotiation, and award. Timelines may be based on the need to do something quickly or on historical experience with other past RFPs. In either event, make sure that enough time is allowed to complete the RFP process efficiently and thoroughly.

An effort should be made to write RFPs as comprehensively as possible to ensure that everything you want to see in a completed contract is included in the RFP. It will give the bidder a clearer and more comprehensive idea of what you are looking for. This saves time on the back end and also helps to bring potential problems out in the open early. Before any RFP is issued it should be reviewed and approved by an organization's legal department or legal counsel. This allows for corrections before issuance, prevents potential problems from arising later, and saves time in negotiations, contract construction, and approval.

RFPs all have different requirements and expectations and will therefore always have differing levels of importance and priority. The majority of those reading this book may have been involved with or written numerous RFPs in their careers. For those who may not have been involved with an RFP process, we will now present an outline generally used for writing appropriate and successful RFPs.

An RFP is appropriate if it addresses a requirement or need of an organization. An RFP is successful if it supplies information needed for an organization to make an informed decision that satisfies the requirements and needs of the organization and adds extra value to the organization. Use the model that will help you write both an appropriate *and* a successful RFP.

Request for Proposal

Introduction or Statement of Purpose

The introduction identifies your organization, defines your primary business, explains your standing in the industry (optional), summarizes what you want to achieve with the proposal, and explains to the bidders why you are issuing an RFP, what you are asking for in the proposal, and when responses are due.

General Instructions and Requirements for Completing the Proposal

This section usually contains what is generally referred to as boiler plate language. It contains the basic instructions for completing the RFP and the obligations of the bidder from a legal standpoint. Although every RFP may be different, this section is usually standard in most RFPs. In addition to the boiler plate, it may also contain the steps required in the submission process, contact and communication protocol, type and number of deliverables required, non-disclosure agreement requirement (if applicable), timeline for RFP due date, evaluation period, and award. It will also include any other instructions or requirements of a general nature.

Evaluation and Selection Criteria

This is the main section and will constitute the bulk of an RFP. Describe in detail the criteria that will be used in the evaluation and selection process. You can elaborate on and define the evaluation and selection criteria outlined in the RFP. This section should include all minimum requirements of the solicitation and scope of work required. A few examples of evaluation and selection criteria that should be included are:

- **Price**—What the bid price should include such as:
  - Price each of the product or service
  - Transportation costs
  - Transportation terms
    - FOB—Free on board (origin or destination)
    - CIF—Incoterm meaning cost, insurance, and freight
    - DDP—Incoterm meaning delivered duty free
- **Duration or term of purchase**—If it is a contract, it should include the dates when the contract would begin and when it would terminate.
- **Delivery schedule**—Specifics of delivery requirements such as:
  - Due dates for individual components of the overall purchase
  - Quantities required and specific dates required (if applicable)
  - Completion dates of individual services or work required (if applicable)
- **Flexibility**—Any allowable variation to schedules outlined
- **Reliability**—Minimum reliability requirements such as:
  - Mean time between failure guarantees of a component or part
  - Warranty guarantees
  - Quality specifications—What are the specific quality requirements and rejection parameters?
  - Tolerances—What the allowable +/− tolerance is for specific components and parts.
- **Diversity requirements (if applicable)**—List any requirements required pertaining to diversity or minority status such as a percentage or set aside participation of minority subcontractors or suppliers to the bidder.
- Any other topic you deem important to the solicitation.

Payments, Incentives, and Penalties

This section outlines all financial requirements and stipulations of an award.

- **Payments**—Describe the payment terms and conditions of payment such as net 30; payment will be made within 30 days of receipt of invoice following the receipt and acceptance of product or service. Also describe how payment will be made, manually or electronically, and conditions of payment.
- **Incentives**—Describe any incentives offered such as:
  - Discount payment terms 2/10 net 30; payment due within 30 days but buyer will receive a 2% discount if paid within 10 days
  - Premiums for exceptional performance
  - On-time deliveries
  - Reliability
  - Reductions in price to supplier/buyer
  - Rebates to buyer
- **Penalties**—Describe any penalties that may apply such as:
  - Late shipments or poor performance
  - Lack of compliance with contract terms and conditions
  - Out of tolerance and/or reject allowable levels
  - Reductions in price to supplier/buyer

These examples may vary from project to project. Some of the examples given may be included in the actual RFP issued or may be withheld and included in the negotiating strategy plan. Since each procurement project is different, it will be up to the issuing organization which items are best suited for inclusion in the RFP. Accepting a response to an RFP does not mean you are obligated to consider it or award the project to a bidder. It is not a contract and you have the right to reject it without consideration to the bidder. This offers a high degree of flexibility for the issuer. Educating bidders on all specifics of the RFP promotes better understanding of what the issuing organization is looking for in an agreement and limits misunderstandings or mistakes on the part of the bidders in preparing their bid responses.

Following the selection of finalists, or if one supplier was chosen for an award, all of the other bidders not selected should be notified officially that they were not selected as a finalist or chosen for an award. This is only common courtesy and appropriate business etiquette. Some people choose to make this type of notification via e-mail but I believe it presents an organization as being more professional if an actual signed letter on company letterhead is sent. Some people call these reject notifications or letters but a more appropriate term would be *notices on nonaward*. Any time that a supplier bids on business and does not receive an award, they will naturally be disappointed. The supplier will most likely be a bidder on other or future business so it is wise to maintain a good relationship. It will also ease the pain if they are sincerely thanked for their participation and the positive points of their bid or proposal pointed out.

15

The Importance of Negotiating the Right Agreement

It has been said that life is a negotiation. This is especially true in business. Negotiations can either be formal, as in the negotiation of contracts and agreements, or informal. Many people do not realize that every correspondence, e-mail, telephone conversation, teleconference, and every face-to-face meeting with suppliers, factory reps, sales people, internal resources, coworkers, and management is a negotiation to some degree. In each instance you are presenting facts, asking questions, and making suggestions to promote your point of view or guide decisions made by others to align with your own ideas. The vogue and general consensus these days is to negotiate contracts and agreements that are win-win. That is, the final agreement is good for both sides and both sides win; they are happy and can make a profit. This is a good philosophy as it does neither side any good to crush the opposing side to the point that they either fail or cannot perform. This usually costs more to overcome in the long run and should be avoided. However, even in win-win agreements, one side always wins a little more than the other and there can rarely be a 50/50, totally even outcome. So take the ego out of your negotiating strategy and replace it with sound business reasoning.

Negotiating successfully is an art. Some people have a natural talent for negotiating, but it is also a technique that can be learned. Whether you consider yourself a skilled negotiator or a beginner, knowing how to negotiate the right agreement for a specific situation is important. Negotiating is an in-depth topic and many books have been written just on this subject alone. But, because of negotiation's crucial role in successful supply management, we will delve into some of its basics here as they pertain to procurement contract negotiations and from a procurement project team and resource perspective.

Developing a negotiating strategy begins with asking a series of questions:

- Is this a one-time or special buy?
- Will this negotiation ever repeat itself, in some form, at another time?
  - Is it likely that you would ever repeat this particular purchase?
    ○ Determine what characteristics used in this negotiation would be similar and used in other negotiations.
- Is the negotiation for a long-term contract or some other type of agreement?
  - Is it a term purchase contract, strategic alliance, procurement partnership, vendor managed inventory agreement, or other special agreement?
- Internally, how many stakeholders and resources will be involved and who are they?
  - Pick the right stakeholders and resources for the project team.
    ○ Know who is critical and who will add the most knowledge and advantage.
- Is there a timeline requirement or deadline (drop dead) date for completion?
- What is the financial or other impact of this negotiation?
  - What value will it bring to the organization?
    ○ What is the value weight of the procurement project?
    ○ What is the priority weight of the procurement project?

By asking and answering these questions you can establish the broad requirement of the procurement project and have an idea of the parameters that will be needed for negotiations. Here is a negotiations model I developed and use for planning negotiations:

- Ask questions pertinent to the situation.
- Identify the issues.
- Assess the situation.
- Establish preliminary objectives.
- Assess strengths and weaknesses of the procurement project.
  - Determine and assign a priority weight to the procurement project.
- Assess strengths and weaknesses of the company and persons with whom you will be negotiating.
  - This is important! Know your counterparts and understand their negotiating approach and tactics.
- Begin pre-negotiation preparation.

- Assemble required data.
- Establish optimum and minimum requirements.
- Determine the size and make-up of the negotiating team.
  - How many team members and their roles
  - How many resources and their roles
- Select the team.
- Define the responsibilities of the team.
  - Team leader
  - Team members
- Develop a preliminary negotiation strategy plan.
- Start a negotiation tracking log.

Now, let us break down each step in the model.

Most of the questions you will need to ask are covered in the initial questions listed. These questions will establish the importance and scope of the procurement project. Other questions specific to the situation may be required.

Identify the issues:

Define the specific issues of the procurement project that will lead you to determine the particular requirements of the negotiation strategy. Perform any additional research that might be required.

- Will the negotiation be a result of competitive bidding process or a single source requirement?
- Will adequate resources be available to conduct and complete successful negotiations?
- Is adequate information and data available about internal specifics and requirements as well as the opposite negotiating company and team members?

Assess the situation:

- What is the importance and priority of the procurement project?
- Is this a must buy?
- Is there a short completion time limit?
- How much research (data mining) will be required?

Again, many of these questions will have been identified in the initial questions you asked.

Establish preliminary objectives

Obviously, both the preliminary and final objective of any negotiation is to win an acceptable agreement that meets or exceeds your minimum requirements and satisfies the basic requirements of who you are negotiating with. Preliminary objectives are just that, preliminary. As the strategic negotiating plan develops, the preliminary objectives may evolve into more defined or hybrid objectives. Examples of preliminary objectives may include:

- Minimum requirements are met.
- Negotiations are completed within the required timeline.
- Value will be gained for the organization.
- Process and activity improvement will be realized.
- Risks are minimized.

Assess strengths and weaknesses of the procurement project

- How much value will be gained for the organization?
  - In terms of money saved, costs reduced
  - In terms of process improvement
- How much time and resources will the procurement project tie up or require?
- Is the procurement project a stand-alone project or can it be linked to other procurement requirements to create additional leverage?
- Assess strengths and weaknesses of the company/persons with whom you will be negotiating.
- What is the level of competition of the company you are negotiating with?
  - Several qualified competitors
  - Sole source company
- What are your organization's key objectives in negotiations?
  - Are your organization's objectives realistic and achievable?
- What are the key objectives for the company you are negotiating with?
  - Are the objectives of the company you are negotiating with realistic and achievable?
- What are the consequences to each side if negotiations fail?
  - This is important if negotiations fail. What effect will failure have on you? You must have an alternative and backup plan.
  - What are the consequences to the company you are negotiating with? You may be able to use the possibility of failure to your advantage. This should be taken into account in developing your strategy.
- Can you develop a profile for who you will be negotiating with?
  - Have you ever negotiated with this person or team before?
    - Recall negotiating strengths, weaknesses, and tactics.

- Can you find out from industry colleagues who have knowledge of the strengths, weaknesses, and tactics that the person or team uses that you will be negotiating with?

Begin pre-negotiation preparation

- Assemble any and all data required to formulate a negotiating strategy. This might include:
  - Purchase histories
  - Supplier performance
  - Reliability performance
  - Industry standing
  - Risk analysis
  - Breakeven analysis
- Establish what your minimum requirements are for accepting a deal.
- Establish what your optimum desires are.
  - What would you like to achieve over and above minimum requirements?
- Determine the size and makeup of the negotiating team. Who is a necessity and who will benefit as a resource? Determine what role each will play in the negotiations; who will speak on what topics and who will be support only.
- Select the team.
  - It may be beneficial to develop a profile for each potential team member to determine their strengths, weaknesses, and what they might add to the negotiations.
- Select a team leader.
  - Determine the most qualified person to lead and manage the negotiating team.
- Define the roles and responsibilities of the team leader and each of the team members.
  - Assign roles and responsibilities for each and make sure everyone understands them.
- Develop a preliminary negotiation strategy plan.
  - This initial plan should be revised as negotiations progress if circumstances change or the situation warrants. An example of the negotiation strategy plan the author uses is presented in Table 15.1.
- Start a negotiation tracking log.
  - Often negotiations will require more than one formal negotiating session, it may even require the company you are negotiating with to submit additional revised bids. A negotiation tracking log is useful in

Table 15.1 Negotiation strategy planning matrix

Negotiating strategy planning sheet	
Most desired outcome (MDO)	List all of your heart's desires, what the very best you could hope for such as a 35% overall reduction in prices, extended warranties, reliability, penalties, etc.
Least acceptable agreement (LAA)	List all items you are willing to settle for and at what levels. This could be minimum requirements or something more.
Best alternative to a negotiated agreement (BATNA)	If an agreement cannot be reached, list what acceptable alternatives would be. This could be do nothing and continue status quo, revise requirements and rebid, add additional bidders, etc.
Assumptions	Make assumptions based on known facts and list them all. Examples are: bidder must make a sale, bid can be linked and leveraged to other purchases, bidder has technology edge over competition, etc.
Don't Knows	List all that you do not know such as financial condition of bidder, bidder's supply chain, forecasts of bidder's raw material costs, etc. An effort should be made to answer "Don't Knows" before negotiations begin.
Probes	List all questions that can be safely asked to determine possibilities for discounts, reductions, extentions, etc. These are leading questions that will help you determine what concessions you might realize.
Must haves (non-negotiable)	List what you absolutely must have. These are the minimum requirements at the least.
Trade-offs (concessions)	List any concessions you might be willing to make for an offsetting gain.
Options for mutual gain (creative trades)	These usually go hand-in-hand with "Trade-Offs" but can also be selectively separate. List points you might bring up that are not part of the original offering but could be mutually beneficial to both parties. Examples might be extending the term of the agreement for increased discounts, doing vendor managed inventory (VMI) to reduce in-house inventory levels and costs, etc. This is your chance to be creative.
Obstacles and biases	List any perceived obstacles and biases to a successful agreement. Examples might be, stakeholder preference for another bidder, reliability issues that would have to be overcome, etc.
Risks	List all perceived risks. Develop alternatives to mitigate those risks, and develop a risk management plan.

tracking changes to the initial and subsequent revised bids for comparison and strategy. Comments can be added that aid in revising strategies, and the tracking log, as a whole, is beneficial as a reference for other future negotiations. An example of the negotiation tracking log is presented in Table 15.2.

Table 15.2 Negotiation tracking log

Negotiation Tracking Log

Procurement Project: Ergonomic DooJiggy Stamping Machines

Type of Buy (Term/Spot): Spot

Type of Bid: RFQ sent to 6 bidders

Tentative Awardee: Ergorific Manufacturing

Meets Minimum Requirements of Bid: Yes

Negotiation key elements	Intial round date:	2nd round date:	3rd round date:
Number of units wanted	5	NA	NA
Price per machine FOB our plant	$275,000	NA	NA
Alternative qty offered by bidder	NA	8	7
Alternative Price FOB our plant	NA	$260,000	$255,000
Delivery lead time	10 weeks	10 weeks	10 weeks
Bidder supplies onsite installation	No	Will pay 50% costs	Yes
Bidder supplies onsite training	Yes	Yes	Yes
24-hour support hot line	Yes	Yes	Yes
Spare parts inventory supplied and spares discounts	All spares at 10% discount	Critical spares less 15% other spares 10%	Critical spares free other spares 15%
Engineering services available	Yes	Yes	Yes
Warranty	12 mos.	18 mos.	24 mos.

Continues

Table 15.2 (continued)

Comments:

First Round

1) It was apparent that Ergorific wanted to make this sale and establish a relationship.

2) Feelers and probes were used to determine the extent Ergorific might reduce price and make concessions.

3) Ergorific was asked to propose a revised bid taking into consideration an increase in quantity, a reduction in per unit cost, on-site installation expense, spares discount and cost, and extension of warranty.

Second Round

1) Ergorific's revised bid included an increase in quantity, a reduction in price, concessions on spares, and an extension of warranty.

2) Ergorific was told we were close to a deal but that further concessions would be required. We were willing to buy 7 units instead of the initial 5 units but the price needed to reduce further. Installation costs would have to be bore solely by Ergorific, we wanted critical spares to be supplied initially at no cost and a higher spares discount. They were also advised we required a 24 month warranty.

Third Round

1) Ergorific submitted their final offer that included compliance with a quantity of 7 units, a further reduction in the per unit price, concessions on spares and discounts, and acceptance of an extended warranty.

2) Erorific's offer was accepted and tentative award made.

3) Specifics and results of negotiations were turned over to legal for review before issuance of a purchase order.

Negotiations to attain the right agreement that adds the most value to your organization may be approached in several ways. When people think of negotiating a procurement agreement, they think of the final negotiations with an apparent winner of a competitive bidding process. An RFQ or RFP is issued, analyzed, and a tentative winner is chosen, and then negotiations begin. That is often the case, but sometimes there are also opportunities to negotiate your way to a final negotiation. There will be procurement projects you may have already done, or will do in the future, where negotiations are based on the proposals or bids submitted by two or more companies who were considered finalists in the bidding process. In this scenario, more than one company submitting a bid met or exceeded minimum requirements, had a bid price close to the others, and each had offered something unique from the other finalists. Some procurement professionals prefer to inform companies that they are a finalist in the bidding process and request a revised bid or proposal from them in hopes of gaining reduced prices and other considerations. This is perfectly acceptable and may be the best approach for certain circumstances. In other situations though it may be useful and beneficial to invite each of the finalists in separately for a bid review. This has benefits at several levels.

- It allows you to learn more about the product or service you will be buying.
- It allows you to learn more about the company you may be buying it from.
- It allows you to see who you might be conducting final negotiations with and what their negotiating style and techniques are.

This all plays a significant part in developing a successful negotiating strategy.

16

Successful Contract Management

Many procurement departments and individuals do a fantastic job of constructing and issuing requests for proposals (RFPs), negotiating, awarding, and building a contract that brings great value to their organizations. But once the contract is signed they stop there and forget about it. Contract management is a primary ingredient of best-in-class strategic supply management. It does not do any good if great value is gained in the contract creation process and not implemented or used effectively during the life or duration of the agreement.

A case in point is a company that had negotiated a multimillion dollar product/service contract with a supplier. Using the strategic supply management concept of linkage, they were able to leverage a contract for the supply of one type of part from one of the supplier's brand divisions and another separate and distinct part from another division. By linking the two together they were able to leverage a better cost structure and realize more value adds than if they would have simply issued RFPs for each of the individual parts and awarded contracts separately. Linkage and leverage are both important examples of best-in-class strategic supply management.

The contract was worth several hundred million dollars over a three-year period. But here is the most significant issue; the supplier offered an annual percentage rebate based on annual sales volume and amount. There was also a penalty clause for late guaranteed deliveries (past a specified date) for some parts and warranty repair/replacements. Sounds pretty good doesn't it? The problem was that during its term no one took ownership of managing and enforcing the provisions of the contract. At the end of the three-year period preparations began for a new RFP and bid process. One of the analysts on the new procurement project team was reviewing the existing contract, purchase, delivery, and reliability histories and asked a simple question, 'How much did the organization realize in rebates each of the three years?' Nobody could answer the question because nobody knew. Accounting was contacted to find out the amounts. Accounting's answer was . . . you guessed it . . . zero! Because no one had ownership for the management of the contract, none of the provisions were enforced. After reviewing the purchase history it was discovered that approximately $23 million qualified as rebates that could have been realized and claimed but wasn't. Wow! That was a big cookie and a costly mistake. Many people got upset and there were a lot of sore toes that got stepped on as a result.

The organization tried to recoup the whole amount but was only able to qualify for a small portion that applied in the latter stages of the contract. The provisions for what qualified for rebate, when it qualified, and how to apply for the rebate were all spelled out in the contract. The fact that the organization did not choose to apply for the rebates nullified their entitlement to the rebates after certain dates and they missed the opportunity. This actually happened and the example is used because it exemplifies how not practicing best-in-class strategic supply management can affect an organization's bottom line. Yes, the organization realized better prices and value on the front end, but it missed opportunities for overall cost reduction and extra value on the back end. No doubt the individuals involved thought they were practicing good procurement and supply management but in reality they were only practicing basic supply management. Practicing best-in-class, strategic supply management is what separates the men from the boys, the winners from the losers, and organizations that realize their maximum potential from those that do not. After the dust settled and the tears dried, the organization in this example decided it needed a system and process for managing all its contracts and took steps to put one in place.

Now you should understand the importance of managing contracts. But who should actually manage contracts—accounting, procurement, or legal? The answer is all of the above, or at least all should play a part in the management of contracts. In the case of the example of the rebates, accounting would have been the logical entity to manage the rebate portion of the contract. Knowing what qualified for rebates and when they must be applied for, accounting could then issue invoices for them at the appropriate times. The problem with our example organization is that nobody notified accounting of the possibility of rebates or supplied them with a copy of the contract or the specific provisions. They did not know so they could not comply. Legal should also be kept in the loop. Any time there is a change, variation, or problem, it should be reviewed with the legal department to determine any appropriate course of action. Procurement should have been responsible for the overall management of the contract as the majority of the stipulations and provisions pertained to the supply of parts, delivery requirements, warranties, reliability, and repairs. There must be communication between any and all parties that have a responsibility for or may be affected by the performance of a contract (see Figure 16.1).

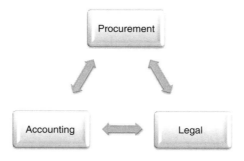

Figure 16.1   Contract management responsibility

As mentioned, procurement should have overall responsibility of the management of the contract. Day-to-day management and responsibility of the individual aspects of the contract are overseen by different entities or individuals within the procurement department's personnel structure. Coordination and management of these responsibilities is required. Figure 16.2 shows an example of contract management responsibility flow down.

There are several off-the-shelf contract management software programs available on the market to help in overseeing and managing contracts. There are also contract management services that can be retained for a fee. But an organization can usually design and implement a successful contract management process themselves. The key ingredients are defining and delegating areas of authority and then assigning individual responsibilities. The primary stakeholder in contract management has to be procurement as they have ultimate responsibility over the details and specifics of the contract and are involved in the day-to-day activities of the contract. Procurement is the entity most knowledgeable regarding the details and mechanics of the contract because they negotiated the terms of the contract and awarded it.

In computer software contract management scenarios, event flags, milestone points, or other types of triggers are programmed to identify when specific events or goals are reached in the contract. The responsible individual(s) are then notified so that appropriate action can be taken. Most computer-based contract management software programs also have the ability to generate data and reports, either at prearranged points in time or on demand. Whether commercial off-the-shelf software, internally designed programs, or fee-based services, computer-assisted contract management programs can make a supply manager's life easier and greater value can be gained for the organization.

If an organization elects to manually manage contracts, a comprehensive management plan will need to be designed and implemented in order to be truly effective. Clearly defined responsibilities will need to be assigned and responsible parties held accountable. Although entirely workable, manual

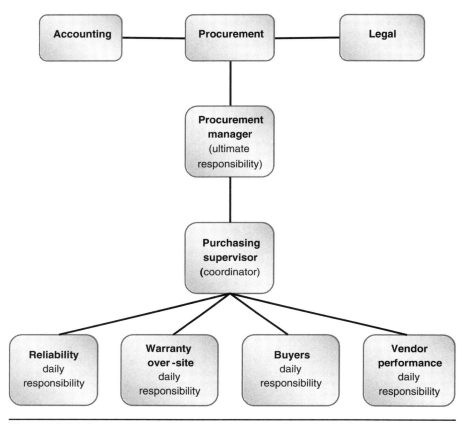

Figure 16.2   Contract management responsibility flow-down chart

management of contracts carries a higher cost value from an employee time and effort standpoint. It is, however, preferable to no contract management at all.

Back to computer-based—or driven—software programs. Some contract management software programs are only part of the software program capabilities. Many of these programs are also used to analyze and manage an organization's overall spend of procurement dollars. This is referred to as spend analysis and management and is another best-in-class strategic supply management technique and process. By analyzing what an organization spends, and what they spend it on, they can identify areas of criticality and importance. It can also identify opportunities and areas for spend improvement.

Organizations work on budgets, that is, monies allocated by accounting and finance to man and operate individual departments within the organization.

Procurement budgets include wages and benefits of employees, overhead (normal operating expenses), and projected costs of purchased parts and services. Spend analysis can help the supply manager know and understand where procurement dollars are being spent and identify opportunities for improvement. Not only does it help the supply manager stay within budget and meet goals that have been set, but it can also aid in establishing new, value added goals.

17

Supply Management and International Trade

With globalization, more companies are trading with companies in other countries, and it is important that supply management and procurement professionals understand the nuances of international trade. Many factors are involved in international trade, including language, culture, monetary exchange, international law, time zone differential, governmental stability, logistics, and transportation. Many companies find it advantageous to buy and sell their products in other countries. But selling internationally is a whole other topic and because this is a book about supply management and procurement, we will only look at international trade from a purchasing point of view. Several chapters within this book use procurement of goods involving raw materials or parts from other countries as examples. The Chinese drywall example that we discussed in Chapter 3 is a good illustration of what can go wrong if sound supply management and procurement principles are not practiced. In this chapter we examine the importance of knowing how to trade effectively with other countries, what the benefits are, and what the ramifications can be.

Before a company embarks on doing business with a company in another country there are many things they should know, understand, and consider. Doing business internationally is easier than it used to be although some of the same pitfalls and obstacles still exist. Two things that have made international trade easier are the Internet and the fact that so many companies have established operations in different countries. The Internet has made communications and transactions so much easier and faster. Before the Internet, written correspondence had to be handled entirely through the mail. Even with airmail there was a substantial lag time between delivery and response. Due to the diversity in time zones, verbal communication involved scheduling telephone and conference calls at unusual and often at inconvenient times, for example, in the middle of the night. Although this is still the case, the Internet and e-mail have made communication and correspondence much easier. The Internet has also reduced the amount of travel required when a face-to-face meeting is required for presentations or negotiations. This can now be handled in large part through video conferencing and live streaming. Another thing that has made international trade easier is the fact that many corporations and companies have established actual operations in different countries or have established trading partnerships with foreign companies. This makes doing business with these organizations much easier because they have already overcome many of the barriers and obstacles present in international trade by establishing and practicing standard practices that transcend boundaries and borders. It has smoothed the road, if you will. But keep in mind, there are still differences and nuances and always will be. Never assume that the way you do business in your home country is the way they do business in other countries.

Trading internationally can offer substantial rewards by reducing costs and increasing profits, but it may not be right for every company or situation. In recent years there was a rush by many companies to buy from low-cost country providers that created an explosion of commerce in many countries such as India, Pakistan, countries in the Asia Pacific, and others. Cheap labor was the main driving force although technology runs a close second. The rush has been curbed somewhat and a pulling back to some degree has occurred. This is the result of a global recession and many problems encountered with quality and reliability issues. But there are still plenty of opportunities available. There are four reasons for an organization to consider trading internationally:

1. A desire to decrease operating costs
2. A way to access available new markets
3. A way to keep pace and stay technologically and cost competitive
4. A way to obtain competitive advantage over competition

Before considering doing business with a company in a country other than your own, you should consider several things. The key concerns of trading internationally are:

- Cultural compatibility—Know the culture of the country in which you are considering doing business and any language barriers. Also learn what the customs are. For instance, in Japan you should only hand your business card to someone with the information (lettering) facing them. Addressing someone by their name, either vocally or in correspondence, should be followed by *san*. This is a sign of respect to the person you are addressing. Larger and more sophisticated foreign companies have websites that offer language options, but if they do not, this can be a real barrier if you, or someone in your organization, does not speak that language.

- Political and economic stability—Know the political and economic climate of the country you are considering. It should be a stable government and susceptibility to terrorism should be considered. The recession has caused uncertainty in many global markets so make sure the company and the country you want to do business with/in has a sound economic policy. You want to be assured that any goods shipped to or from a country will arrive safely and on time.

- Financial and legal—Financial and legal considerations are important. Know the monetary exchange rate because this is important when entering into agreements and contracts since rates change daily. Predetermine at what point price will be established. This could be the bid price, the price at the time the agreement is made, or the price at the time goods are shipped or received. You can be sure of one thing, the price for all of the examples given previously will not remain the same due to fluctuations in exchange rates. You must know what the legal considerations are and the governing laws of the country you want to do business in. Know how you will pay or get paid. Establish terms for sale, conditions, and financing options in advance of entering into an agreement and make sure you understand all of them. Know what export/import documentation and licensing requirements and procedures are.

- Taxes, tariffs, and duties—Know what taxes, tariffs, and duties are for the goods you want to purchase. Many countries have trade agreements in place that forego many taxes, tariffs, and duties. Others have extra taxes that may apply such as a value added tax (VAT) applicable in the European Union.

- Geographical, logistical, and transportation accessibility—Whether shipment will be made by land, sea, or air, lead times are extended when trading for international goods no matter the location or mode of transportation. Take this into consideration when looking at a country with which to trade. Accessible shipping facilities are an important factor to consider as well.

- Openness to foreign investment, local, and international trade—This is an added plus when conducting business internationally. Most companies in other countries want to do business internationally as much as you might want to do business with them. Many countries make it easier to do so than others. Look for countries with policies of openness and inclusiveness and that have programs in place that support and encourage international trade.

Make certain the foreign company you are considering offers products that are compatible and comparable to the type you require. The old marketing adage let the buyer beware certainly applies when trading internationally.

There must be a thorough understanding by all parties of the requirements and specifications and a quality control system in place, on both sides, that is comprehensive and subscribes to the same standards of testing. Some companies have been burned because they took a seller's word for quality and ended up with cheap knock-offs of substandard quality products that were made with inferior or toxic materials. The quality and reliability of a product should always be a main concern.

Answers about the political, financial, and economic stability of a country can be obtained from a variety of sources. The U.S. government has many agencies that can be helpful in supplying information. Many other countries also have government offices dedicated to promoting foreign trade and business enterprise. The Internet can be a prime source of information as well. Whenever the World Trade Center is mentioned most people think of the tragic events that happened on September 11, 2001, but many do not know what the World Trade Center was, and still is, or what it has to offer in the way of promoting and facilitating international trade. The World Trade Centers Association is a business organization headquartered in New York, but administers approximately 300 offices in 100 countries. They provide services that support companies desiring to enter, or that are involved in, international trade. Services offered include counseling, translation assistance, market research, cultural training, international trade seminars, trade missions, business referrals, and many other services. Their website is www.wtca.org.

Some companies employ agents in foreign countries to help them determine what is required for doing business in that country and to help in establishing business relationships. This is a common practice, especially when a company is new to international trade or seeking new trading partners. Foreign trade agents usually have a physical presence in the country being considered, in-house legal counsel familiar with the laws and customs of the country, and people who can aid in other areas such as financial, demographics, geography, and logistics. Companies also employ freight forwarding agents who aid in customs documentation and requirements, relieving the company of that responsibility. Additionally, they arrange for and oversee the logistics and actual movement and transportation of goods from the origin to the final destination.

During my tenure in the coal industry I was involved with exporting U.S. coal and coke to nine countries—Spain, Ireland, Egypt, Nigeria, Mexico, Sweden, Belgium, Japan, and Norway. I also negotiated a contract to export railroad sleepers (the wood timber cross ties that steel rails rest on) from the U.S., Canada, and Colombia, South America to a third-party country. During my 14 years at UPS airline, I solicited and purchased aircraft parts and services, negotiated and managed contracts internationally with companies in Japan, Singapore, Canada, Germany, France, England, Ireland, Norway, and New Zealand. Through my dealings I became familiar with the culture and customs of many countries and can personally testify that trading internationally can be a rewarding and profitable endeavor.

After soliciting bids and negotiating the basic agreement for the purchase of goods, there are other particulars that need to be addressed and included in a final agreement. One important item is determining at what point the title transfers from the seller to the buyer. This defines the risk points and the amount of risk exposure to both parties and can be either simple or complicated, depending on the type of goods involved and how much and what type of transportation and handling is involved. In the example that follows we use coal as an example to illustrate some of the complexities of transportation and handling that may be encountered.

Coal is considered a bulk cargo and is loaded into the holds of ships when moving across oceans. Smaller ships carry 25,000 and 35,000 metric tons but most carry full loads of 55,000 metric tons. These are PanaMex class vessels. The PanaMex size classification is bestowed on the largest ships that will fit through the Panama Canal. There is significant logistics involved on both the United States and the final destination end of exporting coal. Raw coal is transported by truck from the mine to a processing tipple where it is sampled and analyzed for quality. It is then classified, crushed, sized, and loaded into rail cars where it is sampled and analyzed again. Some export movements are shipped via rail cars and loaded directly into vessels at Norfolk, Virginia where final sampling and analysis is performed. Other export coal movements are shipped via 80, 90, and 100 ton rail cars and off-loaded into 2,500 to 3,000 ton barges. The coal is sampled and analyzed again at this transfer point and each loaded barge is also sampled and analyzed.

There is a substantial amount of coal involved in a 55,000 metric ton movement and significant logistical coordination is involved. The maximum weight allowed for movement by rail is 10,000 tons per train. A minimum of five 10,000 ton trains would be required if it was moved to a port by land. The maximum size tows that are allowed on the Ohio River is fifteen barges and the maximum size on the Mississippi is 30 barges so that more than one tow would be required for enough coal to fill a vessel. This is due to the size and number of locks that barges must pass through on the Ohio River. Actually, because of the amount of time required to load a barge, they would continually be added to passing tows in increments of 3 to 10 barges as they made their way down to the port. The barges traversed three different rivers—the Big Sandy, Ohio, and Mississippi—and have to navigate river locks at various points along their path. Finally, the barges arrive at Darrow, Louisiana between Baton Rouge and New Orleans and must be loaded midstream onto the ocean going vessel. Final sampling and analysis is performed as the coal is loaded into the ship. A variation of this whole process is repeated when the coal arrives at its final destination port. The coal would still need to be off-loaded from the vessel and transported to the end user or buyer by some transportation method.

This example was used because it is an excellent way to show the complexity involved in some types of commodities and what can be involved in delivering a product (in this case a bulk product) that must be handled (transferred from one transportation conveyance to another) multiple times and how much logistical coordination is involved. You probably noticed how often the coal was sampled and analyzed. Final acceptance and payment was based on the samples and analysis performed when the coal was loaded into the vessel. All the other times the coal was loaded and sampled were for backup and arguing points, or averaging data. Coal is a combustible material that is comprised of several chemical and mineral ingredients, primarily moisture, ash, volatile matter, sulfur, and fixed carbon. Fixed carbon is what actually burns and heat value is rated in British thermal units (BTUs), which is a heat index. Several things affect the amount of heat that coal produces such as moisture, ash, and sulfur content. Volatile matter are the gases that are emitted when burned. Ash and sulfur are impurities left over after burning that must be disposed of. There are two kinds of moisture, inherent (which is contained within the coal) and surface moisture. Inherent moisture does affect the level of BTUs, but surface moisture can be deceiving. The higher the moisture content, the lower the BTUs. Since coal is purchased based on specific chemical and heat specifications, analysis is the determining factor for acceptance, rejection, assessed penalties, and procurement. If it rains (as it often does in the warm months in Louisiana) on the coal as it is being loaded, surface moisture increases and BTU content decreases. Of course, as the coal dries the BTUs come back up but if payment was based solely on that sample taken in the rain the seller could take a huge financial hit. That is the reason for all of the other samples and analysis along the coal's journey. It is backup proof that the product loaded is actually the product contracted for and delivered.

Now let us look at a couple of other examples. From a logistics standpoint petroleum works much the same way as coal does with a few exceptions. The chemical analysis requirements and specifications for petroleum are exactly the same as coal, including moisture, ash, sulfur, and BTUs. In fact, leave oil in the ground under pressure long enough and it turns into guess what, coal—both are fossil fuels. The major difference between coal and petroleum is that coal is a solid and petroleum is a liquid. That means that instead of rail cars, barges, and open hold vessels, transportation requires tanker trucks, pipelines, and tanker ships. Most of the readers of this book are probably more familiar with goods not measured in weight but rather in individual quantities of pieces and lots, although transportation costs may still be by weight. Logistics of these types of goods are substantially different from bulk products. Depending on geographic proximity of the trading countries and the type of cargo being shipped, transportation may be by land, sea, or air. Trade between the United States, Canada, and Mexico, along with the various countries in the European Union, might be by land only using trucks and/or rail shipments.

Transportation covering long distances between trading partners might be shipping by sea or air. In both these instances land conveyance will also be a factor for the delivery to the final destination. Transportation by sea constitutes a large percentage of all international transportation movements. Commodities and goods other than bulk shipments are usually containerized. Ocean going containers are those big steel boxes you so often see everywhere. The advantages of containerized cargo are many. They not only protect goods from the weather and elements, but offer a secure way to transport goods. Containers may contain a whole consignment to a single destination or be made up of several consignments independent of each other. But the greatest advantage is the ease of handling. Containers are loaded with goods at the point of origin and transported by truck to the port where they can be off-loaded from the trailers onto specially designed vessels called container ships. At the destination port the containers are off-loaded onto trailers again for transport to their final destination or onto flatbed railcars for intermediate shipping if required.

There are several different transportation and title transfer designations that may come into play when buying or selling internationally. These are called Incoterms. Staying with our coal example, all of the shipments involved in our example were negotiated and sold loaded, stored, and trimmed (LST) in the vessel's holds. At that point, based on the acceptance of the analysis at loading and other contractual requirements, the title transferred to the buyer who was also responsible for contracting for and paying the charter of the vessel, insurance after title transferred, all docking and undocking fees, pilot services (port in and port out), unloading at the destination port, and all transportation requirements to the final destination. There are many ways that goods might be handled, transferred, and shipped in an international trade movement and many different title points where title could possibly transfer. This is why it is important to know and understand what and where these points are and make a determination which ones are the most advantageous for your organization from a time, knowledge, and cost standpoint and which offer the greatest advantages as well as which points carry the greatest risks.

There are 13 primary Incoterms that are used in international trade. A chart has been prepared from a buyer's perspective for ocean freight and cargo movement and is presented in Table 17.1. It shows what each Incoterm usually involves, who pays the cost (buyer or seller) at various points and functions, and at what points title might transfer. This chart was prepared to help in understanding international movements and determining what designations are the most advantageous from a cost and time standpoint as well as which offers the lowest risk for particular transactions and situations. A "YES" indicates a cost that is usually paid by the seller or exporter and a "NO" indicates a cost that is usually paid by the buyer or importer. Remember, all of these points are negotiated terms and conditions of sale and may vary from what is presented here.

Table 17.1 Incoterm acronym requirements

Incoterm acronym	Loaded on truck	Export duty paid	Shipment to point of embarkation	Off-load at port of origin	Transport to buyer's port (ocean passage)	Port landing charges	Off-load onto trucks at buyer's port	Transport to final destination	Insurance paid by seller	Point of entry customs clearance	Import duties and taxes paid
DDP	Yes	Yes	Yes	Yes	Yes	Yes	Yes	Yes	No	Yes	Yes
DDU	Yes	Yes	Yes	Yes	Yes	Yes	Yes	Yes	No	No	No
DEQ	Yes	Yes	Yes	Yes	Yes	Yes	No	No	No	No	No
DES	Yes	Yes	Yes	Yes	Yes	No	No	No	No	No	No
DAF	Yes	Yes	Yes	Yes	Yes	No	No	No	No	No	No
CIP	Yes	Yes	Yes	Yes	Yes	Yes	Yes	Yes	Yes	No	No
CPT	Yes	Yes	Yes	Yes	Yes	Yes	Yes	Yes	No	No	No
CIF	Yes	Yes	Yes	Yes	Yes	No	No	No	Yes	No	No
CFR	Yes	Yes	Yes	Yes	Yes	Yes	No	No	No	No	No
FOB	Yes	Yes	Yes	No	No	No	No	No	No	No	No
FAS	Yes	Yes	Yes	No	No	No	No	No	No	No	No
FCA	Yes	Yes	Yes	No	No	No	No	No	No	No	No
EXW	No	No	No	No	No	No	No	No	No	No	No

Incoterms is an abbreviation for International Commercial Terms. They are international standards established by participating countries to simplify the terms of sale for international commercial trade and sales transactions. They are published by the International Chamber of Commerce (ICC) and are based on the U.N. Convention on Contracts for the International Sale of Goods initially written in 1936 and periodically updated. Before the standardization and adoption of Incoterms, countries had different interpretations of terms and conditions of sale that sometimes led to uncertainties, misunderstandings, and disputes that arose from the sale and transportation of goods. Incoterms were designed to describe and define the rights and obligations of all parties in a contract of the sale and delivery of goods. Although similar to the domestic terms of sale (FOB terms of sale), Incoterms involve more than just the designation of point-of-title transfers, they also define responsibilities and who pays for which costs at various points of the transportation chain.

Incoterm definitions:

- DDP—Delivered duty paid (at destination port of entry). This term stipulates that the seller pays for all transportation costs and bears all risk until the goods have been delivered to their destination and all applicable duties have been paid. DDP is also sometimes used interchangeably with the term *free domicile*. This term is the most comprehensive term of sale for the buyer. Some importing countries may access additional taxes for imported goods such as (but not limited to) VAT and excise taxes. Although usually prepaid by the buyer or importer, they are considered a recoupable cost because they are usually recovered against sales to customers within the internal local market. An exception to this would be parts and components used to make a finished product that is then sold at another price. In this scenario the cost of the taxes would be considered as another cost within the total purchase cost and as part of the transportation and importation costs.

- DDU—Delivered duty unpaid (at the destination port of entry). This term stipulates that the seller delivers the goods to the buyer to the named place of destination in the contract of sale. The goods are not cleared by the country's customs for import or unloading from any type of transport (ship, aircraft, railcar, or truck) at the place of destination. The buyer bears the responsibility to pay for all costs for the unloading and is responsible for all risks associated therewith. The buyer or importer is also responsible for any subsequent delivery requirements beyond the place of destination landing. If the buyer or importer desires that the seller should bear these responsibilities, costs, and the risks associated with import clearance that includes payment of duties, and the unloading and subsequent delivery beyond the place of destination landing, then they would need to be negotiated and agreed to in advance and prior to the shipment being initiated.

- DES—Delivered ex ship (at destination port of entry). This term stipulates that when goods are delivered ex ship, risk is not passed from the seller or exporter to the buyer or importer until the ship has arrived at the destination port and all goods are made available for unloading to the buyer. An example where this term is used is at a port that is small or extremely busy. Even though the vessel has arrived at the destination port, it must queue up and anchor until its designated turn to dock and off-load. The seller or exporter pays the same freight and insurance costs as would be expected in a cost, insurance, and freight arrangement. The seller or exporter agrees to bear all costs associated DES and bear risk and retain title until the arrival of the vessel at the port dock. All costs for unloading the goods and cargo, along with any duties and taxes, are the responsibility of and paid for by the buyer or importer. This arrangement is frequently used in shipping some bulk commodities such as coal, cement, dry chemicals, or grains where the seller or exporter either owns or has chartered for the vessel.

- DEQ—Delivered ex quay (at destination port of entry). This term is similar to DES with the exception that risk is not passed until all goods and cargo have been off-loaded from the vessel at the port of destination.

- DAF—Delivered at frontier (or delivery place). This term refers to a classification used when goods and cargo are transported by road or rail. The seller pays for transportation to a named place of delivery at the border or frontier as it is commonly called. The buyer or exporter is responsible for customs clearance and pays for any and all transportation from the frontier to the buyer's final destination. Title and risk is transferred from the seller to the buyer at the frontier.

- CIP—Carriage and insurance paid (to destination port or point of entry). This term is used for containerized goods and cargo and is the transportation multimodal equivalent of CIF. In this arrangement the seller or exporter pays for carriage (transportation) and insurance to a designated destination port or point of entry. Title and risks are passed when the goods or cargo are handed-off to the first carrier required and used for final delivery.

- CPT—Carriage paid to (a destination port or point of entry). This term is used when the seller or exporter pays for transportation and carriage to a designated port or point of entry and can be applied to containerized, multimodal, and general goods and cargo. In this arrangement the seller or exporter pays for carriage (transportation) only, and title and risk are passed to the buyer or importer when the goods or cargo are handed-off to the first carrier required and used for final delivery.

- CFR (also called CNF)—Cost and freight (to destination port of entry). This term is used for maritime or ocean-going freight and cargo only and designates that the seller or exporter is responsible for and pays the costs and freight to bring the goods and cargo to the destination port of entry. Title and risk is transferred to the buyer or importer when the goods or cargo have been off-loaded (said to have crossed the ship's rail). Insurance for the goods and cargo is not included and is the sole responsibility of the buyer or importer.

- CIF—Cost, insurance, and freight (to destination port of entry). This term is used for maritime or ocean-going freight and cargo only. The conditions of this term are the same as those for CFR with the exception that the seller or exporter must additionally secure and pay for insurance on behalf of the buyer or importer. A variation of this term is CIF-free out that means that the vessel has off-loaded, undocked, and piloted out of the harbor.

- FOB—Free on board (at designated port or point of loading). This term is used for maritime or ocean-going freight and cargo only and does not apply to containerized or multimodal cargo or air transport. It signifies that the seller or exporter is responsible for and must load the goods or cargo aboard the vessel designated by the buyer or importer themselves. This can also be handled by the seller contracting and paying for a stevedoring service to perform the loading. Two good examples of this situation are those used earlier in this chapter. One was the coal exported. It was loaded by a stevedoring company midstream in the Mississippi River using bucket elevators and cranes using clam shell buckets to off-load from the barges pulled alongside the ship. The other example was the wood railroad sleepers from Columbia, South America. In this instance there was not a modern port available and native labor loaded the sleepers onto rafts and they were actually floated out to the vessel anchored in a bay. The ship's booms were used to hoist the cargo and place in the holds. This actually happened. Even though we live in a modern world, there are still places that are less advanced where methods may not be what some are accustomed to. In an FOB arrangement, risk and cost both transfer when the cargo crosses the ship's rail. It is the responsibility of the seller or exporter to clear the goods or cargo with customs for export. The buyer or importer must charter the vessel and inform the seller or exporter of all details regarding the vessel and also the port of origin loading details.

- FAS—Free alongside ship (at designated port of loading). This term designates that the seller or exporter is responsible for placing the goods or cargo alongside the vessel at a designated port. The seller or exporter is also responsible for clearing the goods or cargo through customs. This is another maritime and ocean-going transportation arrangement used for the movement of bulk or heavy-lift cargo only and does not apply to containerized or multimodal sea transportation. An example is heavy equipment and machinery that is not containerized.

- FCA—Free carrier (to designated place). This term refers to the arrangement where the off-seller or exporter transfers goods or cargo into the custody of the first carrier designated by the buyer or importer at a specific designated place after it is cleared of customs and ready for export. This term can be applied to all modes of transportation, including carriage by road, rail, air, and containerized or multimodal ocean transportation. It is also applied to freight collect situations regarding shipments of goods and cargo in ocean-going containers regardless of whether they are full or less than container load).

- EXW—Ex works (at a designated place). This term refers to an agreement whereby the seller or exporter makes goods or cargo available to the buyer or importer at the seller or exporter's premises such as a warehouse, mill, or factory. The buyer or importer is responsible for all applicable costs and charges required to deliver the goods or cargo to its end destination. This arrangement places all of the responsibility and risk on the buyer or importer. There is minimum obligation on the seller or exporter except to make the goods or cargo available to the buyer or importer at a designated time and place. This term is often used for making an initial quotation for the sale of goods before any other costs are known, have not been determined, and/or added. In this arrangement the buyer or importer is responsible for and pays all transportation, handling, and insurance costs and bears all risks for transporting and delivering goods or cargo to its final destination.

- Additional charter terms that may be attached to and used in conjunction with various Incoterms are:
  - *Free in* is used to indicate that the entity chartering a vessel is responsible for all costs associated with the loading of goods and cargo onto the vessel.
  - *Free in and out* refers to the pricing that indicates that the entity chartering the vessel is responsible for all costs associated with the loading of goods and cargo and also the unloading of the goods and cargo from the vessel.
  - *Free out* refers to pricing that indicates that the entity chartering the vessel is responsible for all costs associated with the unloading of goods and cargo from the vessel.

Whenever entering into international trade agreements one should fully understand the implications and ramifications for each type of transaction that include conditions of the sale or purchase. As we have discussed in this chapter, there are many ways that transportation and handling, along with the transfer of title and the assumption of risk can be handled. Making the decision of what is right and best for a particular situation can mean the difference between an uneventful and successful transaction and one that can have financial consequences. It is important to choose the right type of transportation arrangement that affords the lowest cost and safest way to receive purchased goods. Anyone contemplating acquiring goods internationally should first obtain a copy of Incoterms 2010, or the latest revised copy. It is an easily obtainable publication from the ICC and is a good reference in helping to make the right decisions on which transportation model to negotiate for and incorporate into international trade agreements.

18

Make versus Buy Decisions

There are times when situations arise, or present themselves, that a consideration of whether to make goods and perform services in-house or purchase from outside sources becomes necessary. The decision to do one or the other—make versus buy—is based on the satisfaction of a required need an organization has for goods and services. The objective is to make a decision that maximizes utilization of capabilities, resources, and strengths that will best contribute to fulfilling the organization's requirement. Many organizations prefer to purchase all of their required goods and services from outside sources rather than go to the added expense of making or performing them in-house. This does make total sense in many situations, but in other situations a decision to make or perform is driven by necessity or value opportunity. In this chapter we explore what make versus buy decisions are, how to determine their feasibility, and how to determine their value opportunity.

In the case of service requirements, there are many instances where the decision to perform a required service internally or outsource it are based primarily on convenience more than cost, although other factors certainly have a bearing. Let us look at several examples to see the different criteria and requirements that might go into making a decision to perform a service internally or contract for it outside the organization.

Example 1: Let's make this a duel example—janitorial/cleaning and cafeteria food service. An organization could most certainly perform both services but would need to consider the time, effort, and resources required to oversee and manage both services. The addition of staff to actually perform the services and management to supervise the work would need to be added. The primary cost here would be wages and benefits along with purchasing the required supplies to support the services. This seems like a relatively simple decision to make: calculate the costs of performing in-house, solicit bids for the service, compare what the difference would be, establish a convenience factor, and make a decision. If the cost difference for outsourcing was lower or close to what the cost of performing in-house then the convenience factor for not adding additional staff and doing it in-house would probably be the deciding factor.

Example 2: This is a manufacturing example. Transportation is required in the acquisition of raw materials, parts, components, supplies, and the distribution of finished goods. An organization must make the decision either to contract or perform the services in-house for all or part of their transportation needs and requirements. Some organizations whose procurement departments contract for outside services at some level have dedicated transportation sections within their procurement departments that do nothing but purchase transportation. Others require the buyers to purchase transportation along with their other duties.

Example 3: This is an airline industry example. The FAA requires periodic, mandatory maintenance checks of all types of aircraft based on time (flight hours or in-service time) and usage (landings and takeoffs). These are classified as A, B, C, and D checks. The basic work or inspection requirements are set by the manufacturer of the aircraft and the FAA. They vary by size and/or fleet type of individual aircraft. Check A is a minimum maintenance check performed at predetermined intervals in flight hours or takeoff and landings, perhaps every 500 flight hours. It is performed by local aircraft mechanics at an airport and requires a series of tasks predetermined by the manufacturer such as checking fluid levels, lubricating certain parts, opening panels for visual inspection, among others. Check B is performed approximately every three months and is somewhat more comprehensive than Check A. It is also performed by local aircraft mechanics at an airport and requires tasks similar to Check A, but it is a more detailed inspection and involves more tests of systems and components. Checks C and D are referred to as heavy checks and are far more comprehensive and thorough, requiring specialized facilities, tools, parts, labor, and materials. Some airlines perform Checks C and D at their own main maintenance hub while other airlines contract for these services from other companies located at remote facilities. All heavy checks require an aircraft to be out of service while the checks are being performed. Check C requires extensive tests of parts, components, instruments, and systems. Specialized tools, test instruments, and personnel are required. Check D is the most comprehensive check of all and deals extensively with structural aspects of the aircraft. Some aircraft may even be partially disassembled to inspect and test portions of the airframe, fuselage, flaps, stabilizers, and so forth.

Now let us look at true make versus buy decisions. Whether an organization decides to make something or buy it from someone else, these decisions are basically driven by two philosophies, value opportunity or necessity. From a value opportunity standpoint, the criteria for make decisions are:

- Availability access—Which course of action offers the best access to supply and inventory availability?
- Control of inventory—Which course of action offers the best control of inventory levels?
- Cost differential between make and purchase—What is the exact cost difference and total cost of ownership (TCO) between purchasing from outside suppliers and producing in-house?
- Control of costs—Which option offers the greatest ability to control production and other associated costs?
- Strategic factors should be considered—Are there any strategic factors that should be considered? Can a technological advantage be gained? This would probably be a consideration in our example. Keeping design specifications and production in-house might offer a technological competitive advantage.
- Quality control—Which option can assure the highest degree of quality control?
- Reliability improvement—Which option offers the greatest opportunity for reliability improvement?
- Labor considerations and organizational restrictions—Do current outside suppliers offer stable workforces that are reliable and trained? Are there any union versus nonunion issues that should be considered? Labor and benefits make up a large percentage of production costs for both outside suppliers and in-house production.
- Experience level of production—Obviously the outside supplier already producing DooJiggys, used in the example later in this chapter, has an existing experience level. Can moving production in-house develop an equivalent level of experience that meets or exceeds that offered by the outside suppliers?
- Support capability—What is the current support capability of the outside suppliers and can moving production in-house generate higher support capabilities?
- Long-term implications—The long-term effects and implications of make versus buy decisions over an extended period should be considered. Can an organization live with potential supply shortages and interruptions, limited control, higher prices, and increased inventory levels, or does it make economic sense to move to in-house production? Remember, the freedom to select suppliers will be lost. Will reduction

in TCO and the assurance of supply that might be gained offset this loss of freedom?
- Risk (interruption or control of supply)—Risks should be identified for raw material supply and other factors. An evaluation should be made to compare those risks and determine which option offers the lowest risk threats and which are more easily mitigated.

Not everything required to produce something could, or should, be made internally. The great industrial innovator Henry Ford found this out the hard way. Henry Ford introduced many innovations that revolutionized manufacturing. The assembly line is probably the most well-known, but he was responsible for many other innovations as well. Early in the company's history he decided that every single part and service required to build his automobiles should either be made or performed by his own company. That way the company would have total control over everything and not be reliant on, or at the mercy of, anyone or any other company. He even opened the Rouge River steel plant and foundry that made all of the metal parts for his automobiles. Total control sounds reasonable enough in theory, and it was effective in practice initially. But what Henry Ford found out the hard way was that so many parts and services were required that it became a management nightmare. In essence, instead of managing one company, it was like managing hundreds of separate companies and coordination of supply lines became convoluted. So, being the smart business man that he was, he reorganized his company. The company still made some crucial and critical items but contracted for most other parts and services. Why give this example? It demonstrates that an organization must decide what makes the most sense for their individual situation and what brings the most value to their organization.

How do you determine when to make and when to buy? As stated previously, it is based primarily on value opportunity or necessity. What is value opportunity? Simply put, it consists of two ingredients: (1) the value of what doing something has and (2) the availability to do it. Strategic supply management and procurement has a critical role in any make versus buy decision process. The evaluation and ultimate decision by an organization to either make an item or perform a service internally or acquire it from an outside supplier involves careful research and analysis. Procurement has the proper tools and expertise at their disposal and should always have a seat at the decision table and be involved in the decision-making process. Procurement can obtain and evaluate the costs of the raw materials, supplies, parts, components, and equipment by performing a make versus buy analysis. An example of this analysis is presented in Table 18.1. It is a basic and simplistic example that uses a value impact rating to access each criterion. Other make versus buy analyses may be constructed more comprehensively. In either circumstance, research

Table 18.1 Opportunity analysis for a make versus buy decision

Criteria	Description	Value rating impact		
		Low	Medium	High
Start-up costs (initial costs)	What impact initial funds required would have taking into consideration amortization			
Investment required	How much money is required to fund			
Facilities	Expansion of existing facilities			
New equipment	New equipment required			
Employees	Number of additional hourly employees and staff required			
Training	Cost of initial and ongoing training			
Financing	Impact of initial funds invested			
Production costs (ongoing costs)	Cost less to produce each piece in-house vs. buying from outside sources			
Product availability improvement	Value of having greater product availability and lower stock inventories			
Product reliability improvement	Value of having greater control over reliability and reliability improvement			
Consistency of supply	Value of having uninterrupted, consistent supply			
Technology improvement	Value of having greater technological control and able to make improvements quicker			
Flexibiity	Value of having greater flexibility in all aspects of supply			
Quality	Value of having improved overall quality of product and greater control of inspection and testing			
Risk	Risk of making in-house			

may be required to determine cost factors and totals for individual criteria that may include obtaining quotes, cost figures, and feasibility information from industrial engineering, and it may be necessary to canvass suppliers.

Let us assume that an organization presently makes a product—a Widget—and wants to determine if it can make a primary component of the Widget—a DooJiggy—in-house for less cost with more availability and reliability than continuing to purchase from an outside supplier. The reason this issue has surfaced is based on the following factors:

- DooJiggys are critical to the manufacture of Widgets.
- Engineering has made design changes to the Widget that will require totally new DooJiggy specifications that are not presently available in the marketplace.
- DooJiggys are made of a particular metal alloy that is outside most industry standards.
  - Current suppliers have experienced raw material shortages in the past that have slowed or caused disruption of DooJiggy production. This has forced the organization to adjust their on-hand inventory levels higher than production schedules dictate in order to establish safety stocks and avoid shortages or stock-outs.
- The organization has had quality and supply problems in the past because there are only a handful of qualified companies that are willing to make and supply DooJiggys to the organization's tight specifications and quality requirements.
- All of these factors make the cost of purchasing DooJiggys inherently high.

Now that we have the facts and the reason for considering a change to the present process, let us begin our evaluation. The first step in the make versus buy analysis is to establish the parameters within which the analysis will be conducted. This process starts off and works much like many of the strategic supply management and procurement projects and decisions we have discussed. Start by determining basic requirements and asking some fundamental questions:

- Identify the need or quantify the objective.
  - What is the need?
  - Why is it needed?
  - What quantities are required?
- What are the decision criteria to be considered?
  - Cost
    - Start up
    - Ongoing production
  - Availability (of product)
  - Reliability
  - Consistency of supply (of raw materials)
  - Technology improvement
  - Investment required
    - Equipment

- Facilities
- Employees
- Training
- Financing
- Labor requirements and constraints
  - Union vs. nonunion
  - Number of employees and staff required
- Flexibility and Versatility
- Quality
- Risk

Next, determine who should be involved in the decision process. Determine who the stakeholders are and who have additional resources that might contribute to the evaluation process by contributing data, information, and expertise. This will be the evaluation and decision team and will probably include one or more people from the following groups:

- Procurement—stakeholder
- Finance—stakeholder
- Engineering—resource
- Quality control—resource
- Operations—stakeholder
- Industrial engineering—resource

In this particular example procurement has been picked to lead the evaluation team. They are considered one of the stakeholders of this project. They will be a major player in determining whether the cost benefits of making the new DooJiggy in-house is feasible or if the organization should contract with an outside source to make it. If the decision is to make internally, many factors will need to be considered:

- Expansion of existing facilities
- Addition of new equipment
- Addition of employees and supervisory staff
- Training programs (initial and ongoing)

Finance is considered a stakeholder because they will be responsible for approving and budgeting the money required to pay for the items listed. Engineering is considered a resource because they are the entity that decided a design change was necessary and actually developed the new design of the DooJiggy. Engineering also will recommend what new equipment will be required, or at least advise what the new equipment should be capable of doing. Quality control is considered a resource because they will be responsible for the inspection and testing of the new DooJiggy regardless of whether it is made in-house or purchased from outside sources. Operations is a primary stakeholder because they would have the ultimate responsibility of making the new DooJiggy. Industrial Engineering is an important resource because it will be responsible for supplying such things as time studies and facility layout. There you have the evaluation team and what their responsibilities are. Now it is time to begin the evaluation and analysis process.

Throughout this exercise we will not be using specific numbers. Since this scenario is all hypothetical and fictitious, we will instead present generalities and assumptions. What I want is for the reader to grasp the basic concept of what is involved in a make versus buy decision. Why is it a component of strategic supply management and procurement and a part of a best-in-class philosophy? A key ingredient of a make versus buy analysis is a feasibility study. The initial questions asked to quantify the objective have been asked and answered:

- What is the need? Widgets are made of many parts and components, many of which are already made by the organization. Existing DooJiggys are made by and purchased from outside suppliers. The question has been asked whether it is feasible to make DooJiggys in-house or continue to purchase from outside sources.

- Why is it needed? A new Widget requirement has forced the redesign of existing DooJiggys. There have been supply problems with existing suppliers in the past and costs have become out-of-line with normal component costs.

- What quantities are required? Production quantity requirements essentially will be the same as the old DooJiggys although improvement in inventory levels are hoped for if made in-house.

Now our attention turns to determining costs and whether a move to in-house production is feasible. There are two types of cost considerations that must be evaluated: (1) initial start-up costs and (2) ongoing production costs. There are several make versus buy criteria that require analysis and evaluation:

- Cost—Analysis should be conducted that compares in-house production to an outside purchase. The cost analysis should include both start-up and ongoing production costs. In-house cost of production should include elements such as cost of raw materials, supplies, salaries and benefits, and all other associated requirements, activities, and functions.

- Investment—Analysis should be conducted that looks at all initial costs such as primary and support equipment and/or re-tooling of existing equipment required to produce DooJiggys, facility expansion or re-design, addition of employees and staff, training requirements, and financing requirements and costs, that is, will available on-hand cash be used or loans secured requiring an interest charge.

- Technology—What technology requirements are involved. Will new technology need to be purchased? Is existing technology already owned by outside suppliers? Examples might be computer programmable laser cutters or stamping machines.
- Quality—Are outside suppliers capable of ensuring and supplying consistent quality levels that comply with the organization's specifications and requirements? Is the organization capable of ensuring consistent quality?
- Flexibility—Would in-house production be in a better position to respond and react to the organization's needs than an outside supplier? Service levels and rapid response times are considerations as well as the willingness to make changes.
- Consistency of availability and supply—One of the issues that prompted the consideration of make versus buy in our example was the inconsistencies in the availability and supply of existing DooJiggys by present suppliers. This was primarily a result of specialized requirements and shortages of raw materials. Would in-house production increase the availability of supplies and be able to reduce current safety stock inventory levels?
- Differentiation—Differentiation is a strategic approach to supply management and procurement that takes into consideration the ability to reduce costs while meeting organizational and customer needs. A comparison of this ability between outside suppliers and in-house production should be considered.
- Regulatory considerations—Are there any existing or proposed governmental regulatory requirements that would add additional costs to the production of the redesigned DooJiggys, from both an in-house and outside supplier standpoint? If additional costs are anticipated they should be identified and defined for both, then an evaluation of what changes would be required and the effects of those changes from an in-house point of view.

Any decision to make a part or perform a service in-house will require a make versus buy analysis. This should not be confused with the opportunity analysis mentioned earlier in this chapter. Opportunity analysis is performed to determine if a feasible and viable opportunity exists to do something different. One aspect of opportunity analysis is determining the cost factors involved such as cost to produce/perform and cost savings/increased profits. But these determinations are a high-level estimation and not usually based on actual facts and data but rather on more general or generic information. An opportunity analysis is just a way to determine what possible opportunities exist. If an opportunity presents itself, the next step would be to perform a more detailed make versus buy analysis.

Make versus buy analysis are detailed and based on factual and researched data. It is a comparison of the actual costs and requirements of producing goods or performing services in-house compared to buying goods and services from outside, independent sources. An important part of any make versus buy analysis is a break-even analysis. Any make versus buy analysis will include a feasibility study and that study will include a break-even analysis. A break-even analysis is important in determining the viability (feasibility) of making DooJiggys in-house as opposed to buying from outside sources. Obviously, after calculating all of the costs involved (both fixed and variable), if the example organization cannot make DooJiggys for less than they can buy them from an outside source, the only determining factors left on which to make that decision are reliability and availability. Break-even analyses have importance to organizations in making other decisions and planning strategies other than deciding to produce something in-house. This is especially true for start-up companies, new product development, and marketing promotions. It is important that procurement be included in this process because of their expertise in research, analysis, analytical philosophies, techniques, and methodologies. Interdepartmental collaboration and cross-functionality are earmarks of a best-in-class organizational philosophy.

What is a break-even analysis? It is required when developing a strategy to make or produce something. This can be a strategy for determining the sale price in the context of a business plan or a marketing plan. Simply put, it is the point at which you break even, that is, where the cost to make or do something is equal to the market cost or sales price; it is a zero point on the economic or cost scale. This is called the break-even point or BEP where costs, expenses, and revenue are all equal to one another with no net loss and no net gain. Determining the break-even point of something is relatively easy to determine. The basic formula used for this calculation is:

Fixed Costs/(Unit Selling Price – Variable Costs) = BEP

In the example used in this chapter, the per unit selling price would equate to the price that the organization is presently paying for DooJiggys or that it would expect to pay for the newly designed DooJiggy. Fixed costs are basically the overhead of a company—the costs that do not vary with output and remain constant within a relevant range for a specified period of time, independent of variations or fluctuations in production total volume increases or decreases. Variable costs are costs or expenses incurred as a result of the item being produced. They change when the amount or volume of an item produced increases or decreases. Variable costs in our DooJiggy example would be fluctuations in raw material prices and other supply costs, utilities, and labor. There are limitations to the example formula we use for our make versus buy analysis. The example formula listed is a supply side (costs only) formula. Assumptions are made such as fixed costs are constant, the quantity of DooJiggys produced would equal the quantity of DooJiggys required and is constant, and the average variable costs would be constant within the range of quantities required. Variations in the form of other formulas to determine unit contribution margin, margin of safety, and cost-volume-profit analysis can also be used to calculate break-even points for anything from determining optimum or desired sales profit margin and production cost levels, to currency transactions.

Why is break-even analysis important? Break-even analysis is important because you must know what something costs before you can determine the profitability and advantage of doing something. Break-even lets you know the minimum financial requirement or cost of doing it. Break-even analysis is also a great tool and useful in performing what-if scenarios for determining how to price a product initially or what increasing production for a sales promotion would decrease costs and impact profit margins. In the case of our example, if there were other markets available for the sale of DooJiggys in addition to the organization's requirement, the opportunity would exist to increase production to points exceeding internal consumption requirements. This opportunity would thereby reduce the overall cost of DooJiggy production substantially and create an additional revenue stream.

Break-even analysis is a tool that can be used extensively for a variety of purposes. It can be used to not only calculate the cost of internal production but to estimate the cost incurred by the competition. Knowing the point at which certain quantities of production would be required to reach a break-even or zero point after all applicable costs were calculated and applied allows the determination of various degrees of profitability. Break-even analysis can be invaluable when developing strategies, determining financial requirements, and setting sales prices. Normal or average supply management and procurement operations do not have the opportunity or occasion to use break-even analysis that often and, in fact, may never have a need to use it. It does have direct applications in make versus buy situations and is a useful tool to know how to use even if it is used infrequently. It is part of a critical thinking, resourceful, creative, strategic, and best-in-class mentality and philosophy.

The example used in this chapter evaluated the decision to move DooJiggy supply requirements from a purchase acquisition from outside suppliers to in-house production. However, most make versus buy decisions considered by organizations pertain to moving in-house production to an outsourced production arrangement or purchasing from independent outside suppliers.

19

Best-In-Class Strategies, Tools, and Techniques

If you research best-in-class you will not find much written about it, which is one reason I decided to write this book. So exactly what is best-in-class and how can it benefit you as a supply management and procurement professional and, more importantly, your department and organization?

My definition for best-in-class is: The highest current level of performance achievable for an organization in a specific market or industry. Within an organization it is the highest level of performance achievable for a business activity or process that can be achieved. Just like the U.S. Army slogan, it is being all that you can be, in other words, being the best you can be at what you do.

The concept of best-in-class is most commonly associated with best practices and total quality management. A best-in-class organization, or one or more of an organization's business activities or processes, are often used as benchmarks for quality or process improvement by other organizations or by other departments within an organization. Best-in-class represents the top of the mountain or pinnacle of successful achievement and efficiency in something that is done.

Being best-in-class becomes a part of an organization's culture. Achieving a best-in-class philosophy is difficult and takes time, effort, and a strategy of how to get there. One way of achieving a best-in-class philosophy and culture is to have upper management put emphasis on it and by nurturing an environment of progressive, creative, and forward thinking. It also requires openness with, and inclusiveness of, all employees to create an atmosphere of teamwork and their desire to be the best at what they do. Ongoing training is another essential. Being best-in-class requires an acceptance of change and being able to adapt and assimilate new ideas and techniques into current processes or perhaps even replacing them. Once a department or organization achieves best-in-class status it does not ensure that it will always be so. To sustain success and best-in-class, there must be a willingness to continue to seek improvement. This can be accomplished through continuous monitoring and adjustment.

Working with substantial numbers of professionals and organizations, I have been struck by just how little basic formal business knowledge and training some people in authority actually have. Please do not think I am criticizing or being disparaging to anyone. Even if someone is super fantastic at what they do, they may not possess all of the skills, experience, or knowledge to fully grasp some concepts and, thus, are unable to immediately see what the implications, ramifications, or benefits of adopting and implementing a new philosophy would have to the organization or what would be required to make it happen. I have seen instances where a manager who has attended a workshop gets inspired about a new technique or philosophy and wants to institute it in the organization. That's great, but the problem is that they—or their employees—do not possess the basics of overall business knowledge that is needed to operate effectively before the process is changed. Understanding what you want to do, why you want to do it, and how you will do it are essential questions that must be asked before attempting any change. Training in specific areas related to what is going to be changed is an absolute necessity. Individuals who understand the effect of the change on their specific job or area of responsibility, their department, and the organization as a whole are in positions to make extraordinary contributions to the organization's efforts. It should be stressed that the importance of individuals continuing their education at some level only improves that individual's marketability and also increases their value as an asset to the organization. Whether it is college courses, formalized training courses, or self-training, it will increase their knowledge base and stimulate their cognitive and creative thought processes. Organizations that invest in their employee's education and training reap great rewards in the long run.

So far we have discussed what best-in-class is and what it represents. Now let us discuss some of the tools, techniques, and concepts available that can be used to achieve best-in-class supply management and procurement. As mentioned several times, there is no cookie cutter or standard answers for what tools and techniques to use in order to achieve best-in-class supply management and procurement. Each procurement project is different. Procurement departments and organizations are also different, each having their own supply management and procurement philosophy, requirements, processes, and procedures. With this book you have at your disposal a best-in-class toolkit from which you can select the best tools to do any specific job. Some tools are specific to certain jobs or projects while others can be used in a variety of situations.

This chapter lists the various tools and techniques available that can be used to attain best-in-class in supply management and procurement. The choice of which tools and techniques to use is up to you. The tools listed are in no specific order:

Basic price analysis—This is a simple comparison of prices for the same goods or services. In a basic procurement environment, this may be the only analysis performed. In a best-in-class strategic supply management and procurement environment it is a quick look to determine the range or spread of pricing that is received from a bid or from on-line catalogs to aid in the prequalification of bidders, develop a strategic plan for negotiating, or to determine a short list of bidders.

Total cost analysis—TCA analysis takes into consideration costs other than the cost per piece or function. Costs for transportation, receiving, quality control, stocking, taxes and/or import and export duties, and other associated costs that might add to the total cost of goods and services purchased.

Total cost of ownership—TCO analysis is a financial estimate to determine both direct and indirect costs of goods and services. It takes into consideration all life cycle costs associated with an item from its initial acquisition (birth) until it is dispensed to the production floor or disposed of by picking, packing, and shipping (death). It contains all of the cost considerations found in TCA as well as inventory carriage costs, lease payments, finance charges, shelf-life expiration, and haz-mat documentation and disposal that are involved throughout the life cycle.

Usage cost analysis—UCA looks at the usage and cost aspects of goods to determine how effectively they are being purchased. It is most commonly associated with, and a part of, a purchase history analysis, but sometimes it is performed as a stand-alone analysis to determine how effectively shelf-life items are being bought and used, the number of out-of-spec or out-of-tolerance items being received and rejected in a given time period, and so forth. UCA can also be beneficial in discovering commonality of parts being purchased. There are situations where separate sections of a procurement department are basically buying the same part but under various part numbers from different suppliers. This is an example of inefficiency at its best. Many suppliers assign their own part numbers to the parts that they buy from manufacturers, even though different suppliers may buy from the same manufacturer. By buying basically the same part from different suppliers, a company is obviously paying varying prices. This is due to the price structures and profit margins of the various suppliers but can also be affected by quantity or volume purchase discounts. When various individuals and/or sections of procurement departments purchase the same parts from different suppliers, they lose volume leverage by not using a standardized part number and combining buy requirements. Part of an effective UCA is a review of specifications and requirements to look for commonality and opportunity for standardization.

Vendor financial analysis—VFA is most often used to prequalify potential bidders as to their financial soundness. Financial data and information can be obtained on a corporation or company from several sources:

- Balance sheets show the financial position of a company at a specific point in time.
- Income statements reveal the financial earnings of a company in a specified time period (usually one year). It reconciles earnings from sales against cost of goods sold to show the net income for that time period.
- Audited annual reports are generated by publicly held and traded companies at the end of each fiscal year. It contains balance sheets, income statements, 10-K reports, and other statements and information. Annual reports are the most comprehensive financial information you can obtain.
- 10-K reports are required by the Securities and Exchange Commission for all publicly held companies and foreign companies doing business within the United States. It contains more detailed financial information on assets, liabilities, and earnings than annual reports. They can be obtained via the Internet by navigating www.sec.gov.
- Dunn and Bradstreet is a service-for-fee provider of credit information on a company as well as organizational, management, and payment histories. Its rating system assigns ratings to a variety of categories and is useful.
- Financial advisory reports provide a variety of information on a company such as the ranking within their industry and factors that are affecting particular industries. Financial advisory reports are provided by companies such as Standard & Poor's, Bloomberg, Hoover's, and Moody's and can be accessed via the Internet.

There are many tools that can be used in measuring, assessing, and analyzing an organization's financial soundness and viability. Information provided in balance sheets, income statements, and 10-Ks can be used to calculate the level of performance of a company. Some of the most frequently used tools (in the form of financial formulas) are:

- Working capital shows how much money is being held in reserve by a company and is calculated by subtracting current liabilities from current assets. (current assets – current liabilities)
- Gross profit margin gives the ratio between net revenue from sales to cost of goods sold. (gross profit ÷ net sales)
- Current ratio indicates the liquidity of a company by comparing the amount of current assets to current liabilities. (current assets ÷ current liabilities)

- Debt to asset ratio offers information about a company's ability to absorb asset reductions when incurring losses. (total liabilities ÷ total assets)
- Long-term debt to working capital ratio gives some insight into a company's ability to pay long-term debt with current assets after the liabilities are paid. This information can usually be found in the current liabilities section of the balance sheet.
- Debt to equity ratio gives an indication of how protected creditors are in case of insolvency. (total debt ÷ total equity)
- Acid test is a measurement that indicates the liquidity of a company. (cash + marketable securities + accounts receivable ÷ current liabilities)
- Cash turnover shows how effective a company utilizes its cash. (net sales ÷ cash)
- Accounts receivable turnover shows how liquid a company's receivables are. (net sales ÷ average gross receivables)
- Return on sales (also known as net profit ratio) reveals how much income is generated for every dollar of sales and is calculated as follows: net income (before tax and interest) ÷ net sales.
- Return on investment (ROI) is used to determine how efficiently a company is investing its money. (ROI = net income [annual operating expense] ÷ total capital invested [long-term liabilities + equity])
- Margin analysis is used to determine the profitability of a company in relation to its sales. (net operating margin = total operating income ÷ total sales)

These are just a few of the many financial formulas that can be used to analyze an organization's efficiency and soundness. Some procurement departments prefer to have their finance and accounting departments perform financial analysis of suppliers while others make it a part of their normal operating procedure. It does take some knowledge of accounting practices and procedures and an understanding of how to read financial statements, but all of it can be learned and perfected with practice. With publicly traded companies, required financial data is readily available, but you may find obstacles when trying to determine the financial standing of a privately held company. There may be objections to divulging financial information from some suppliers. A company's right to privacy should be respected but, when it comes to awarding a critical or multimillion dollar contract, one should insist on knowing the financial position of the supplier. To overcome this and avoid the issue arising later in the negotiating process, it can be made a requirement in a request for proposal solicitation in applicable situations. A requirement that financial information be included in, and made a part of, a bidder's proposal response would not be out of order. Appropriate confidentiality guarantees could be made, but if a bidder did not choose to comply it should be considered a red flag and a warning sign that the bidder should not be considered a qualified bidder and should be removed from the solicitation.

Sometimes a technical analysis is needed to review and compare offerings from different vendors. Goods and services that have specific specifications and tolerances, are complicated, have a variance in the type of offering made, or require other special considerations are all candidates for a technical analysis. Examples of such technical analyses are:

- Software or program designs. Study and analysis are required to determine cost benefits, programming requirements, testing timeline and requirements, implementation time, training, and so forth.

- A heavy maintenance program in the airline industry. Some airlines perform their own heavy maintenance of periodic FAA mandated inspections and checks, but the majority contract these services out to third-party maintenance providers. Comparisons of what specific services are performed and how (procedures), what parts are scheduled for replacement or repair, whether replacement parts and costs are included in the service fees, location of the service provided, and length of time required (how long an aircraft will be out of service) are all components of this analysis.

- Another airline industry example is the purchase of Class D full flight simulators (FFS) used to train and certify aircraft pilots and crews without actually flying an airplane. A Class D FFS consists of an enclosed aircraft cockpit with both actual and replicated parts and instruments, either hydraulically or electrically driven. There are only three qualified manufacturers of Class D simulators in the world. Due to the complexity, variation in design, and actual controls and instruments versus replicated parts, a technical analysis is absolutely necessary to analyze and compare variations in the offerings.

PEST (political, economic, social, and technological factors) analysis is usually not a regular analysis performed in a normal supply management or procurement project unless circumstances require it. It is an environmental strategic management component. PEST analysis is beneficial to determine factors involved with trading in a third-world country when considering the use of first-time, low-cost country providers. But there could be other instances where PEST would be applicable in a standard procurement environment.

SWOT (strengths, weaknesses, opportunities, and threats) analysis is useful and is used to help identify potential risks and value adding opportunities as well as process improvement. It is usually performed as a prelude to a formal risk analysis and the development of a risk management plan and should be performed in all major buy projects.

Risk analysis takes SWOT analysis to the next logical level. Risk analysis identifies all potential risks to a procurement project by defining what the risk is and assigning an estimated impact value to the chance it will happen, what the impact to the project might be, and what priority it should be assigned.

Some individuals only identify risks and stop there. The thought here is that knowing potential risks exist is enough. This is asking for trouble. Once risks are identified a plan to mitigate (deal with and overcome) those risks should be developed. A risk mitigation plan requires brainstorming and doing what-if scenarios to determine potential outcomes. This process usually requires information obtained from other types of analysis to provide accurate and up-to-date data on which the mitigation plan will be based. The plan also identifies the primary stakeholder responsible for each risk. Once a risk mitigation plan is developed, a plan of how it will be managed and by who should be made.

Many functions and activities of business are sensitive to internal and external forces and events that can have either a positive or negative effect on projects and/or processes and activities within an organization. Sensitivity analysis is a process and technique used to determine the possible outcome of a situation on which a decision and/or plan is or will be made if a key ingredient such as a prediction, forecast, or an event result turns out to be in error. It may also be used to determine the outcome of a situation given a set of different events or variables.

An environmental scan is an analytical tool used by best-in-class organizations to gather and analyze data externally to determine factors that might affect the organization and how it conducts business. Findings of the scan and analysis can then be used to perform SWOT or risk analysis and then used to formulate goals for both tactical and strategic plans for the organization. An example of an external environmental scan might be determining the percentage of potential customers for a particular product by demographics and consumer trends. When Apple's iPhone was being developed, environmental scanning would have most likely been used to determine if a market might exist for the product and who target customers might be.

Environmental scanning is used externally but can also be used internally to analyze the specifics of the organization's business processes and procedures and to determine the capabilities of the organization as they exist today and if they will be adequate to fulfill the needs of the organization in the future. Internal environmental scanning can be used in some procurement situations, for example, as it might apply to value chain management (VCM). The data obtained from environmental scanning must be analyzed to be useful. This requires screening of the data to eliminate unnecessary data. Questions asked when analyzing will aid in fine tuning the data to maximize its usefulness. For example, the purpose for VCM is to determine the efficiency of primary and secondary business activities of an organization and to determine if any opportunities exist for improvement. Therefore, an environmental scan is done (in this case both internally and externally) to gather data about how business activities are performed, who performs them, what factors affect how they are performed, and how the competition performs these same activities. A few of the questions that might be asked are:

- How am I performing each of the business functions?
- What are the outer limits to what I can do?
- Will—or should—changes to the external environment affect the way this function is performed?
- How does my competitor perform this function?
- Is my competitor's way better than mine?
- Does it cost less?
- Does it provide more value to my company and customers (internal and external)?
- Does what I am doing in one activity or process fit with what I am doing in other activities or processes?
- Do I really have an integrated strategy?
- What are the overall cost drivers?
- What is the cost for each link of the supply chain?
- What are the cost-restructuring opportunity options?
- What is the estimated cost for each opportunity option?
- What are the different reengineering configuration opportunity options at critical links?
- What is the cost-restructuring compared to competitors costs?
- What are the economies of scale?
- What is the capacity utilization?
- Is there any linkage between activities and/or functions?
- What is the relationship between business units?
- What is the degree of vertical integration?
- What is the time to market?
- Are there any institutional factors (regulations, union activity, taxes, etc.) to consider?

One of the most difficult things to accomplish is seeing inside your competition. It is easier scanning an industry overall to gain some insights into the state of the industry and how it operates in general. Many people do not understand that if you want answers to some of the questions that need to be asked then research will be required. The Internet was a big boon to research and it is free. All it costs is the time of the researcher. One can view most industry journals, newsletters, and trade magazines online. Many have free subscriptions and can be delivered automatically via e-mail. A Google of specific topics and competitors by name can yield significant useful information. If someone in a competitor company has written an article or a paper that has been published, it can offer real insights into what they have done and how they did it. If a competitor is a publicly traded company their annual report can be enlightening. Manufacturer reps are also a key source of information on competitors as well. You would be surprised what can be learned from reps if you know how to do it and what questions to ask.

Although environmental scans are most often used by an organization to determine data and information externally of the organization, there are specific reasons for a supply management or procurement department to do internal environmental scans. Internal environmental scans are a good way to identify activities and processes of other departments within an organization and determine the effectiveness and efficiency that procurement adds to the overall operations. In addition to being used for generating data for a decision or plan that needs to be developed, they should also be performed periodically to aid in strategic planning processes. Most organizations develop their strategic plans for 5- to 10-year periods, but it is important to remember that plans may change as circumstances warrant and they would need to be revised. The recent financial crisis and current recession is probably prompting many organizations to revisit and revise their strategic plans. Environmental scans, both external and internal, may be one of the tools they use to do so.

The continuous development of computer software and their capabilities continue to offer new and better ways to improve how business is performed. One such opportunity is electronic data interchange (EDI), the electronic exchange of information between two organizations or entities. Some organizations that have intimate, long-term relationships with other organizations establish an Extranet that is a Website used exclusively by the participating parties to allow access to and sharing of information between the organizations. It can also be utilized by contracting with an independent EDI service platform to initiate the exchange of data between parties. There are real cost-saving advantages of using EDI to transfer information, and even funds, between parties.

Supply chain management is a significant value adding technique when practiced effectively. By identifying links in the supply chain and effectively managing them, more opportunities for cost reduction and process improvement will be developed. It is a necessary requirement to achieving best-in-class.

Understanding what and who makes up the supply chain is the foundation of practicing strategic supply chain management. Supply chain mapping is a visual way of portraying individual entities, or links, in the supply chain. It is discussed in detail in other chapters and examples of how to develop a process map are given.

Value chain mapping is not always used or practiced in supply management and procurement but a short version sometimes is used if a particular project warrants it. It is used much the same way as supply chain mapping to identify the primary and support activities of an organization's operations. The purpose for doing value chain identification and mapping is to allow the supply manager to look for opportunities for cost reduction and process improvement. Value chain mapping can prove to be an important and valuable tool in determining and developing cost-saving and process improvement activities.

Process and activity mapping can be used in any and all aspects of an organization's operation, in any or all business functions. Anywhere there is a business function, activity, or process, a process and activity map can be developed to identify the steps and sequence. From a supply management and procurement standpoint, process and activity maps provide a way to help the supply manager and procurement professional see how something currently works. It also helps identify possible areas where opportunities exist for process and value improvement. Process and activity maps can be used in conjunction with supply chain and value chain management to understand how a department, process, or activity works.

The purchase history query is widely used to identify past procurement activity within a defined time period. Information is taken from the organization's databases to reflect past procurement activity. What was purchased, how many, when, and from whom are all components of a purchase history query. This information is helpful in developing future procurement requirements, developing RFPs, and establishing minimum requirements.

A reliability history query is used to track and identify the reliability of certain parts and components purchased by an organization and used in their operations or production. Reliability tracking involves such things as quality control and reject rates, mean time before failure rates, quality assurance standards, out-of-spec tolerances, and a wide variety of measureable variables that might affect goods purchased. Databases must be set up and maintained to record, track, and analyze these elements. In a basic procurement environment, reliability history and tracking probably would not be used, but in a best-in-class environment, it most certainly would.

Weighted Decision Matrix—All decisions, whether made by a single individual or by a group, are subject to influence by prejudice or preference. These biases are inherent to all human natures and, no matter how hard we try to make unbiased decisions, we still run the risk of being unduly influenced. The weighted decision matrix is one tool that can be used to eliminate, or at least limit, bias from creeping into the decision process. An example of using a weighted decision matrix is discussed in detail in other chapters of this book.

Many organizations use vendor qualification assessments such as vendor score cards to track and grade (or rate) vendors that they are currently doing business with. When issuing bids for the purchase of goods and services, it is important to identify whether a bidder is qualified or not. Qualifying vendors should also include an evaluation of their reliability records—on-time and late deliveries—if it is not already part of a vendor tracking and scoring program. If a vendor has never done business with an organization in the past, they still should go through a qualification process that would include a financial fitness evaluation, industry performance history, and vendor visits and inspection. Awarding business to a vendor who may later fail can have adverse consequences so it is important to know if a vendor is both capable and qualified.

Determining a supplier's financial soundness is important before entering into agreements, particularly long-term ones. This is especially true when an organization has not previously done business with a company, but it is also prudent business to evaluate companies with whom you are familiar, have done business with in the past, or is recognized in their industry. Tough economic times, recession, and even mismanagement can have adverse effects on companies that may not be readily apparent. Financial analysis is doing due diligence and part of a strategic supply management philosophy.

Some segments in business are required to meet quotas or have set-aside business guaranteed for companies designated as minority or disadvantaged. Best-in-class organizations, whether required to allocate a portion of their business or not, realize the importance of openness and inclusiveness. These organizations make attempts to identify and include qualified minority and disadvantaged businesses in all bid offerings as a matter of every day procedure.

Knowing inventory levels, turnover rates, and usage and specification requirements are all necessary to analyze and evaluate inventory levels. This is usually a function of procurement and is monitored by inventory planners and/or buyers. Increases or decreases in usage require adjustments to minimum and maximum inventory levels. Inventory level analysis should be performed at regular, predetermined dates or when changes occur or are anticipated in usage requirements.

Many electronic systems and software programs exist to monitor and manage inventory. From receipt to dispersal, bar codes and scanners can be used to record and automatically adjust inventory levels. Software programs such as MRP, MRP-II, and ERP automatically manage inventories and offer visibility to many segments and departments of an organization. One relatively new concept is electronic vendor managed inventory (VMI), a system and process whereby inventory is electronically managed by a partner vendor from a remote location, usually for high usage and common or consumable parts and components. As inventory is scanned at various process points, data is collected and dumped at predetermined times daily to a vendor who makes adjustments to inventory levels (minimum and maximums), schedules replenishment shipments, and prepares reports on behalf of the company being managed. Advantages to this type of system are reduced costs in time and personnel.

One of the key components in practicing strategic supply management and procurement and best-in-class supply management is tracking prices and the supply of commodities used in an organization's operations. Best-in-class supply management and procurement organizations use this information to predict (forecast) what prices and supply availability might be in the future. Commodity price forecasts are discussed in detail in other chapters of this book and show the many advantages of practicing this valuable strategic tool.

To make the best decisions for future strategies, best-in-class organizations pay close attention to the state of their economy and the economies of other nations if they are trading internationally. Some larger organizations employ their own economists to track and forecast economic trends. Other organizations rely on periodicals, financial experts, and independent economists for evaluations. The Institute for Supply Management *Report on Business* that is revised and available each month is another valuable resource.

Industry forecasts are helpful in predicting the direction of an industry that an organization participates in or that they rely on for supplies. Identifying trends, markets, suppliers, obstacles, and risks helps an organization develop and/or adjust their strategic plans and goals. This is another tool that best-in-class organizations use to identify opportunities and obstacles in order to make the best, most informed decisions for their future.

Just-in-time (JIT) inventory does not work for every organization or situation. But where it may have applicability, it can be a viable opportunity if practiced efficiently. JIT inventory control pays substantial dividends in reducing inventory carrying, financial purchase, and operating costs and providing process efficiency improvement. JIT is a strategic supply management tool that can be determined by doing a VMI candidacy evaluation that is an analysis to determine the cost-benefit-viability aspects of JIT for given goods or services.

VMI is occasionally a viable opportunity. In those instances where it is doable, a vendor, usually on a long-term contract, monitors inventory usage and adjusts inventory levels on behalf of an organization. This may require that a vendor place staff on-site at an organization or make regular, periodic visits. Advances in information technology also offer the opportunity for remote electronic access to inventory databases so that a VMI supplier can see inventory usage and the status without actually having a body at a location. This is a strategic supply management tool that can be determined by doing a VMI candidacy evaluation that is an analysis to determine the cost-benefit-viability aspects of VMI for a given situation.

A negotiation strategy matrix is a helpful tool when planning for negotiations. It allows for brainstorming and recording thoughts, expectations, and desires. This allows an orderly development of how negotiations are perceived and should be executed. Elements of a negotiation strategy matrix are declaring what the most desirable outcome is, as well as the least acceptable agreement and the best alternative to a negotiated agreement. Other elements that are listed are assumptions, don't knows, probes, must haves, trade-offs, options for mutual gain, obstacles, biases, and risks.

Negotiations rarely can be completed in one round or one sitting, therefore it is important to record the particulars of each round of negotiations in order to revise and adjust strategy for the next round. Used in conjunction with a negotiation strategy matrix, a negotiating tracking log is a good tool to use as a comparison reference, both in current negotiations and in future negotiations whether it is the same, similar, or different type of project. The negotiating tracking log allows the supply management and procurement professional to see what worked and what did not, learn from mistakes and build on successes, and view what and how others within the organization conducted their respective negotiations.

After a best-in-class strategy is developed it then has to be implemented. This is where plans oftentimes fall short. The strategy can be a perfect one but if it is not implemented correctly it can still fail. Two things are important at this stage: (1) how the plan is implemented and (2) when it is implemented. Designing a plan to implement a strategy is in fact a strategy within itself. Both the strategy and the action plan must be communicated effectively to everyone affected by the plan. It should first be explained why the plan is necessary and what benefits it presents to the organization. Since action plans may require some type of change in philosophy and/or process activity, knowing why doing something new is required goes a long way in securing stakeholder and employee buy-in.

The plan should also be designed to be easily transitioned and workable. Every detail should be thought out in advance and viewed from the standpoint of those doing the work or managing the process. Training is an important aspect and everyone involved should be trained and made to understand what is required before the plan is implemented. Timing is important and can mean everything to the success of the plan. There should be a sequence of implementation and a timeline established for initiating the various stages of the plan. Contingencies should be thought out in advance and be ready to activate in case of unforeseen events that might jeopardize the implementation process. The smoother a plan is implemented, the greater its success will be.

We have discussed several types of analyses available, including sensitivity analysis. Many aspects of business are sensitive to internal and external forces that can have either a positive or negative effect. In many situations a sensitivity analysis is an absolute necessity when developing contingency plans to deal with these forces or when developing a strategy to present to an organization to justify philosophical or process changes. They are part of the what-if scenarios one would run in determining what the best options and alternatives are for action. By taking a set of circumstances and applying different scenarios that might have an effect on the outcome, one can predict to some degree what the eventual result might be. Knowing the alternatives allows for planning of reactions to a certain set of circumstances or events, ergo, contingency plans.

Sensitivity analysis is a process and technique used to determine the possible outcome of a situation on which a decision and/or plan is made if a key ingredient (prediction or forecast) actual result turns out to be in error. It is a systematic evaluation and analysis of what the effects might be on predicted outcomes and assumptions. It is also the determination of what the degree of sensitivity might be to outcomes based on predictions and assumptions. In other words, sensitivity analysis shows us what effects might be if a forecast, projection, or plan turns out to be wrong and how likely (the degree of sensitivity) it is that something might happen.

We have discussed SWOT and risk analysis previously and the important roles that they play in developing appropriate supply management and procurement strategies and decisions. Both are also part of a best-in-class operating process. SWOT and risk analysis are required prerequisites to a comprehensive and successful sensitivity analysis.

Many software programs have been developed that greatly facilitate various operating functions within organizations. MRP, MRP II, and ERP are the most recognizable of these. The purpose of these operating systems is to increase efficiencies of specific job functions and increase the productivity of operations overall. MRP stands for material requirements planning and is specific to individualized operations. Its purpose is to make sure that materials required for production or services are available when and as needed. It does this by computer-aided planning and scheduling of manufacturing and procurement activities as well as operating schedules for production and delivery. It also is designed to insure that inventory levels are kept low but still maintained and available.

MRP II stands for manufacturing resource planning and is a software information system that integrates all aspects of the manufacturing process. It is an extenuation of (and includes) MRP but with an emphasis on manufacturing activities. It also includes such functions as decision support, distribution, and accounting. MRP II is a centralized system that uses real time data to plan, support, and schedule labor and materials.

ERP stands for enterprise requirements planning and is an expanded software planning system that includes elements of MRP and MRP II but is fed and accessed by all business functions of an organization. ERP integrates real-time data from both internal and external sources across an entire organization, including manufacturing, operations, marketing, logistics and distribution, service, accounting, and finance. It facilitates the flow and availability of information by multiple business functions that are part of an organization.

Questions are necessary if one wants to find the answer to something. There are all types of questions that can and should be asked when practicing strategic supply management and procurement in order to attain best-in-class. One must know what information they want to extract from data because it will help in designing the appropriate questions to ask. Asking questions will lead to a greater chance for success in any endeavor. Appropriate questions need to be asked at the beginning and throughout each new buy project as well as for different aspects of normal daily operations. Asking questions as part of your regular discovery process gives an edge to your effectiveness.

Not many people know about the 5-whys or practice it. Many times people think they know the answer to a question or know what the root cause of a problem is, but really they do not because they have not dug deep enough. Using the 5-whys regularly will serve one well in getting to the bottom of things and determining the real reason for something. The following example demonstrates how identifying a problem and asking five sequential questions usually ends in identification of a root cause. Once the true root cause is determined, an appropriate solution can then be proposed.

Widgets are failing (this is the identified problem):

- Why are Widgets failing? One of the component parts is bad.
- Which component part is bad? The DooJiggy part.
- Why is the DooJiggy part bad? Some of the specifications are out of tolerance.
- Why are out-of-tolerance parts getting to the production line? There is no quality control testing procedure in place.
- Why isn't there a quality control testing procedure in place? The organization has limited resources and does not have the ability or equipment to test DooJiggys. Quality requirements are the responsibility of procurement.

Finally, the root cause is identified. So what is the solution to resolving this problem? There are several alternatives that might be considered and applied:

- Upgrade the quality control department to institute and include the testing of DooJiggys when received and then rejecting out-of-tolerance parts or lots.
- Make sure all quality problems are reported to procurement so that they can be added to the vendor management and reliability databases for quality tracking purposes.
- Procurement identifies who DooJiggys are being bought from.
  - Supplier is immediately notified and steps to correct are initiated.
  - Financial penalties for quality are imposed.
  - Other sources for DooJiggys are explored.
  - Tighter quality and specification requirements are incorporated in purchase orders and contracts.
  - Make or buy analysis is performed.

The goal of asking questions is to avoid making premature assumptions that could lead to wrong decisions being made. Asking appropriate questions develops a trail of cause and effect that allows the decision maker to make more informed and accurate decisions for a situation. Asking questions at the beginning of buy projects are helpful in developing an outline of the larger picture or how the project might fit into the overall procurement plan of what is required or desired of the project. It also helps identify opportunities for process improvement within the buy project itself and in overall procurement strategies. To summarize, the following questions should be asked:

- What do we want to accomplish?
- Why do we want to accomplish it?
- When do we want to accomplish it?
- How can we accomplish it?
- Who will accomplish it?

These are the basic questions that can be expounded on to fit your personal project situation. If the questions do not give all of the answers then more questions need to be asked and research performed to answer them. You can never ask too many questions. Asking questions and discovering answers is the basis for expanding your knowledge base.

Ethics plays an important role in all business practices. Not all companies or their executives have or practice ethics. They will be exposed given circumstances and in time. Both customers and employees expect to be treated honestly and fairly, in other words, ethically. Poor ethics, or the lack thereof, can have a profound effect on an organization. Enron and WorldCom are two notable examples of the absence of any ethics running wild. On a smaller scale, poor ethics can have a negative effect and impact on any organization. Poor ethics affects morale and performance internally and can lose customers and business externally. Best-in-class organizations practice ethical behavior and make it a part of their corporate culture. Supply management and procurement are especially susceptible to ethical practices and procedures. There is no substitute for practicing ethical behavior in conducting business transactions and the procurement professional should be on guard at all times against breaches of ethical protocols.

Supply Management Best-in-Class Check List

In striving to become a supply management and procurement best-in-class operation, one must adopt a strategic management philosophy. Incorporating strategic tools, techniques, and processes in the operation will allow a supply manager a better opportunity of achieving this goal. Not all tools and techniques may apply in all situations but most will. By identifying and implementing tools and techniques specific to a particular situation, the opportunity for additional value and greater success will be proportionately enhanced.

Since all procurement projects have different value, priority, and importance, a check list can be developed to evaluate these criteria and decide what tools and techniques would yield the highest value or the greatest dividends for each procurement project. People do a mental check off of requirements, but it is usually better to have an actual reference checklist available as it provokes more thought and evaluation for each item, criteria, or category being considered. By having a choice of pre-established options to be incorporated or used in each buy project, it avoids the possibility of overlooking something and having to adjust your plan and add it later. The checklist is a time management tool that allows prequalification and prioritization of projects before too much time is spent on them. It uses the initial, sometimes basic, information submitted by a stakeholder or that is already known within the department. Other basic research such as purchase history may be required for some items at this point but would normally be required anyway whether the checklist was used or not.

Now we are going to do an exercise to illustrate how this idea and concept can be used. We will assume that a procurement department in an organization has identified five buy projects that they want to implement:

- **Buy Project 1:** Rebid of an existing three-year contract that is expiring soon.
- **Buy Project 2:** Grouping of chemical-based commodity items to place on contract.
- **Buy Project 3:** Grouping of commodity items with aluminum as the base raw material.
- **Buy Project 4:** Grouping of all office-related supplies to place on contract.
- **Buy Project 5:** One-time purchase of two computer programmable laser-cutting machines and a service agreement to expand manufacturing operations.

Let us start by asking a series of basic questions about each of the individual projects:

- What is the estimated financial size of the buy project?
  - What is the estimated dollar spend?
    - What is the existing annual spend (if applicable)?
  - What is the perceived scope of the project?
    - What is the estimated annual number of items to be purchased?

- o   What is the number of annual purchase orders issued for this item or items?
- • Are the items to be purchased critical to the operation?
- • Does the buy project have a specific or mandatory completion or drop-dead date?
- • Is supply chain management being used to monitor and manage products or services being purchased?
- • Is the buy project a special, one-time, repeat, or term contract buy?
- • What is the percent savings target or other specific goals for the buy project?
- • Are the items required in the buy project candidates for EDI?
- • Are the items required in the buy project candidates for JIT inventory management?
- • Are the items required in the buy project candidates for VMI?

As you can see, most of the basic questions concerning a buy project are covered and other questions particular to a specific buy project may also be added. The next thing to do is determine the buy projects with the highest priority. We do this by constructing a project priority decision matrix to aid in the decision-making process. An initial project priority decision matrix is illustrated in Table 19.1. Keep in mind that priorities may change after conducting additional research, time line requirements, or specifications change.

For clarity, here is a quick explanation of the bases for priority assignment. This organization is in the process of instituting EDI wherever feasible because of the huge cost-saving advantage it offers in issuing purchase orders and invoices over a manual entry and issuing system. Four of the five buy projects offer extended cost savings by moving contract purchased items from a manual purchase order issuing system to EDI and offer substantial additional savings for those buy projects. If the organization was already using an EDI system then the priority assignments would have been based solely on the total estimated savings from contract purchasing only and the priority assignment would have been different.

- • First priority—buy Project 5: One-time purchase of two computer programmable laser-cutting machines and a service agreement to expand manufacturing operations. This buy project was assigned first priority status because operations require two new laser-cutting machines to increase production. There is a specific timeline required to bid, purchase, and install the equipment. A service agreement is also required and some negotiations can be expected and time allocated for them.
- • Second priority—buy Project 3: Grouping of commodity items with aluminum as the base raw material. This buy project was dedicated as the second priority because it offers the highest total estimated savings

Table 19.1 Project priority decision matrix

Buy project	Buy items	Annual # of POs issued	Critical items	Current estimated annual spend	Days available to award	Estimated savings contract vs. spot	Estimated savings (EDI vs. manual)	Total estimated annual savings	Value rank	Priority assigned
		Knowns				**Assumptions**				
No. 1	384	1,629	Yes	$1,265,000	60	$423,000	$244,105	$667,105	2	3
No. 2	258	2,789	Yes	$896,000	60	$245,000	$417,932	$662,932	3	4
No. 3	1424	5,684	Yes	$768,000	60	$232,450	$851,747	$1,084,197	1	2
No. 4	252	917	No	$59,605	90	$8,746	$137,412	$146,158	4	5
No. 5	2	N/A	Yes	N/A	40	N/A	N/A	N/A	N/A	1

Assumption No. 1: Average cost of issuing a manual purchase order is $150.00 per PO.
Assumption No. 2: Average cost of issuing a purchase order via EDI is $.15 per PO.

based on the highest number of items to be purchased, purchase orders issued, and greatest savings from moving purchases from manual purchase orders to EDI.

- Third priority—buy Project 1: Rebid of an existing three-year contract that is expiring. Buy Project 1 was chosen as the third-highest priority because an existing contract is expiring and rebid and award need to be in place before contract expiration and also because it offers the second-highest total estimated savings.

- Fourth priority—buy Project 2: Grouping of chemical-based commodity items to place on contract. Buy Project 2 was assigned the fourth-highest priority because it offers the third-highest total estimated savings but has the advantage of no time constraints other than the sooner it is done, the sooner the organization starts realizing significant savings. There are additional considerations as well. Chemicals also have shelf-life and Haz-Mat disposal issues that will need to be looked at closely. Chemicals may require inventory minimum/maximum levels to be adjusted and be a candidate for JIT and/or VMI.

- Fifth priority—buy Project 4: Grouping of all office-related supplies to place on contract. Although a useful and value adding project, buy Project 4 was assigned the lowest priority because it has the lowest total estimated savings of the five buy projects and can be done at anytime as there are no pressing time constraints.

Now we are ready to do our best-in-class check list. The project priority assignment was performed first so as to give us a list of what buy projects should be done in what sequence. Naturally we would want to do the check list for the highest priorities first or, if time allowed, they could all be analyzed at once as we did in a check list matrix in Table 19.2. This table lists which best-in-class tools and analysis should be used in each project. It also asks some questions to identify if the buy project might be a candidate for a specific service or action. As you study Table 19.2, keep in mind that all buy projects may not require the same tools in every project, and some buy projects may require additional analysis not listed for the five projects used in this exercise.

Table 19.2 should be self-explanatory and used in tandem with Table 19.1, the project priority matrix, along with the facts and data presented in the exercise. For a purchasing manager and/or procurement professional who has the desire to practice best-in-class supply management and procurement, the check list is a simple, time saving, and easy way of prequalifying a buy project and identifying what tools and analysis should be used in carrying out the project. It is a visual way of identifying and portraying this information to aid in building a buy project's requirements and strategy.

Table 19.2 Best-in-class check list

Buy project number	Basic price analysis	TCA	TCO	UCA	Vendor financial analysis	Technical analysis	SWOT analysis	Risk analysis	Sensitivity analysis	EDI candidate	Map supply chain	Map value chain	Process or activity map	RFP or RFQ required	Purchase history query	Reliability history query	Vendor qualification assessment	Vendor minority identification	Inventory level analysis	Commidity price forecast	Industry forecast	JIT candidate	VMI candidate
No. 5	Yes	Yes	No	No	Yes	Yes	No	No	No	No	No	No	No	RFQ	No	No	Yes	Yes	No	No	No	No	No
No. 3	Yes	Yes	Yes	Yes	Yes	Yes	Yes	Yes	Yes	Yes	Yes	Yes	Yes	RFP	Yes	Yes	Yes	Yes	Yes	Yes	Yes	Yes	No
No. 1	Yes	Yes	Yes	Yes	Yes	Yes	Yes	Yes	Yes	Yes	Yes	Yes	Yes	RFP	Yes	Yes	Yes	Yes	Yes	Yes	Yes	No	No
No. 2	Yes	Yes	Yes	Yes	Yes	Yes	Yes	Yes	Yes	Yes	Yes	Yes	Yes	RFP	Yes	No	Yes	Yes	Yes	Yes	Yes	Yes	Yes
No. 4	Yes	Yes	No	Yes	Yes	No	No	No	No	Yes	No	No	Yes	RFP	Yes	No	Yes	Yes	Yes	No	No	No	No

20

How to Implement and Manage Change

Change is inevitable in all things. It can't be avoided because it is going to happen, like it or not. Life itself is fluid and constantly changing and so is business. Change may be required as a reaction to certain unforeseen events or it may be the result of a strategy formed and presented by an organization to increase sales, reduce operating costs, and obtain or sustain competitive advantage. The French Foreign Legion had a saying—march or die. A variation of this can be applied to business—change or die. With this fact of business life, why then are there so many people that are resistant to change? There are several reasons, including:

- People and companies become complacent. Believe it or not, many successful companies can be the most resistant to change. Other successful companies realize that change is a necessity if they are to attain and sustain success. Some responses to suggestions for change are 'If it works why fix it', 'We cannot afford to change', 'We have too much work to do now, and we do not have time to change and do more work', and 'Our structure and processes will not allow us to change'. These are just a few of the common responses and excuses for not making needed changes. What they really mean is that they are afraid of change, they do not know how to change, or they do not understand the benefits of change.
- Corporate culture is antiquated, out of touch, or not in tune with the needs of the organization, their market, or employees. This is especially true for some organizations that have been in business for a long time. They have been successful but have failed to keep up with innovations

or the way business concepts have evolved and how they have developed techniques and processes that allow businesses to become more efficient.

- There is a breakdown of support at various levels of management. Even if upper management is open to and supportive of change, there can be a breakdown of support at other levels of management. And, if upper management is not open or supportive of change, then any change initiatives are doomed from the start. If there is not full agreement and support at all levels of management, the possibility for failure can be very real.

Why Should an Organization Consider Changing Philosophies, Processes, and Procedures?

In Chapter 7 an exercise was presented that identified two new opportunities for placing items that were presently being purchased as noncontract spot buys that could be bid and placed on contract. Both situations presented opportunities for a reduction in purchase costs but also would require a change in operating procedures. This exercise provided a good example of some of the reasons change in the status quo might be required. For background and clarity purposes, let us revisit this exercise.

The procurement department of an organization currently has three existing long-term purchase contracts. It has also identified opportunities for placing items on two long-term contracts that would add substantial additional value by decreasing the number of suppliers and the costs paid for those items. Additionally, it would improve the cost and efficiency of the purchasing department overall. To give you a better idea of what the opportunities represent, see Table 20.1. Here are some facts to consider:

- All existing contract buys are done automatically through an electronic data interchange platform (EDI).
  - The cost of buying items manually on a spot basis is calculated at $150 per purchase order as opposed to a cost of $.15 using EDI.
- The department has three buyers, a purchasing supervisor, and a purchasing department manager. It takes the buyers an average of 30 minutes per spot buy item to research, issue bids, evaluate them, and write and issue a purchase order. Three buyers yield a potential of 16 purchase orders per 8-hour day each—48 purchase orders per day and 240 per week. Remember, these numbers represent a perfect situation that generally does not hold true. The actual number of purchase orders will be lower because of employee vacations or other time off.

Table 20.1 Project priority decision matrix

Contract opportunity	Knowns					Assumptions				
	Items	Annual # of POs issued	Critical items	Current estimated annual spend	Days to award	Estimated savings contract vs. spot	Estimated savings (EDI vs. Manual)	Total estimated annual savings	Value rank	Priority assigned
Existing No. 1	278	1,132	Yes	$875,000	30	$350,000	$169,630	$519,630	3	1
Existing No. 2	380	1,620	Yes	$1,215,000	30	$420,000	$242,757	$662,757	2	3
Existing No. 3	258	1,089	Yes	$746,000	30	$245,000	$163,187	$408,187	5	4
Proposed No. 1	478	1,923	Yes	$948,000	50	$185,000	$288,162	$473,162	4	5
Proposed No. 2	312	4,468	No	$201,000	50	$76,000	$669,530	$745,530	1	2

Assumption No. 1: Average cost of issuing a manual purchase order is $150.00 per PO.
Assumption No. 2: Average cost of issuing a purchase order via EDI is $.15 per PO.

- Researching (finding and qualifying suppliers), issuing bids, and writing POs is not a continuous process. It takes time to receive direct bids and quotes from suppliers. Consequently, the buyers are working several buys simultaneously. Less time is required for retrieving a price from an online catalog or bid request, but the average time per purchase order is calculated at 30 minutes.
- The procurement department issues approximately 1,040 purchase orders per month for all items not presently on contract (based on the numbers we are using).
- There have been 790 items identified that can be considered as candidates for two separate new contracts.
  - Items considered critical to the operation total 478 and 312 of the items are considered noncritical.
- Approximate time to research, bid, analyze, negotiate, and award items on the two new proposed contracts is 50 days for proposed Contract 1 and 30 days for proposed Contract 2.
- Each item on both proposed contracts is being bought multiple times per year.
  - Proposed Contract 1 is estimated to have 1,923 purchase orders being manually issued for purchase per year.
  - Proposed Contract 2 is estimated to have 4,468 purchase orders being manually issued for purchase each year.
- By moving 478 items presently being bought manually to an EDI program, $288,162 can be saved in operating costs annually. These savings are calculated in the total cost savings identified in the previous two bullet points.
- By moving 312 items presently being bought manually to a contract and into an EDI program, $669,530 can be saved in operating costs annually.
- After calculating projected total cost savings for proposed Contract 1, a total of $473,162 can be realized annually covering the 478 critical items.
- After calculating projected total cost savings for proposed Contract 2, a total of $745,530 can be realized annually covering 312 noncritical items.
- The two new contract opportunities combined represent a total cost savings of $1,218,692 and the elimination of 6,391 purchase orders being bid and written manually.

Now here comes the change part. There are two change opportunities: (1) moving contract purchase orders from a manual PO entry process to an EDI automatic PO issuance process and (2) redefining the procurement department's processes and the duties/responsibilities of the buyers. By moving the items to EDI, there will be 6,391 fewer purchase orders per year that will be bid and purchased manually. The three buyers in this example organization have been doing approximately 12,480 purchase orders a year and we are about to eliminate over half of those. I am sure the purchasing manager is thinking he or she will have to eliminate at least one buyer position. That may or may not be the case. With the cost savings involved in this scenario there is no question that these contracts should be replaced with an EDI system. This exercise is simplistic but it was presented to prove a point, that is, circumstances and opportunities predicate the necessity for change. If a buyer position was eliminated that would certainly be a change that reduced operating expense to some degree. But, instead of eliminating a buyer position, why not change the procurement philosophy and processes to bring even more value to this organization?

If you studied this exercise closely you probably see that even though they are realizing some fairly substantial savings from their three existing contracts and will hit a home run with the two proposed contracts, there is still ample room for improvement. For one thing, 100% of the buyer's time has been spent bidding and writing purchase orders, nothing else. It is obvious that this particular organization's procurement department has an order fulfillment philosophy—only bid and write purchase orders and do not worry about anything else. Maintaining inventory levels is the primary concern, thus, they get the best price and issue the purchase order. With the movement of so many items to EDI and the automatic purchase order placement, it will free up a substantial amount of the buyers' time and allow them to perform other proactive and value adding activities.

So what is the purchasing manager of this particular organization going to do? Will he make the recommendation to eliminate one buyer position, reduce his operating costs to some extent, and maintain the status quo? Or will he realize that there is more to supply management and procurement than just bidding and issuing purchase orders? Since this chapter is about implementing and managing change, we are going to assume that the manager has read this book and has come to realize the benefits to the organization of practicing strategic supply management and procurement. Not only does he want to change procurement philosophy, but he wants them to become best-in-class in supply management and procurement. These are two good examples of why this organization should consider change. Now we will look at how that can be accomplished.

How to Promote Change

Exactly what new philosophies and what new processes would you, the reader, adopt and implement for this procurement department and organization? If you said a strategic supply management approach, you are correct. All of the preceding chapters of this book address and discuss, in some way, different aspects and benefits of practicing strategic supply management and procurement to become best-in-class. But what should be done specifically in the case of this procurement department. Let's outline what those changes should be.

A total approach to strategic supply management and procurement should be adopted. This will require a philosophical change in organizational and employee beliefs and behavior. The need and benefits of changing will first have to be sold to the employees and, more importantly, to upper management. An acceptance and buy-in by everyone will be required if changes that are made are to be successful and beneficial. So, the first thing that has to be done is to win the hearts and minds of employees and management. This is no easy task. As we have discussed previously, most people are inherently opposed to change, for whatever reason. We all like to feel comfortable and we want things to stay the same—we do not like the waves that change brings.

Before we discuss how to sell our changes, we first have to decide what changes we want to make. As previously stated this procurement department has only had a bid and buy philosophy in the past. They now want to adopt a strategic supply management philosophy. What will this new philosophy be? The foundation will be a supply chain management approach. If you are just bidding and buying the lowest price from the same suppliers, you are not practicing supply chain management effectively, in fact, you are not practicing supply chain management at all. The first three chapters explain and define what supply management and supply chain management are, their differences, and the benefits of practicing them. We will assume the purchasing manager has grasped the concept of supply chain management and understands how supply chain management should be applied and practiced in this particular situation and environment. This is a list of changes the purchasing manager wants to implement in the procurement department:

- Move from a bid and buy only philosophy to a strategic supply management philosophy.
- Initiate a coordinated supply chain management approach.
- Form three commodity groups and divide all of the items currently being purchased and place them in one of the three groups.
  - One buyer will be placed in each group and other procurement support personnel will also be added to each group.
  - Appoint one supervisor to be responsible for and lead each group.
- Identify and map the supply chain for each commodity or service being purchased that is critical to operations.
- Initiate commodity tracking (tracking prices, supply, and industry trends).
- Initiate a supplier management and assessment system.

- Make the key performance drivers of the new philosophy:
  - Cost
  - Quality
  - Time
  - Reliability
  - Technology
- Initiate and require that research and strategic analysis is part of all procurement decision-making processes.

The items outlined are a general representation of what the purchasing manager will present to upper management. The tricky part will be to first get upper management to accept and support these changes and then to get employees to accept and embrace them. How can this be done? The easiest way to sell an idea to, and get acceptance from, upper management is to show them the money. If you can show the dollar cost savings from improved efficiencies and other benefits, you stand a good chance of winning their support and approval.

In the scenario described in this chapter, moving items purchased from bid and buy to contract and EDI represents huge savings for the organization. This move is actually part of a strategic supply management philosophy whether this procurement department realized it or not. But it is a good place to start and can be used as a springboard to sell and implement other changes that will increase efficiencies, reduce costs, increase profits, and sustain progress and successes.

In preparing a presentation for change to upper management, it will be important to do appropriate research to ascertain the impacts, both positive and negative, of adopting and implementing each of the changes wanted. In this case, the purchasing manager is asking for a complete reorganization of the procurement department. Both a SWOT and risk analysis should be performed and made part of the presentation. The positives and advantages of making the changes should far outweigh any negatives associated with maintaining the status quo. A risk mitigation and management plan should also be prepared and presented. Showing the dollars saved, the efficiencies gained through process improvement, the risks and downsides and how they can be dealt with if they materialize, the purchasing manager has a good shot of getting approval. Face it, we all are a little greedy and if upper management sees opportunities to save money and increase profits it will be hard for them to turn it down. If they do turn it down, this organization has far greater problems than a nonprogressive procurement department.

How to Implement Change

Let us assume that the purchasing manager convinced upper management and won approval to make the changes, now he or she must sell it to the rank and file. Remember, there are more employees in the procurement department who the changes will affect beside the buyers. Employees who currently handle planning and managing inventory, order expeditors, warranty administration, reliability administrators, as well as the buyers will be transitioned and incorporated into commodity groups. Two supervisors will also be added to oversee and lead the commodity groups. There is one existing supervisor who is responsible for the buyers. The other two will be supervisors recruited from other areas of responsibility within the procurement department and each of the three supervisors will head a commodity group. They will be expected to work as teams to fulfill their new responsibilities and reach the defined goals.

For those who have been used to performing their individual tasks and responsibilities the same way for years, and that includes everyone in the procurement department, the changes that the purchasing manager is proposing may seem pretty radical. Many will think they are unnecessary, some will be concerned or fearful, and others will be resistant. Rather than just tell everyone what the changes will be and what their new responsibilities are, it is important to make employees feel a part of and contributors to the changes. Some companies think that the fewer employees who know about how and why they do something the better. Based on actual and practical experience, just the opposite tends to be true. The latter approach has a more proactive and positive result. The more employees know about a company's operation, what part they play, and the importance of what they do to the company's success, the more supportive they are and then are willing to embrace change.

After gaining approval and support from upper management, the purchasing manager scheduled a department wide meeting with all procurement personnel to give an overview and outline of what the new procurement philosophy was going to be, how it would change operating procedures within the procurement department, and how procurement would work with and interact more closely with other departments in the organization. Most importantly, the purchasing manager told the staff why the changes were being made and the benefits to the employees and the organization. Employees should be told that they are all an important part of the changes and that their input, suggestions, and recommendations of how to improve process efficiencies would be solicited and welcomed.

The next thing to do would be to train everyone on their new roles, responsibilities, and how to perform them. The best place to start would be with the commodity group supervisors. They will be expected to lead their respective groups and should have the most detailed understanding of the new concepts and know how to perform each of the jobs included within the commodity groups. Another cornerstone of the new strategic supply management and procurement philosophy is a team-oriented, cooperative, cross-departmental approach. Each commodity group will have total ownership of the commodities and services they are responsible for. They will be expected to interact with other departments within the organization and share information. Moving from a bid and buy philosophy to a strategic supply management and procurement philosophy, when new procurement projects are identified (contracts and special buys), the purchasing manager and supervisor will no longer be the sole participants. Procurement project teams will now be formed that will not only include management, but buyers and other procurement department personnel as appropriate, as well as resources and representatives of stakeholder groups. Everyone will contribute in developing procurement strategies pertaining to the project, request for proposal preparation, and even negotiating.

This example scenario placed emphasis on the formation of commodity groups. It was chosen as an example of the reorganization of an entire procurement department. Although commodity groups are a good concept and can bring a great amount of value to an organization's supply management and procurement efforts, they may not be the best solution or the answer in all situations. There are a wide variety of techniques and tools available to the supply management professional and various philosophies and concepts that organizations can adopt for their specific needs and goals. They are presented and discussed in this book. It is up to the supply management and procurement professionals and organizations to determine what their supply management goals are and how they want to achieve them. They can be basic, best-in-class, or somewhere in between. The choice of the degree of value and success is up to them.

How to Manage Change

The example procurement department manager used in this chapter recognized and understood the benefits of change, designed a strategy to present changes to management and the rank and file to gain approval and support, and developed an implementation plan to make the changes happen. Now he must decide how to manage the changes as the department goes forward. In this section we discuss the most effective ways to manage change.

Since the procurement department completely changed operating processes from basic bid-and-buy procedures to more comprehensive strategic supply management and procurement processes, a plan will need to be developed to oversee and manage those changes to ensure continued improvement and success. The procurement manager has two options at this point: (1) limit the change to just the two that were made, that of forming commodity groups and moving the purchase of contract items from manual order entry to EDI and then forming commodity groups to take ownership and manage families of commodities or (2) continue to adopt more strategic supply management and procurement concepts to add even more value to the organization. The course chosen will determine what type of management plan should be developed.

If the decision made is to only adopt the two new processes, the plan should contain the following considerations:

- After the initial training of management and employees on the concepts adopted and the specifics of the process and job functions, a continuous training plan should be developed and initiated that provides additional periodic employee training to keep everyone updated and maintain enthusiasm for the new processes.
- Begin setting goals and benchmarks for the processes. Prior to the beginning of each fiscal year and parallel with budget preparation, the manager should meet with the commodity group supervisors to set goals and strategies for the year and identify projected requirements.
- The manager should also hold quarterly meetings with the commodity group supervisors to review performance, evaluate successes, discuss problems encountered, and make any adjustments warranted.
- The manager should also meet with the commodity group supervisors at the end of each fiscal year, and prior to the next year's planning meeting, to discuss what went right and what went wrong in the year. They should then collaborate to develop solutions to institute in the forthcoming year. These might include changes in actual process and may require additional training requirements that would need to be included in the new budget. This is even more important if the decision made is to expand supply management and procurement philosophies even further.
- The manager should document and report successes resulting in the philosophical and process changes to upper management. This serves as justification and verification that making the changes was the appropriate and smart thing to do. It also sustains and/or promotes increased support for the changes made and any new changes the procurement manager might propose in the future.
- The manager should also hold periodic meetings that include the entire procurement department to report on successes, ask for input and suggestions for additional improvement, and explain any new changes in procedures and processes that might be coming. It also offers opportunities to sustain momentum and enthusiasm for the changes previously made.

If the decision made is to expand supply management and procurement philosophies even further by instituting other strategic supply management and procurement concepts and techniques, a more comprehensive plan will need to be developed. The manager must decide if additional process improvements should be added all at one time or phased in over a period of time. Whether added all at one time or phased in over a period of time, the plan should have the following considerations:

- Additional training of management and employees on each of the new concepts and activities adopted and the specifics of the process and job functions should be scheduled to coincide with the commencement of the new processes and job activities. A plan for continuous training should also be developed and initiated that provides additional periodic employee training to keep everyone updated and maintain enthusiasm for the new processes.

- Set goals and benchmarks for each of the new activities and processes. Prior to the beginning of each fiscal year and parallel with budget preparation, the manager should meet with the commodity group supervisors to set goals and strategies for the coming year and identify projected requirements.

- The manager should also hold quarterly meetings with the commodity group supervisors to review performance, evaluate successes, discuss problems encountered, and make any adjustments warranted. If required, establish or revise activity implementation and employee training for the next quarter if not already completed.

- The manager should document and report successes resulting for any new process and activity implemented to upper management. This will justify and validate that making the changes was the appropriate and smart thing to do. It also sustains and/or promotes increased support for the changes made and any new changes the procurement manager might propose in the future.

- The manager should also hold periodic meetings that include the entire procurement department to report on successes, ask for input and suggestions for additional improvement, determine the effectiveness of training programs, and explain any new changes in procedures and processes that might be forthcoming. It also offers opportunities to sustain momentum and enthusiasm for the changes previously made.

Other Strategies to Promote, Implement, and Manage Change

Understanding an organization's culture is important for several reasons. It gives insight into why the organization does the things that it does, the way it does them, and is also used as a guide by many individuals in determining what they do and how they do it. This can be a good or a bad thing because many times individuals think they understand the organizational culture but really do not. Knowing and understanding an organization's culture is especially important when developing strategies. Two situations an organization might face in managing the strategy-culture relationship is that (1) a new strategy might require the organization to adopt its culture and processes to accommodate the strategy or (2) the strategy might require the organization to change its culture entirely.

There are many factors that need to be considered when implementing a best-in-class strategy in an organization or, for that matter, any degree of strategic supply management and procurement philosophical or activity and process change. These factors include structural, leadership, and cultural considerations. The structure of an organization is both vertical and horizontal. Vertical structure denotes descent of responsibility, of personnel, and business or operational functions. Everyone is familiar with this in the form of an organizational chart, that is, the management, division, or department hierarchy. Horizontal structure is the linkage between management, division, department, and business activity or function. This might also be portrayed in an organizational process or flowchart.

Considerations that should be given to organizational structure is the effect that implementing a strategy would have on others. For a strategy to be implemented successfully it must be supported from the top down, and each of the tiers in the descent must have a full understanding of the strategy and the impact it will have on each level and each successive level. There is interconnectivity here that many people do not understand. Oftentimes managers at one level only see the effect on their level and fail to see the relationship to other levels or the effect that they have on those levels. For a strategy to be successful there must be a concentrated and coordinated effort on all levels.

Leadership is an important consideration. Strong leadership is required for a strategy to be successful. The right leader should be chosen to lead the strategy implementation. This leader must inspire those affected by the strategy to embrace the vision and motivate them to accept change and overcome obstacles. Leadership must also have the capacity to support the implementation. Even so, the best laid plans sometimes fail. Even if the strategy does not fail altogether, it can be partially ineffective, take longer to work efficiently (as originally designed), and cause employee dissatisfaction. It can also cause a lack of trust. Some plans never recover. It is a sad waste of time and effort, and the resulting higher costs that could be avoided if the strategy were completely thought out and a workable implementation plan and time line developed in advance of rollout. Communication and training are key factors. Trust is a significant factor in the success of a change to a new philosophy. An organization must trust its managers and employees, and employees must trust their managers and the organization, the river of trust flows both ways. Lack of trust leads to low morale and loss of productivity. 'They don't care about me so why should I care about them' and 'Why do we need to change, it just means more work on us' are fairly common responses to proposed changes in philosophy.

But business is continually changing and new strategies and plans are continually being developed to react to circumstances or to make an organization more competitive. Making strategies and plans are part of a manager's job description and it is incumbent on them to make that happen efficiently and successfully. Organizations that practice paying incentives for individual projects are asking for trouble. It promotes jealousy and envy and, if it comes to be expected and it doesn't happen, an organization runs the risk of getting less than a manager's best efforts.

Communication is one of the key factors of success. The more you know, the better you understand. It helps in understanding how the pieces of the puzzle fit together (the big picture as it were), how other departments and divisions approach and perform their duties (gives ideas for process improvement in your own department or division), and helps you to understand why something is done. The most common reason that some managers do not share information is simply that they do not understand the importance and benefit of sharing this information with the organization and other departments. They do not understand that information shared might inspire someone to make suggestions for improvements or develop beneficial new ideas. Other reasons for not sharing is a fear of exposing their deficiencies to others or not caring (I do my job and I'm not going to help somebody else do theirs).

You might interpret cultural considerations to be the culture of the organization. The culture of an organization includes the values and ethical standards by which management and employees are expected to adhere and operate under. In many instances there may be disparity between what an organization purports to believe in and how it wants to operate and how employees actually behave. Therefore, it is important that a strategy be in line with the organizational culture, and that it is explained and reinforced with employees.

For a strategy to be successful it must be shared with all members of the organization. It should start with members of management at all tiers. It is important that management fully understands and signs on to the strategy first, then it should be shared with all employees directly affected by the strategy and then with the rest of the organization. Information should be disseminated that explains the purpose and value of the strategy and the mechanics of how the strategy will be implemented and supported.

Organizational culture could be considered the personality of the organization that includes organizational behavior, image, products or services, and strategies, just to name a few. It is what management and employees think and feel about the organization and how they act on those feelings.

People probably get tired of me bringing this up, but in the initial development of strategic plan options a review and analysis of the supply chain and value chain are absolutely critical. By performing these two analyses, process efficiencies/deficiencies and opportunities for improvement are identified. Knowing this information is crucial in developing strategic plans that fit the mission and vision of the company. They also point out the direction in which the organization needs to go. They also offer details necessary for designing specifics of the plan and how and when to implement them.

Let's say that hypothetically you have a decision to make or that you need to develop a plan. Before you do anything it is important to clearly define

what you want to do and what you want to accomplish. Once you clearly define these two things the next step is to ask yourself how you can accomplish
them or, more specifically, what do you need to do to accomplish them. Next,
research is required and a determination needs to be made as to which tools
would be desirable and applicable to the situation.

After all of this information is gathered and an analysis is performed (you
must have all this information first) you should be ready to evaluate, brainstorm to determine all options, and make a decision or develop a plan.

There will always be more than one option or alternative. Which option or
alternative would have the most value for the organization is what you should
be looking for. If two or more people are involved there is usually a difference
of opinion. In many cases these people will have biases that influence their
opinion as to which option should be chosen. One proven way around this
issue is to use a weighted decision matrix to help make an impartial decision.

As an example, let's say that we needed to develop a plan to reduce patient
time in the emergency room of a hospital. We've done all the research and
analysis, including a financial analysis to determine the effect of increases or
decreases in cost (adding or reducing staff, etc.) for each of the options (cost-
benefit analysis). Now it is time to make a decision.

There is so much to consider in determining a long-term goal or objective and even more in developing a strategic plan to achieve it. A tremendous
amount of work is involved in coming to the conclusions needed to achieve
these endeavors.

The qualities that would be required to characterize a sound long-term
objective would be anything that helped to attain and sustain success. What
is the purpose of performing research, scans, surveys, and analysis as they cost
time, effort, and money to perform? The purpose(s) is to achieve an advantage
for the organization such as advantages in growth, technology, and operational
efficiencies, market share and market independence, profitability, and competitive advantage to name a few. But any quality considered must also be
achievable. That is why so much work is required in determining not only
what qualities should be considered, but if they can be achieved and what the
cost benefit is to the organization. In achieving these varied qualities, it is also
important to develop ways to sustain them.

Make sure the risks are calculated and that you have all the information
needed to make a good decision. Life and business is a crap shoot. Even the
best plans can get hit by the unexpected, so you also have to plan for the unexpected by having contingencies available. That is what risk analysis is for—to
determine what the risks are and determine how they can be mitigated. People
or organizations that are not willing to take risks now and again and are satis-
fied with just playing it safe never get anywhere and are usually passed by
their competition.

Appendix A

Case Study Answers

Case Study 1—Made Better Manufacturing

1. Based on the research findings discovered in the case study, which supply chain links and value chain activities did you identify that might be candidates to add more value? The answer: all six links. They are:
   - Raw rubber distributor
   - Inbound logistics
   - Purchasing
   - Production operations
   - Inventory warehousing
   - Outbound logistics

2. List those opportunities:
   - Made Better is currently only purchasing rubber raw materials from one supplier on a spot buy or as needed basis. Raw synthetic rubber is derived from petroleum. Therefore, the cost of crude oil has a major effect on the synthetic rubber supply availability and prices. Made Better should do two things:
     i. Issue a request for proposal (RFP) for the purchase of raw synthetic rubber on a three- to five-year contract to several reliable suppliers. The negotiated contract should include escalator and de-escalator clauses to compensate for the up and down fluctuations in crude prices.
     ii. Expand their supply chain map to include the raw synthetic rubber distributors' suppliers as well as the material source,

223

which in this particular situation would be the cost per barrel of crude oil at the well head or at the point or port of debarkation. This will allow tracking of what the distributor is paying and keep them honest.

1. Begin tracking the price of crude oil per barrel to build a price history so they can forecast and/or anticipate up and down price fluctuations in the future. This would enable them to anticipate, plan for, and control future operating costs more effectively.

3. Are any of the activities and functions you chose candidates for outsourcing? YES.

4. List all opportunities:

   - Inbound transportation—Made Better is currently paying for all goods and materials on a free on board (FOB) destination bases and is allowing each supplier to contract for transportation that is then added to their invoices and submitted to Made Better. Consolidation of transportation carriers might be an opportunity for cost reduction.

   - Outbound transportation—Made Better currently contracts for transportation from one independent carrier and also uses their own trucks for regional deliveries.

     i. Inbound transportation might also be combined with outbound transportation bidding to obtain even better rates from a single carrier.

     ii. A cost and comparison study and analysis could be performed to determine if opportunities exist to eliminate the use of Made Better owned transportation equipment and outsource all transportation needs and requirements.

5. What links in the supply chain and operational activities are candidates for outsourcing? Inbound and outbound transportation, warehouse storage, and inventory management are all candidates for outsourcing to independent companies. To make the most informed and the best decisions about outsourcing, a value opportunity or value chain analysis should be performed. Since Made Better only practices basic procurement activities and previously did not even practice any formal supply chain management, value chain analysis is probably something they would not attempt. There is enough information available to them, however, that they could consider some outsourcing decisions.

6. Explain why they are new opportunities. Anything different from the current processes or changes made to them would be considered new opportunities. An explanation of these opportunities follows:

- Transportation—Better bidding and contracting for all transportation (both inbound and outbound) might produce better rates for Made Better and the number of transportation companies might be reduced to a single carrier.

- Warehouse storage—Made Better might explore the possibility of contracting warehouse and logistical services with an independent company such as UPS Supply Chain Solutions or someone that offers similar services. In this outsourcing scenario, Made Better would contract for warehouse and distribution services at a centrally located distribution hub. In this scenario, outsourcing logistics would eliminate the need and cost for inventory storage and picking of manufactured, finished DooJiggys. Since all DooJiggys would be sent to a single outside storage and distribution point, completed DooJiggys coming off the production line could be packaged, palletized, and loaded directly into box trailers for transport to that location. This could eliminate the need for some warehouse shipping personnel and finished inventory carrying costs. It would also eliminate the need to bid and negotiate transportation to Made Better's customers as transportation bidding and costs would be handled by the outsourcing company.

- Inventory management—Made Better might also consider several types of inventory management and control systems. Some of the possibilities are:

  i. Instituting an electronic inventory software system such as an MRP system that could more effectively manage incoming supplies and materials as well as finished products. Inventory minimum and maximum levels set would be triggered electronically (and automatically) to issue reorder requisitions and manage finished products.

  ii. Instituting an electronic data interchange system (EDI) that would automatically issue some purchase orders and transmit them to suppliers electronically and could even pay invoices.

  iii. A form of vendor-managed inventory arrangement (either physical or electronic) might be worth exploring for selected materials and supplies obtained from a single supplier whereby the vendor (supplier) managed Made Betters' inventory and initiated stock replenishment orders.

7. Give a brief description of your thoughts on how the links and activities you identified might be candidates for process improvement. Each and all of the links identified are candidates for some form of process improvement.

- Raw rubber distributor—Expand the supply chain map to include the raw synthetic rubber distributors' suppliers. Bid a three- to five-year contract with escalators and de-escalators.
- Inbound logistics—two options:
  i.   Negotiate a contract for services with lower transportation costs.
  ii. Bid a contract for both inbound and outbound transportation with combined lower costs.
- Purchasing should do the following:
  i.   Institute a computerized inventory system for both preproduction and post production items. Barcoding and scanners automatically adjust inventory. It is faster, cheaper, and more accurate than older manual systems.
  ii. Install an e-procurement system that uses EDI. Automatic purchase order generation for inventory replenishment, acknowledgment, shipping notices, and invoicing are cost-savings benefits of 80 to 90% from that of manual systems.
- Production operations—two options:
  i.   Consider installing an enterprise resource planning (ERP) system that ties all of the organizations operating functions together. This includes production operations, purchasing, warehousing, and inventory control.
  ii. Consider moving to a just-in-time (JIT) material supply system to reduce on-hand inventories and reduce overall costs.
- Inventory warehousing. Several options are available:
  i.   Install an electronic inventory system using barcode labels and scanners. This automatically adjusts inventory levels for materials received and finished products that are shipped.
  ii. Set up a minimum/maximum electronically automated inventory system. Whenever a minimum inventory level is reached, a request to buy is automatically generated to purchasing.
  iii. Consider moving to a JIT material supply system.
  iv. Consider an ERP system to connect with purchasing, production operations, and other connected departments.
- Outbound logistics—three options:
  i.   There are three transportation companies being used, two inbound, one outbound in addition to Made Better's own trucks and drivers. Two have limited capabilities and one can do everything. An RFP should be issued for one carrier to handle all transportation needs, both inbound and outbound. If XYZ

Express is given the opportunity to do both, it could reduce both inbound and outbound transportation costs.

ii. Outsource the portion of outbound transportation that Made Better performs with its own fleet of trucks and drivers. This would dramatically reduce the total portion of outbound transportation costs. A logical decision would be to include that portion of transportation in the RFP for one carrier to handle all transportation needs, both inbound and outbound.

In addition to the supply chain map developed for the raw rubber distributor, supply chain maps should be developed for the other critical parts and supplies required in DooJiggy manufacture.

All of the possible options listed here are process improvement techniques that are proven successful alternatives that generate cost savings and improve process efficiencies. You may have even come up with some additional ones not addressed here. Many times organizations are reluctant to look at alternative process methods because they are comfortable with existing processes and how they work. Best-in-class organizations take the approach that business is fluid and constantly changing and to maintain a competitive advantage new ways to reduce costs and improve process efficiencies must continually be researched and considered. Ways to promote change and gain support for moving from a basic procurement philosophy to a strategic supply management philosophy is addressed throughout this book.

Case Study 2—Ship Right Transportation (SRT)

In Case Study 2 a purchase request scenario by a stakeholder department was presented to Ship Right's procurement department. A procurement initiative team was assembled with procurement leading the group. Research and fact gathering were performed after which the results were analyzed, evaluated, and presented to the team for consideration. You were asked to make a best value decision to present to Ship Right based on the information provided.

1. What do you see as the best courses of action for Ship Right? There are four courses of action that would add value to SRT:

   a. The first is the best value buy obtained from the request for quote (RFQ) that was issued to qualified bidders. In this case, KLM proved to be the best value purchase based on their offer, capability and comparison analysis, and weighted decision matrix that was used.

   b. The second is negotiating master purchase agreements with a metal distributor and GE for fabrication of Lexan panels. The negotiated prices could be offered to the shipping container manufacturer who was awarded the bid and the savings passed to Ship Right in the form of a lower purchase price of unit load devices (ULDs).

c. The third option is that SRT could negotiate master purchase agreements for the metal and polycarbonate and have the original manufacturers fabricate to Ship Right's specifications. Ship Right could then contract with a company to assemble the containers and deliver to them. Both options (b) and (c) would substantially reduce costs for Ship Right with (c) offering the lowest costs and highest visibility and control.

d. The fourth option would be to not buy any new shipping containers but instead use the inventory of open door containers acquired in a purchase of another shipping company. Approval would have to be obtained and signed off on by the operational stakeholder and approved by other appropriate departments within Ship Right.

2. Are there any alternatives to buying more shipping containers? Yes, there are several alternatives to purchasing new containers. The best course of action that offers the most value is to use the existing inventory of full open front doors. The open front configuration is different from Ship Right's normal specifications, but operations has stated that since all other specifications such as dimensions, weight, and alloy/temper of the metal and polycarbonate meet their requirements, then they are usable. The acquisition of the 2000 shipping containers as part of the purchase of another company resulted in them not being included on the asset books as part of operation's existing inventory. If operations agrees, the 2000 shipping containers can be added to the inventory and the required 100 used immediately—no lead time and at no cost to Ship Right. It also means that operations can draw on the balance of the 1900 remaining containers whenever future requirements dictate at no additional cost to Ship Right. This is a tremendous savings. Although the RFQ bids produced a new supplier that offered a substantial reduction in purchase costs, you still can't beat FREE. Since the 2000 shipping containers acquired in the purchase of another company were never placed on the asset books, accounting and finance would have to assign a value if they were used. The case study purchase history report showed that SRT had been paying an average of $4299 per each ULD. By accepting the variant configuration of the 2000 shipping containers for future needs and demands, Ship Right could ultimately realize a savings of $8.598M dollars in deferred purchases.

3. If purchase is chosen, which vendor offers the best overall value? KLM proved to be the lowest priced purchase option by far and offered the most value based on the results of the weighted decision matrix.

4. Based on the evaluations and analysis that were performed, which supply chain links did you identify that might be candidates to add more value? The answer is that every link identified in the supply chain maps developed for the metal, Lexan, and repair supply chains as illustrated in the research results section of the case study would be candidates. Any process or activity is a candidate for improvement at any time. Processes and procedures should be continuously monitored and whenever an opportunity for improvement presents itself, action should be initiated for value adding improvement. A few examples relating to the supply chain links are:

   a. Monitoring and tracking prices and inventories of the raw materials required to make the key products and components.

      i. The price of aluminum ore at the mine, at the smelter and mill, and at the extruder (if different from the mill).

      ii. The price of raw crude oil per barrel at the well head and at the refinery for specific, processed by-products such as polycarbonate.

   b. There are several services available for purchase that track commodities for you and report the results. This allows you to see price trends as they develop, and it also allows you to forecast the direction that prices are heading in the future. This is a useful tool in developing strategies for future projected costs, budget development, contracts, and negotiation.

5. Based on the evaluations and analysis you performed, which value chain activities did you identify that might be candidates for process improvement, outsourcing and/or reengineering that would add more value?

   a. Negotiating a master purchase agreement with an aluminum extruder to make the individual parts to Ship Right's specifications needed for the shipping containers.

   b. Negotiating a master purchase agreement with GE for the fabrication (cutting and drilling) of Lexan panels to Ship Right's specifications for parts that are required for the assembly of shipping containers.

   c. There are many others but, for the purposes of this case study, those determinations will be left to the reader.

6. Are any of the activities and functions you chose candidates for outsourcing? Yes, contracting with a third party (outsourcing) (other than the established ULD suppliers that bid) for the assembly of parts and components into shipping containers.

7. In retrospect, is there anything in Ship Right's current procurement philosophy and processes that could be added to or improved on that would make the procurement department even more efficient and effective in bringing maximum value to their organization? Yes, there are several additional things that SRT should consider implementing in their existing procurement processes.

   a. Immediately review all procurement models to ensure that they meet existing criteria for initiating purchases and set mandatory reviews at periodic intervals. This is something procurement departments should do on a regular basis as requirements and criteria change over time and with circumstances.

   b. Start tracking prices and supply availability of critical and required commodities and raw materials. This builds price and availability histories that can then be used for purposes of forecasting future prices and supply. This strategic supply management concept is useful in establishing supply management goals and in negotiating prices and terms in contracts.

   c. Develop supply chain maps for all critical parts, supplies, and services (not just a select few) and practice total supply chain management.

   d. Map all current procurement and supply management processes and activities to determine current procedures. Evaluate for effectiveness and efficiency. Look for opportunities for process improvement and initiate changes.

   e. Develop a value chain map for current business activities both within and outside the company, and then perform a value opportunity analysis to determine places where extra value and efficiencies may be obtained. Pass information and recommendations of the identified opportunities on to appropriate departments and responsible parties for consideration.

   f. Research and discover what strategic supply management tools and concepts are available and how procurement departments in other companies apply them. Select procurement departments and activities in other companies that are considered best-in-class in what they do. Establish benchmarks as goals and set milestones for performance achievements toward which to work. Make reading *Supply Management and Procurement: From the Basics to Best-In-Class* required reading for management (that would make the author happy and also offer help in building support for changes in procurement philosophies and procedures).

This case study was unique in the type of buy requirement and circumstances surrounding the required item. It also involved many different scenarios that required substantial research, analysis, and evaluation. All of the possible options listed are process improvement techniques that are proven successful alternatives. They can generate cost savings and improve process efficiencies. Many times organizations are reluctant to look at alternative process methods because they are comfortable with existing processes and how they work. Best-in-class organizations take the approach that business is fluid and constantly changing. To maintain a competitive advantage, new ways to reduce costs and improve process efficiencies must be researched and considered continually. In this case study, the procurement initiative team performed comparison analysis of the RFP bids, looked at metal prices from a historical perspective, developed forecasts for future prices, considered negotiating master purchase agreements for metal and polycarbonate, and considered outsourcing assembly. They used information and data gathered in a weighted decision matrix to make an unbiased business decision that offered the best value for Ship Right.

An existing inventory of usable shipping containers was discovered that was unknown before. This turned out to be the best alternative for Ship Right because no money would need to be spent to purchase new shipping containers, now or in the foreseeable future. This scenario was actually based on a project I was involved in with a former employer. The second best scenario was that of negotiating master purchase agreements that chosen suppliers might take advantage of to reduce purchase costs or for using as an outsource opportunity. Both scenarios illustrate and bring home the benefits of practicing best-in-class strategic supply management. These opportunities would never have been discovered if the procurement team had not applied creative thinking, performed research, dug deeper, and been practicing strategic supply management. Ship Right would have simply followed their existing procurement model, gotten three or more bids, and bought more shipping containers.

These are all processes and techniques used in best-in-class supply management and procurement. Some organizations do not practice best-in-class concepts, set benchmarks and goals, or work toward achieving them. This is a mistake if an organization wants to reduce its overall cost and maximize its efficiencies. In these situations a change in processes or corporate culture is required. This is not an easy task in most organizations and can be difficult to say the least. To help readers better understand the importance of change and how to promote and facilitate a change in philosophy as well as gain support, see Chapter 20.

Appendix B

Transportation Terms and Definitions

Domestic Transportation Definitions

The following are common standard transportation terms used domestically in the United States and in some other countries. They differ in some respects to standard international shipping terms and definition due to the complexity involved in international transportation. Domestic transportation designations define the responsibilities of the seller and that of the buyer and address four areas of responsibility.

1. Responsibility of transportation costs
2. Transfer of title of goods
3. Responsibility of filing claims for loss or damage
4. Responsibility of administration and processing of invoices

Domestic transportation terms are generally expressed as free on board (FOB). The six most commonly used FOB designations are:

FOB destination: Freight prepaid—This designation is one of the most widely used, especially with buyers who do not have the ability or resources to purchase transportation themselves. In this arrangement transportation is paid by the seller. The seller retains title of the goods during transit and title does not pass to the buyer until the goods are received and accepted at the buyer's dock. The seller is responsible for filing claims for loss or damage and processing the freight invoices.

FOB destination: Freight collect—In this arrangement the seller retains title of the goods during transit and the buyer is responsible for paying transportation costs. Title passes to the buyer when the goods are received and accepted at the buyer's dock. The seller is responsible for filing claims for loss or damage, but the buyer is responsible for processing the freight invoices.

FOB destination: Freight collect and allowed—The seller retains title of the goods during transit and also pays transportation costs. Title passes to the buyer when the goods are received and accepted at the buyer's dock. The seller is responsible for filing claims for loss or damage, but the buyer is responsible for processing the freight invoices.

FOB origin: Freight allowed—The title transfers from the seller to the buyer when goods are loaded and leaves the seller's dock. The buyer owns the goods during transit and is responsible for filing claims for the loss or damage during transit. The seller is responsible for and pays transportation costs. The seller is responsible for processing the freight invoices.

FOB origin: Freight collect—In this arrangement the title transfers from the seller to the buyer when goods are loaded and they leave the seller's dock. The buyer owns the goods during transit and is responsible for filing claims for the loss or damage during transit. The buyer is responsible for and pays the transportation costs and processing the freight invoices.

FOB origin: Freight prepaid and charged back—The title transfers from the seller to the buyer when the goods are loaded and they leave the seller's dock. The buyer owns the goods during transit. The buyer is responsible for filing claims for the loss or damage during transit. The seller is responsible for and pays the transportation costs and also for processing the freight invoices.

International Transportation Definitions

International commercial terms (Incoterms). Incoterms are international standards established by participating countries to simplify the terms of sale for international commercial trade and sales transactions. They are published by the International Chamber of Commerce (ICC) and are based on the U.N. Convention on Contracts for the International Sale of Goods initially written in 1936 and periodically updated. Before the standardization and adoption of Incoterms, countries had different interpretations of the terms and conditions of sale and that sometimes led to uncertainties, misunderstandings, and disputes that arose from the sale and transportation of goods. Incoterms were designed to describe and define the rights and obligations of all parties in a contract of sale and the delivery of goods sold. Any business contemplating acquiring goods internationally should first obtain a copy of Incoterms 2010, or the latest revised copy. It is an easily obtainable publication from the ICC and is a good reference in helping to make the right decisions for which transportation model to negotiate for and incorporate into international trade agreements.

Delivered duty paid (DDP) (at destination port of entry). Stipulates that the seller pays for all transportation costs and bears all risk until the goods have been delivered to their destination and all applicable duties have been paid. DDP is also sometimes used interchangeably with the term *free domicile*. This term is the most comprehensive term of sale for the buyer. Some importing countries may access additional taxes for imported goods such as (but not limited to) value added taxes and excise taxes. Although usually prepaid by the buyer or importer, they are considered a recoupable cost because they are usually recovered against sales to customers in an importing country within the internal local market. An exception to this would be parts and components used to make a finished product that are then sold at another price. In this scenario the cost of the taxes would be considered another cost within the total purchase cost and part of the transportation and importation costs.

Delivered duty unpaid (DDU) (at destination port of entry). Stipulates that the seller delivers the goods to the buyer to the named place of destination in the contract of sale. The goods are not cleared by the country's customs for import or unloading from any type of transport (ship, aircraft, railcar, or truck) at the place of destination. The buyer bears the responsibility to pay for all costs for the unloading and is responsible for all risks associated therewith. The buyer or importer is also responsible for any subsequent delivery requirements beyond the place of destination. If the buyer or importer desires that the seller should bear these responsibilities, costs, and the risks associated with import clearance that includes payment of duties and so forth, and the unloading and subsequent delivery beyond the place of destination landing, then they would need to be negotiated and agreed to in advance and prior to the shipment's initiation.

Delivered ex ship (DES) (at destination port of entry). Stipulates that when goods are delivered ex ship, risk is not passed from the seller or exporter to the buyer or importer until the ship has arrived at the destination port and all goods are made available to the buyer for unloading. An example where this is used is at a port that is small or extremely busy. Even though the vessel has arrived at the destination port, it must queue up and anchor until its designated turn to dock and off-load. The seller or exporter pays the same freight and insurance costs as would be expected in a cost, insurance, and freight (CIF) arrangement. The seller or exporter agrees to bear all costs associated with DES and bear the risk and retain the title until the arrival of the vessel at the port dock. All costs for unloading the goods and cargo, along with any duties and taxes, are the responsibility of and paid for by the buyer or importer. This arrangement is frequently used in shipping some bulk commodities such as coal, cement, dry chemicals, or grains where the seller or exporter either owns or has chartered for the vessel.

Delivered ex quay (DEQ) (at destination port of entry). This is similar to DES with the exception that the risk is not passed until all goods and cargo have been off-loaded from the vessel at the port of destination.

Delivered at frontier (DAF) (or delivery place). Refers to a classification used when goods and cargo are transported by road or rail. The seller pays for transportation to a named place of delivery at the border or frontier as it is commonly called. The buyer or exporter is responsible for customs clearance and pays for any and all transportation from the frontier to the buyer's final destination. Title and risk is transferred from the seller to the buyer at the frontier.

Carriage and insurance paid (CIP) (to destination port or point of entry). Used for containerized goods and cargo and is the transportation multimodal equivalent of CIF. In this arrangement the seller or exporter pays for carriage (transportation) and insurance to a designated destination port or point of entry. Title and risks are passed when the goods or cargo are handed-off to the first carrier required and used for final delivery.

Carriage paid to (CPT) (a destination port or point of entry). Used when the seller or exporter pays for transportation and carriage to a designated port or point of entry and can be applied to containerized, multimodal, and general goods and cargo. In this arrangement the seller or exporter pays for carriage (transportation) only and the title and risk are passed to the buyer or importer when the goods or cargo are handed-off to the first carrier required and used for final delivery.

Cost and freight (CFR [also called CNF]) (to destination port of entry). Used for maritime or ocean-going freight and cargo only and designates that the seller or exporter is responsible for and pays the costs and freight to bring the goods and cargo to the destination port of entry. Title and risk is transferred to the buyer or importer when the goods or cargo have been off-loaded (said to have crossed the ship's rail). Insurance for the goods and cargo is not included and is the sole responsibility of the buyer or importer.

Cost, insurance, and freight (CIF) (to destination port of entry). Used for maritime or ocean-going freight and cargo only. The conditions of this term are the same as those for CFR with the exception that the seller or exporter must additionally secure and pay for insurance on behalf of the buyer or importer. A variation of this term is CIF—free out, which means that the vessel has off-loaded, undocked, and piloted out of the harbor.

Free on board (FOB) (at designated port or point of loading). Used for maritime or ocean-going freight and cargo only and does not apply to containerized or multimodal cargo or air transport. It signifies that the seller or exporter is responsible for and must load the goods or cargo aboard the vessel designated by the buyer or importer. This can also be handled by the seller by contracting and paying for a stevedoring service to perform the loading. One example would be the coal that I exported. It was loaded by a stevedoring company midstream in the Mississippi River using bucket elevators and cranes using clam shell buckets to off-load from the barges pulled alongside the ship. Another example is the wood railroad sleepers from Columbia, South America. In this instance there was not a modern port available and native labor loaded the sleepers onto rafts, and they were actually floated out to the vessel that was anchored in a bay. The ship's booms were used to hoist the cargo and place in the holds. This is true, I kid you not. Even though we think we live in a modern world, there are still places where things are done a little less advanced than we have become accustomed to. In an FOB arrangement, the risk and cost transfer when the cargo crosses the ship's rail. It is the responsibility of the seller or exporter to clear the goods or cargo with customs for export. The buyer or importer must charter the vessel and inform the seller or exporter of all details regarding the vessel and the port of origin loading details.

Free alongside ship (FAS) (at designated port of loading). Designates that the seller or exporter is responsible for placing the goods or cargo alongside the vessel at a designated port. The seller or exporter is also responsible for clearing the goods or cargo through customs. This is another maritime and ocean-going transportation arrangement used for the movement of bulk or heavy-lift cargo only and does not apply to containerized or multimodal sea transportation. An example might be heavy equipment and machinery that is not containerized.

Free carrier (FCA) (to designated place). Refers to the arrangement where the off-seller or exporter transfers the goods or cargo into the custody of the first carrier designated by the buyer or importer at a specific designated place after it is cleared of customs and ready for export. This term can be applied to all modes of transportation, including carriage by road, rail, air, and containerized or multimodal ocean transportation. It is also applied to freight collect situations regarding shipments of goods and cargo in ocean-going containers regardless of whether they are full container loads or less than container loads.

Ex works (EXW) (at a designated place). Refers to an agreement whereby the seller or exporter makes goods or cargo available to the buyer or importer at the seller or exporter's premises such as a warehouse, mill, or factory. The buyer or importer is responsible for all applicable costs and charges required to deliver the goods or cargo to its end destination. This arrangement places all of the responsibility and risk on the buyer or importer. There is minimum obligation on the seller or exporter except to make the goods or cargo available to the buyer or importer at a designated time and place. This term is often used for making an initial quotation for the sale of goods before any other costs are known, have not been determined, and/or been added. In this arrangement the buyer or importer is responsible for and pays all transportation, handling, and insurance costs and bears all risks for transporting and delivering goods or cargo to its final destination.

Additional charter terms that may be attached to and used in conjunction with various Incoterms are:

- Free in—Used to indicate that the entity chartering a vessel is responsible for all costs associated with the loading of goods and cargo onto the vessel.
- Free in and out—Refers to pricing that indicates that the entity chartering the vessel is responsible for all costs associated with the loading of goods and cargo and also the unloading of goods and cargo from the vessel.
- Free out—Refers to pricing that indicates that the entity chartering a vessel is responsible for all costs associated with the unloading of goods and cargo from the vessel.

Appendix C

List of Formulas

Supply management and procurement professionals are not accountants so they are not required to keep the general ledger or perform other accounting functions. Neither are they practicing mathematicians, cranking out volumes of mathematical information to solve an abundance of problems. They are, however, managers, caretakers, and users of large amounts of data, much of which is numerical and financial in nature. When practicing strategic supply management and procurement, it sometimes requires the use of certain procedures involving formulas and equations to determine particular information. This information is used to perform an analysis, determine the financial soundness of suppliers and bidders, calculate tracking results to create charts and graphs, perform an array of different analysis, and determine certain economic or financial conditions. For this reason I have included a list of useful formulas with examples and explanations. But first, let us look at a few definitions that are important to the procurement function.

Costs

In the procurement function it is all about costs; what something costs to purchase, make, use, or provide, what it costs for transportation, warehousing (carry inventory), handling (receive, pick, package, ship, etc.), what it costs to perform activities and processes, what it costs to pay invoices, and so on and so on. Everything has a cost associated with it, therefore it is important to know how to calculate the costs of various things. Procurement departments in some organizations put little emphasis on the use of mathematics for determining useful and valuable information from raw data. These types of organizations practice what I refer to as basic procurement. But organizations that practice strategic supply management and procurement recognize the importance, value, and necessity of using mathematics to interpret raw data and information that can be used in a variety of analysis, forecasting, and strategic planning. What follows are discussions, examples, and explanations of different costs encountered in the procurement function.

A cost can be defined as a value expressed in time or money. A cost can be positive or negative; when used, it is gone and no longer available, but it may produce or be replaced with something of value. In procurement, there are several types of costing and calculations for determining what something costs. These are:

Standard costs—The specific cost used as a basic unit of measure of something. All standard costs are pre-established or predetermined based on current, historical, or expected future conditions, prices, or costs. Standard costs are often used as benchmarks that allow a comparison to something such as preparing budgets, estimating and forecasting, or as a comparison to actual costs incurred or received. If you purchased something for less than standard cost, you did an excellent job. If the purchase was more than standard cost, you did not do as good. In procurement, standard costs relate to what it costs to purchase one each of something or what it costs to perform a task or process. In manufacturing, standard costs relate to what it costs to make or produce one each of something under normal operating conditions. Standard costs are also used as a total to assign a value to such things as labor, overhead, and freight. *Example:* The cost of Widgets (catalog price) is $2.00 each. If you were to buy a large quantity of Widgets and were able to negotiate a lower than standard cost price of $1.65 each, you would be under budget for the projected cost of purchasing Widgets (saving money is always a good thing). If, however, the cost of raw materials unexpectedly increased and the cost of Widgets increased to $2.35, you would be over budget. The manufacturing costs of Widgets required would increase and the production department would not be very happy with you.

Direct costs—Direct costs are those costs that are directly identified with or attributable to something such as a cost of an object, product, or a department. In procurement, direct costs would be wages and benefits for employees in the department, utilities, supplies, and so on. In manufacturing, direct costs can be several things such as materials costs, wages, and benefits. Direct costs have a broad application. They can be counted as individual costs or combined, for example, the combined direct costs of a department. *Example:* The costs to produce an automobile are made up of many different items all of which are specific direct costs that, when combined, make up the total cost of the finished product.

Indirect costs—Indirect costs are broad categories of common costs not directly identified with anything specific such as a product, activity, function, or department. Indirect costs can be incurred for a joint or common purpose (shared costs) and can also be fixed or variable. They can include such things as taxes, building or plant maintenance, technical services, and rent or mortgage, and are sometimes referred to as overhead. *Example:* Our IT department is currently writing two new software programs for the procurement department. It is taking longer than expected because they are doing it in conjunction with other duties, including the maintenance of existing programs and maintaining the trouble desk. Time is money and in this example it sounds like there was not enough money in the IT or procurement budget to hire additional programmers or outsource the programming. Therefore it is taking longer than hoped. The time required to write the two programs is a variable cost and is also an indirect cost because it is combined with all of the other costs incurred by the IT department.

There are also other categories of costs such as activity, opportunity, and relevant or irrelevant costs. These categories are usually defined and included in one or more of the examples shown but can be looked at separately for evaluation and analysis purposes.

Why is it important to understand what costs are? Because costs make up and determine so much of what procurement does. They can be used as benchmarks for the comparison of process or activity efficiency and profitability to plan for improvement, or they can be used to determine total costs of products, services, activities, and processes for budgetary or reengineering justification. There are many free online calculators that can be used to aid in calculating costs and many other mathematical functions can be found in Microsoft Excel. What follows is an accumulation of useful formulas that can be used in supply management and procurement.

Total cost (TC) is calculated: X (TC) = A (Average Fixed Cost) + B (Average Variable Cost) × C (Quantity Output) or $X = A + B$

Average total cost (ATC) is calculated: X (ATC) = TC (Fixed Costs + Variable Costs)/Q (Output Quantity) or $X = TC / Q$

Total fixed cost (TFC) is calculated: X (TFC) = A (TC) – B (Total Variable Cost) or $X = A - B$

Total variable cost (TVC) is calculated: X (TVC) = A (Average Variable Cost) × B (Quantity Output) or $X = A \times B$

Total product cost (TPC) is calculated: X (TPC) = C (Product Cost) × D (Variable Costs) or $X = C \times D$

Average product cost (APC) is calculated: X (APC) = A (TPC)/B (Variable Costs) or $X = A/B$

Breakeven point (BEP) is calculated: X (BEP) = A (Fixed Costs)/(B (Unit Selling Price) – C (Variable Costs)) or $X = A/(B - C)$

Financial Analysis Formulas

When qualifying suppliers, a financial analysis should be performed to determine the financial soundness and stability of the candidate. Several types of financial information are required to perform the various financial calculations to determine the resources and capabilities of a company. This information can be obtained from income statements, balance sheets, or 10-K reports. Formulas that can be used to calculate valuable information when evaluating suppliers are:

Return on investment (ROI)—Indicates the standard return on an investor's equity:

Annual Operating Income/Total Capital Invested

Net operating margin—Measures how well a company controls its costs and how profitable it is: Total Operating Income/Total Revenues

Gross profit margin—Amount of earnings required to pay fixed costs and profits generated from revenue. It reveals the relationship between revenue from sales and costs of goods sold. It is a good indicator of a company's financial health and pricing strategy:

Gross Profit/Net Sales

Acid test ratio or quick ratio—Measures liquidity, the amount of cash on hand or immediately available to satisfy short-term debt:

(Cash + Marketable Securities + Accounts Receivable)/Current Liabilities

Asset turnover ratio—Measures the inefficient use of fixed assets. This may be the result of over capacity or the interruption of the supply of parts and/or raw materials:

Net Sales/Net Fixed Assets

Cash ratio—Measures the amount of cash (liquidity) on hand or immediately available that is required to satisfy short-term debt:

Cash & Equivalents + Marketable Securities/Current Liabilities

Current ratio—Used to evaluate the ability of a business to meet short-term debts:

Current Assets/Current Liabilities

Unit contribution margin—Indicates the profitability generated by individual products (units):

C (Unit Revenue) = P (Unit Price) – V (Unit Variable Costs) or $C = P - V$

Debt/income ratio—Also called the debt-to-equity ratio, it indicates if creditors are protected if insolvency occurs: Total Debt/Total Net Income (Equity)

Long-term debt ratio—Shows the number of years required to retire long-term debt from net income:

Long-term Debt / Net Income

Risk Analysis Calculations

Risk identification, assessment, mitigation, and management are all essential functions of successful strategic supply management and procurement. Chapter 12 discusses the subject of risk in detail and has examples of a risk assessment index. Both qualitative and quantitative values can be assigned to individual risks to identify potential and probability. Risk assessment can be conceptual (high-, medium-, or low-risk factors) or expressed mathematically by assigning number values. The mathematical formula for a composite risk index is:

Composite Risk Index = Impact of Risk Event × Probability of Occurrence

Process Capability Formulas

Cp stands for inherent process capability. Cp is a statistical tool used to determine the normal distribution of a population range of data and has a variety of applications from supply management and procurement to production processes. Cp is used in total quality management, Six Sigma, and other quality and process improvement philosophies. Cp can be expressed mathematically as a ratio:

Cp = (Upper Specification Limit – Lower Specification Limit)/Six Sigma (Standard Deviation)

Cpk is a statistical tool used when specifications are one-sided and/or the mean (average) shifts and Cp cannot be used. In this instance, k becomes a factor and Cpk is used. Cpk has applications in determining process capability and performance to prevent shipping or receiving marginal quality products and has a variety of other applications. It is a tool used in total quality management, Six Sigma, and other quality and process improvement philosophies. If a processes mean (average) shifts with respect to design or specification, the process capability is then adjusted with a factor of k, and then becomes Cpk.

Determination of what the k factor is can be expressed as: k = Process Shift/(Design Specification/2). The formula for Cpk is then:

$$Cpk = (Upper\ Specification\ Limit - Mean)/Three\ Sigma$$
$$(Standard\ Deviation)$$

and can also be calculated as:

$$Cpk = (Mean - Lower\ Specification\ Limit)/Three\ Sigma$$

Sigma in process capability is defined as the standard deviation of a normal distribution.

Inventory Cost Formulas

Inventory carrying rate—Determines the cost to carry inventory and is performed in several stages. First, define all of the annual inventory costs such as administrative, storage, handling, damage, and loss (expired shelf-life, etc.) and calculate the total cost. Second, divide the total average inventory costs by the total inventory value. Third, calculate the opportunity cost of capital. This is the return you could expect if the money was used elsewhere plus taxes and insurance. Lastly, add the percentages determined in steps two and three to determine the inventory carrying rate:

Annual Inventory Costs/Average Inventory Value + Opportunity Cost

Example: $4,500/$35,000 = 13% + 18% = 31% Inventory Carrying Rate

Average inventory calculation—This calculation determines the average number of days it takes to move inventory (ship):

Average Inventory = (Beginning Inventory + Ending Inventory)/Average Number of Days to Move

Inventory turnover—Determined for a specified period of time by calculating the cost of goods sold and dividing by the average value of inventory for that time period:

Inventory Turnover = Costs of Goods Sold/Average Value of Inventory

Other Useful Formulas

Customer value ranking—A value ranking can be assigned to suppliers or customers developing a matrix and assigning numerical values for various requirements or criteria. This action has value in performing purchase decisions and contract awards. It can be a prerequisite to the supplier or vendor assessment portion of an overall procurement decision matrix:

Value = Quality + Service + Lead Time + Technology/Price

Price elasticity of demand—Measures how much consumer buying decisions respond to a change in price:

Elasticity = (Percentage Change in Quantity)/(Percentage Change in Price)

If prices increase and consumers respond by decreasing purchases, the equation calculates the elasticity coefficient. This results in a negative elasticity if the increase in price (a positive number) prompts a decrease in purchases (a negative number). Price elasticity of demand is said to be inelastic whenever the elasticity coefficient is less than one and elastic whenever it is greater than one.

Present value (PV) of cash flow—Used to calculate what the value of money will be after a determined amount of time at a constant discount rate. To find PV of a number (say $100) at 10% interest for three years:

$$PV = \$100/(1 + 10\%) \text{ for 3 years} = \$75.13$$

Index